Speech and Language Processing: Computational Linguistics and Natural Language Processing

Speech and Language Processing: Computational Linguistics and Natural Language Processing

Edited by Elsa Harrington

STATES
ACADEMIC PRESS
www.statesacademicpress.com

States Academic Press,
109 South 5th Street,
Brooklyn, NY 11249, USA

ISBN: 978-1-63989-493-2

Cataloging-in-Publication Data

Speech and language processing : computational linguistics and
natural language processing / edited by Elsa Harrington.
p. cm.
Includes bibliographical references and index.
ISBN 978-1-63989-493-2
1. Computational linguistics. 2. Speech processing systems. 3. Applied linguistics.
4. Cross-language information retrieval. I. Harrington, Elsa.
P98 .S64 2022
006.35--dc23

For information on all States Academic Press publications
visit our website at www.statesacademicpress.com

STATES
ACADEMIC PRESS

Contents

Preface

The interdisciplinary field that deals with the computational modeling of natural language is known as computational linguistics. It studies various computational models that are used to answer linguistic questions. Some of the theoretical frameworks which are used within this field are linguistic production, structural linguistics, linguistic comprehension and developmental linguistics. The discipline makes use of concepts from other fields such as computer science, mathematics, philosophy, psychology, artificial intelligence, cognitive psychology, psycholinguistics, etc. The field helps in the development of speech recognition software. The objective of this book is to give a general view of the different areas of computational linguistics, and its applications. It strives to provide a fair idea about this discipline and to help develop a better understanding of the latest advances within this field. Students, researchers, experts and all associated with speech and language processing will benefit alike from this book.

The information shared in this book is based on empirical researches made by veterans in this field of study. The elaborative information provided in this book will help the readers further their scope of knowledge leading to advancements in this field.

Finally, I would like to thank my fellow researchers who gave constructive feedback and my family members who supported me at every step of my research.

Editor

1

Evaluation of automatic updates of *Roget's Thesaurus*

Alistair Kennedy[1] *and Stan Szpakowicz*[2,1]
[1] School of Electrical Engineering and Computer Science
University of Ottawa, Ottawa, Ontario, Canada
[2] Institute of Computer Science
Polish Academy of Sciences, Warsaw, Poland

Keywords: lexical resources, Roget's Thesaurus, WordNet, semantic relatedness, synonym selection, pseudo-word-sense disambiguation, analogy

ABSTRACT

Thesauri and similarly organised resources attract increasing interest of Natural Language Processing researchers. Thesauri age fast, so there is a constant need to update their vocabulary. Since a manual update cycle takes considerable time, automated methods are required. This work presents a tuneable method of measuring semantic relatedness, trained on *Roget's Thesaurus*, which generates lists of terms related to words not yet in the *Thesaurus*. Using these lists of terms, we experiment with three methods of adding words to the *Thesaurus*. We add, with high confidence, over 5500 and 9600 new word senses to versions of *Roget's Thesaurus* from 1911 and 1987 respectively.

We evaluate our work both manually and by applying the updated thesauri in three NLP tasks: selection of the best synonym from a set of candidates, pseudo-word-sense disambiguation and SAT-style analogy problems. We find that the newly added words are of high quality. The additions significantly improve the performance of *Roget's*-based methods in these NLP tasks. The performance of our system compares favourably with that of *WordNet*-based methods. Our methods are general enough to work with different versions of *Roget's Thesaurus*.

1 INTRODUCTION

Thesauri and other similarly organised lexical knowledge bases play a major role in applications of Natural Language Processing (NLP). While *Roget's Thesaurus*, whose original form is 160 years old, has been applied successfully, the NLP community turns most often to *WordNet* (Fellbaum 1998). *WordNet*'s intrinsic advantages notwithstanding, one of the reasons is that no other similar resource, including *Roget's Thesaurus*, has been publicly available in a suitable software package. It is, however, important to note that *WordNet* represents *one* of the methods of organising the English lexicon, and need not be the superior resource for every task. *Roget's Thesaurus* updated with the most recent vocabulary can become a competitive resource whose quality measures up to *WordNet*'s on a variety of NLP applications. In this paper, we describe and evaluate a few variations on an innovative method of updating the lexicon of *Roget's Thesaurus*.

Work on learning to construct or enhance a thesaurus by clustering related words goes back over two decades (Tsurumaru *et al.* 1986; Crouch 1988; Crouch and Yang 1992). Few methods use an existing resource in the process of updating that same resource. We employ *Roget's Thesaurus* in two ways when creating its updated versions. First, we construct a measure of semantic relatedness between terms, and tune a system to place a word in the *Thesaurus*. Next, we use the resource to "learn" how to place new words in the correct locations. This paper focusses on finding how to place a new word appropriately.

We evaluate our lexicon-updating methods on two versions of *Roget's Thesaurus*, with the vocabulary from 1911 and from 1987. Printed versions are periodically updated, but new releases – neither easily available to NLP researchers nor NLP-friendly – have had little effect on the community. The 1911 version of *Roget's Thesaurus* is freely available through Project Gutenberg.[1] We also work with the 1987 edition of *Penguin's Roget's Thesaurus* (Kirkpatrick 1987). An open Java API for the 1911 *Roget's Thesaurus* and its updated versions – including every addition we discuss in this paper – are available on the Web as the *Open Roget's Project*.[2] The API has been built on the work of Jarmasz (2003).

---

[1] `http://www.gutenberg.org/ebooks/22`

[2] `http://rogets.eecs.uottawa.ca/`

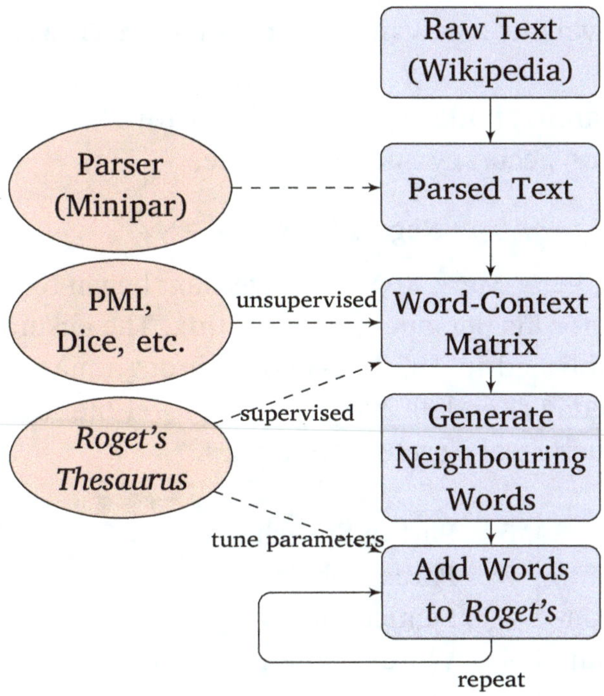

Figure 1: The process of adding new words to *Roget's Thesaurus*

Figure 1 outlines the process of updating *Roget's Thesaurus*. We work with Wikipedia as a corpus and with the parser *MINIPAR* (Lin 1998a). Raw text is parsed, and a word–context matrix is constructed and re-weighted in both a supervised and an unsupervised manner. The nearest synonyms of each word in the matrix are generated and a location for them in *Roget's Thesaurus* is deduced using it as a source of tuning data. The last step can be applied iteratively to update the lexicon of *Roget's Thesaurus*.

This work makes six main contributions:

- apply the supervised measures of semantic relatedness from (Kennedy and Szpakowicz 2011) and (Kennedy and Szpakowicz 2012) to the updating of *Roget's Thesaurus*, and evaluate it carefully;
- propose and compare three methods of automatically adding words to *Roget's Thesaurus*;
- build the updated editions of the 1911 and 1987 versions of *Roget's Thesaurus*;
- create new datasets for pseudo-word-sense disambiguation and the selection of the best synonym;

- propose and evaluate a new method for solving SAT-style analogy problems;
- compare semantic similarity calculation with *Roget's Thesaurus* and *WordNet* on accuracy and on runtime.

1.1 *About Roget's Thesaurus*

In the early 1800s, Peter Mark Roget, a physician, began to categorise terms and phrases for his personal use in writing. The ensuing *Roget's Thesaurus,* first published in 1852, has gone through many revisions continuing to this day (Kendall 2008). A nine-level hierarchy makes up most of the structure of *Roget's Thesaurus*:

1	Class	6	Part of Speech
2	Section	7	Paragraph
3	Sub-Section	8	Semicolon Group
4	Head Group	9	Words and Phrases
5	Head		

Eight classes are subdivided into Sections and Sub-Sections. There are around 1000 Heads – the main category in *Roget's Thesaurus,* corresponding to major concepts. Heads with opposing or complementary concepts form a Head Group. A Part of Speech (POS) groups all noun/verb/adjective/adverb realisations of the Head's concept. The closest counterpart of *WordNet*'s synsets is a Semicolon Group (SG). An SG contains closely related words (usually near-synonyms); a Paragraph contains related SGs. Note the division by part-of-speech quite low in the hierarchy, not at the very top as in *WordNet.* We define a *Roget's grouping* to be the set of words contained within an instance of any of these levels. A Section or even a Class is also a *Roget's grouping,* but usually we talk about words in the same POS, Paragraph or SG.

Figure 2 shows an example of a Head. Head #586 in the 1911 *Roget's Thesaurus* contains terms pertaining to language. A number before a word refers to a Head in which that word-sense may also be found. Although a thorough update of *Roget's Thesaurus* should include such *cross-references,* they are beyond the scope of this work.[3]

[3] They do not figure in any of the applications we consider here to test the quality of the updated versions of the *Thesaurus.*

Class 5: Intellect: communication of ideas
Section 3: Means of communicating ideas
Sub-Section: Conventional means
Head Group: 586 Language
Head: 586 Language

N. *language*; *595* phraseology; *608* speech; tongue, lingo, vernacular; mother tongue, vulgar tongue, native tongue; household words; King's English, Queen's English; *589* dialect.

confusion of tongues, Babel, pasigraphie; *sign 576* pantomime; onomatopoeia; betacism, mimmation, myatism, nunnation; pasigraphy.

lexicology, philology, glossology, glottology; linguistics, chrestomathy; paleology, paleography; comparative grammar.

literature, letters, polite literature, belles lettres, muses, humanities, literae humaniores, republic of letters, dead languages, classics; genius of language; *scholar 516* scholarship.

VB. *592 express by words.*

ADJ. *lingual*, linguistic; dialectic; vernacular, current; bilingual; diglot, hexaglot, polyglot; literary.

Figure 2: Head 586: Language from the 1911 *Roget's Thesaurus*

1.2 *Where to add new words to Roget's Thesaurus*

The number of Heads and POSs per Head have changed little between the 1911 and 1987 versions of *Roget's Thesaurus*. We can aim to add new words in three different ways:

- in an existing SG,
- in a new SG in an existing Paragraph,
- in a new SG in a new Paragraph.

Evaluation of a new semantic distance measure should then be useful at identifying words in the same POS, Paragraph and SG.

2 PREVIOUS WORK ON UPDATING THESAURI

There have been few attempts to expand the lexicon of *Roget's Thesaurus* thus far. Cassidy (2000) added manually a few hundred words to the 1911 edition of *Roget's Thesaurus*. Kennedy and Szpakowicz (2007) disambiguated hypernym instances in the 1987 *Roget's Thesaurus*. Both projects augmented *Roget's Thesaurus*, but did not offer insight into how to update the lexicon automatically.

Other related work includes mapping word senses between *Roget's Thesaurus*, *WordNet* and *LDOCE* (Procter 1978). The contexts where a word appears, whether it is words in the same Paragraph, *WordNet* synset or an *LDOCE* definition, are used to deduce which words are likely to be related (Kwong 1998a,b; Nastase and Szpakowicz 2001).

2.1 *Updating WordNet*

The automatic expansion of *WordNet*'s lexicon has been attempted several times. Snow *et al.* (2006) extracted thousands of new words from a corpus for possible inclusion in *WordNet* (though that expansion never materialised in practice due to its low accuracy). Many of the new terms were proper nouns found in a corpus by a machine learning system (Snow *et al.* 2005) which was used to discover IS-A relations using dependency paths generated by *MINIPAR* (Lin 1998b).

Pantel (2005) created semantic vectors for each word in *WordNet* by disambiguating contexts which appeared with different senses of a word. The building of semantic vectors is described in (Pantel 2003). *WordNet*'s hierarchy was used to propagate contexts where words may appear throughout the network. A word sense was then represented by contexts from its semantic vector not shared with its parents. Pantel did not attempt to place new words into the resource, only evaluated the method on existing words. This technique was only examined for nouns. It presumably applied to verbs as well, but could not be tried on adjectives or adverbs, for which there was no usable hypernym hierarchy.

A folksonomy is a Web service which allows users to annotate Web sites (among other things) with strings of their choice. One such folksonomy was *Delicious* where users categorised Web pages. HYPERNYM/HYPONYM relations can be extracted from folksonomies by identifying tags subsuming other tags. Zheng *et al.* (2008) describe how to use folksonomies to discover instances of hypernymy and so help put new words into *WordNet.*

Not directly applicable but relevant to our work is semi-automatic enhancement of *WordNet* with sentiment and affect information. Esuli and Sebastiani (2006) used machine learning to build *SentiWordNet* by labelling synsets in *WordNet* 2.0 as objective, positive or negative. In *WordNet Affect* (Strapparava and Valitutti 2004), synsets got one or more labels, often related to emotion. An initial set of words marked with emotions was built manually. Next, those emotions were propagated to other synsets via *WordNet* relations. This work was based on *WordNet Domains* (Magnini and Cavagliá 2000), a framework which allows a user to augment *WordNet* by adding domain labels to synsets. No new words were added, but these projects highlight some of the more successful experiments with enhancing *WordNet*.

There is a reasonable amount of work on mining hypernym relations from text, which could then be used to update *WordNet*. This includes using set patterns (Hearst 1992; Sombatsrisomboon *et al.* 2003) or discovering new patterns using a few seed sets of hypernyms (Morin and Jacquemin 1999). Languages other than English for which hypernym mining has been attempted include Swedish (Rydin 2002), Dutch (Sang 2007) and Japanese (Shinzato and Torisawa 2004). There also has been research on hierarchically related verbs (Girju *et al.* 2003, 2006).

2.2 *Wordnets in other languages*

There has been much work on building wordnets for languages other than English, loosely coordinated by the Global Wordnet Association.[4] One strategy is to take the Princeton *WordNet* (Fellbaum 1998) as a starting point. That was the mode of operation in the *EuroWordNet* project (Vossen 1998), an early initiative meant to build wordnets for several European languages. One of its offshoots is *BalkaNet.*[5]

The other wordnet-building strategy is to avoid the influence of Princeton *WordNet*. Polish *WordNet* (Piasecki *et al.* 2009) is one such resource built from scratch. Its development was supported, among others, by *WordNet Weaver*, a tool which helps increase the vocabulary of a wordnet. The tool implements a two-phase algorithm. Phase I identifies a network vicinity in which to place a new word, while phase II connects possible candidate synsets. Phase II is semi-automatic: it is the linguists who decide what additions are ultimately made to the growing Polish *WordNet*.

[4] See `http://globalwordnet.org/wordnets-in-the-world/` for an up-to-date list of available wordnets.

[5] "The Balkan WordNet aims at the development of a multilingual lexical database comprising of individual WordNets for the Balkan languages." (`http://www.dblab.upatras.gr/balkanet/`)

Lemnitzer *et al.* (2008) discuss adding semantic relationships between nouns and verbs to *GermaNet*, a German wordnet. Those were verb–object relationships believed to be useful in applications such as text summarisation or anaphora resolution. Sagot and Fišer (2011) present an automatic, language-independent method (tested on Slovene and French) of extending a wordnet by "recycling" freely available bilingual resources such as machine-readable dictionaries and on-line encyclopaedias.

3 MEASURING SEMANTIC RELATEDNESS

Distributional measures of semantic relatedness (MSRs) use a word's context to help determine its meaning. Words which frequently appear in similar contexts are assumed to have similar meaning. Such MSRs usually re-weight contexts by considering some measure of their importance, usually the association between a context and the terms it contains. One of the most successful measures is Pointwise Mutual Information (PMI). PMI increases the weight of contexts where a word appears regularly but other words do not, and decreases the weight of contexts where many words may appear. Essentially, it is unsupervised feature weighting.

Kennedy and Szpakowicz (2011, 2012) discussed introducing supervision into the process of context re-weighting. Their method identifies contexts where pairs of words known to be semantically related frequently appear, and then uses a measure of association to re-weight these contexts by how often they contain closely related words. The method, very general, can work with any thesaurus as a source of known synonym pairs and with measures of association other than PMI. Here, this measure will help update *Roget's Thesaurus*. This section describes in general how this method is applied.

3.1 *Building a word–context matrix for semantic relatedness*

We used Wikipedia[6] as a source of data and parsed it with *MINIPAR* (Lin 1998a). The choice of dependency triples instead of all neighbouring words favours contexts which most directly affect a word's meaning. Examples of triples are $\langle \textit{time}, \textit{mod}, \textit{unlimited} \rangle$ and

[6] A dump of August 2010.

$\langle time, conj, motion \rangle$: "time" appears in contexts with the modifier "unlimited" and in a conjunction with "motion". Some 900 million dependency triples generated by parsing Wikipedia took up ≈20GB.

Three matrices were built, one each for nouns, verbs and adjectives/adverbs.[7] For each word–relation–word triple $\langle w_1, r, w_2 \rangle$ we generated two word–context pairs $(w_1, \langle r, w_2 \rangle)$ and $(w_2, \langle w_1, r \rangle)$. Words w_1 and w_2 could be of any part of speech. All relations r were considered, with the direction of r retained. When w_1 or w_2 was an individual term, it had to be a noun, verb, adjective or adverb, written in lower case (*MINIPAR* only leaves proper nouns capitalised).

With these constraints we used all of the Wikipedia dump when building the matrices for verbs and adjectives/adverbs, but only 50% for nouns. This limit was chosen both because it was the most data which could be held in a system with 4GB of RAM and because the leftover data could be used in later evaluation.

Very infrequent words and contexts tend to be unreliable, and often appear because of spelling errors. We established thresholds for how often a word or context needs to appear. We measured the quality of synonyms generated for a set of randomly selected words which appear with different frequencies in the matrix. Next, in a series of straightforward experiments, we selected a cutoff after which the quality of the synonyms does not appear to improve: 35 for nouns and for adjectives, 10 for verbs. Also, an entry must appear in a context at least twice for the context to count. Table 1 shows the counts of words and contexts in each matrix before and after the cutoff. Non-zero entries are cells with positive values. While the reduction of the matrix dimensionally was quite large, the decrease in the number of non-zero entries was very small. So, we lost little information, but created a much denser and more informative matrix.

3.2 *Measures of semantic relatedness*

We explored two complementary methods of re-weighting the word-context matrix. An unsupervised method measures association between words and contexts; a supervised method uses known pairs of synonyms in *Roget's Thesaurus* to determine which contexts have a

[7] We have decided to work with *MINIPAR*'s labelling system, which does not distinguish between adjectives and adverbs.

Table 1: Counts of the rows, columns and non-zero entries for each matrix

POS	Matrix	Words	Contexts	Non-zero entries	% non-zero
Noun (≥ 35)	Full	359 380	2 463 001	30 994 968	0.0035%
	Cutoff	43 834	1 050 178	28 296 890	0.0615%
	(% of full)	*(12.2%)*	*(42.6%)*	*(91.3%)*	
Verb (≥ 10)	Full	9 294	2 892 002	26 716 709	0.0994%
	Cutoff	7141	1 423 665	25 239 485	0.2483%
	(% of full)	*(76.8%)*	*(49.3%)*	*(94.5%)*	
Adj/Adv (≥ 35)	Full	104 074	817 921	9 116 741	0.0107%
	Cutoff	17 160	360 436	8 379 637	0.1355%
	(% of full)	*(16.5%)*	*(44.1%)*	*(91.9%)*	

higher tendency to contain pairs of known synonyms (Kennedy and Szpakowicz 2011, 2012). Supervision can be conducted on each individual context, or on groups of contexts with a syntactic relation in common. It was found that supervision at the context level worked best for nouns and verbs, while grouping contexts by relation worked best for adjectives (Kennedy and Szpakowicz 2012).

Both supervised and unsupervised methods employ measures of association; Kennedy and Szpakowicz (2012) found that in all cases PMI was the most successful. These two kinds of methods can actually be complementary. It is possible to use the supervised method of matrix re-weighting and then apply the unsupervised method on top of it. This was generally found to yield the best results; so this is how we report the results.

To evaluate this work, we created a random set of 1000 nouns, 600 verbs and 600 adjectives and generated lists of neighbouring words for each of them.[8] Those words were left out of the training process. We then measured the precision – how many neighbouring words appeared in the same SG, Paragraph or POS – in the 1987 *Roget's Thesaurus*. Precision was measured at several recall points: the top 1, 5, 10, 20, 50 and 100 words retrieved from the 1987 *Thesaurus*.

Table 2 shows the results for the unsupervised baseline, using PMI weighting and the results for the combined supervised methods using synonyms from either the 1911 or the 1987 version of *Roget's*

[8] There were not enough adverbs to construct such a set. Adverbs will be left for future work.

Table 2: Evaluation results for the combined measure with PMI. Significant improvement over unsuper-vised PMI in **bold**, significantly worse results in *italics*

Year	POS	Group	Top 1	Top 5	Top 10	Top 20	Top 50	Top 100
–	N.	SG	0.358	0.236	0.179	0.130	0.084	0.059
		Para	0.560	0.469	0.412	0.352	0.279	0.230
		POS	0.645	0.579	0.537	0.490	0.423	0.374
	V.	SG	0.302	0.206	0.162	0.126	0.086	0.065
		Para	0.513	0.445	0.407	0.358	0.304	0.264
		POS	0.582	0.526	0.487	0.444	0.396	0.357
	Adj.	SG	0.345	0.206	0.156	0.115	0.069	0.046
		Para	0.562	0.417	0.363	0.304	0.231	0.185
		POS	0.600	0.480	0.431	0.368	0.295	0.247
1911	N.	SG	0.358	*0.225*	*0.175*	0.132	0.084	0.058
		Para	0.568	0.472	0.418	**0.361**	**0.286**	**0.234**
		POS	0.659	**0.588**	**0.548**	**0.501**	**0.431**	**0.382**
	V.	SG	0.310	0.207	0.163	0.124	0.086	0.064
		Para	**0.550**	0.456	0.414	0.362	0.307	**0.268**
		POS	0.605	0.533	**0.500**	**0.455**	**0.401**	**0.362**
	Adj.	SG	0.343	**0.209**	0.157	0.114	0.069	0.046
		Para	0.563	0.422	0.365	0.304	**0.232**	0.184
		POS	0.602	0.484	0.431	0.368	0.296	0.247
1987	N.	SG	0.359	*0.229*	0.177	**0.134**	0.085	0.059
		Para	0.564	0.471	**0.419**	**0.365**	**0.285**	**0.234**
		POS	0.651	0.584	**0.549**	**0.501**	**0.430**	**0.381**
	V.	SG	0.308	0.211	0.167	0.127	0.087	0.064
		Para	0.525	**0.457**	**0.417**	0.362	0.305	**0.266**
		POS	0.588	**0.537**	**0.499**	**0.453**	0.399	**0.360**
	Adj.	SG	0.343	0.208	0.158	0.115	0.069	0.046
		Para	0.565	**0.421**	0.365	0.304	0.232	0.184
		POS	0.603	0.483	0.431	0.367	0.296	0.247

Thesaurus as training data. Statistically significant improvement over the baseline appears in bold, while significantly worse results are italicised; we applied Student's t-test. With a few small exceptions, we found that the supervised system performs better. The number of times the scores were better, unchanged, or worse can be found in Table 3. In general, we concluded that the combination of supervised and unsupervised context weighting created a superior MSR, better suited to

Table 3: The number of statistically improved/unaffected/decreased results for both sources of training data

Resource	Nouns	Verbs	Adjectives	All
1911 *Roget's*	8/8/2	6/12/0	2/16/0	16/36/2
1987 *Roget's*	9/8/1	7/11/0	1/17/0	17/36/1

updating *Roget's Thesaurus* than the unsupervised method alone. We used the supervised method of generating lists of related words when adding new terms to the *Thesaurus*.

4 PLACING NEW WORDS IN *ROGET'S THESAURUS*

In this section, we evaluate a variety of systems for adding new words to *Roget's Thesaurus*. The baseline method places a word in the same POS, Paragraph and Semicolon Group as its closest neighbour in the *Thesaurus*. We improve on this baseline using multiple words to deduce a better location or better locations.

4.1 *Methods of adding new words*

We took advantage of the hierarchy of *Roget's Thesaurus* to select the best place to add words. We found first the POS, then the Paragraph, then the SG.[9] We refer to the word to be added to *Roget's Thesaurus* as the *target* word. A word already in the *Thesaurus* may be an *anchor*, acting as a "magnet" for a given target. For every target word t, we generated a list of nearest neighbours $NN(t)$, along with similarity scores, and identified anchors using $NN(t)$.

We experimented with three methods, evaluated against the following baseline: the target t is placed in the same POS, Paragraph and SG as w_i, where w_i is the first word in $NN(t)$ found in *Roget's Thesaurus*. Since w_i may be polysemous, t can go into multiple locations in *Roget's Thesaurus*. Often w_i will be w_1 if the first neighbour of t is found in the *Thesaurus*. For the values in Table 4, this baseline has been calculated using the MSRs built with combined weighting, trained with the 1911 or the 1987 *Thesaurus*. The results show one number for the count of POSs, Paragraphs and SGs where the target t was placed and the precision of placing the word into the POSs, Paragraphs and SGs.

[9] Identifying the POS effectively gives us the correct Head as well.

The first method is to apply a nearest-neighbour model. X nearest neighbours from $NN(t)$ are identified for each target word t. If W of these X words appear in the same *Roget's grouping*, the target word is placed there. It is a weakness that this method considers – somewhat unrealistically – the same number of neighbours for every target word.

In the second method, scores replace rank. Words with scores of Y or higher are identified. If W of them are in the same *Roget's grouping*, the target word is placed there. This allows for varying numbers of neighbours, but similarity scores partially depend on the target word, so the same score between two different word pairs may indicate different degrees of similarity. A very frequent word which appears in many contexts may have more highly related neighbours than a word which appears in few contexts. Such a frequent word may thus have inordinately many synonyms.

The third method considers relative scores. It assumes that the first similar word w_1 is very closely related to t, then takes all synonyms within Z% of the similarity score for w_1. This means that if w_i has a score of within Z% of w_1, then it can be used as an anchor of t for determining the correct *Roget's grouping*. Once again, if W of these words in the same *Roget's grouping* have a relative score of Z% or higher, then the target word can be placed there as well.

We also considered how to optimise the measures. In placing words into a *Roget's grouping*, the method has two parameters to optimise, W and one of X, Y or Z. One possibility is to base F-measure on the precision with which words are placed in *Roget's Thesaurus* and recall on the number of words from the test set which could actually be placed. Another possibility of counting recall would be to identify the number of places where a word appears in the *Thesaurus* and see in how many of them it *was* placed. This measure has some problems.

For one, rare senses are not well represented by the vectors in the word–context matrix, so synonyms for only the most dominant senses will be found. Also, an even balance of precision and recall is not appropriate for this task. Adding incorrect words could be quite detrimental, so we assume that identifying the POS must weight precision more highly than recall. We set a 0.33 ratio of recall to precision (an F0.33 measure rather than F1). Once the POS has been identified, the Paragraph and SG will be identified using the F1 measure. The

Table 4: Baseline for identifying the POS of a word on the tuning and test data

Year	POS	Data	Words	P	R	F0.33
1987	Noun	*Tuning*	*1000*	*0.281*	*0.486*	*0.293*
		Test	1000	0.295	0.487	0.307
	Verb	*Tuning*	*600*	*0.204*	*0.468*	*0.216*
		Test	600	0.245	0.455	0.257
	Adjective	*Tuning*	*600*	*0.250*	*0.460*	*0.262*
		Test	600	0.232	0.435	0.244
1911	Noun	*Tuning*	*817*	*0.232*	*0.296*	*0.237*
		Test	840	0.267	0.344	0.273
	Verb	*Tuning*	*542*	*0.167*	*0.271*	*0.174*
		Test	538	0.196	0.297	0.203
	Adjective	*Tuning*	*489*	*0.246*	*0.288*	*0.249*
		Test	497	0.201	0.262	0.206

choice of F0.33 is somewhat arbitrary, but favouring precision over recall should mostly bring advantages. A high-precision system is, in theory, more likely to place words in the correct *Roget's grouping* at the cost of lower recall. Any method of adding new words to *Roget's Thesaurus*, however, could be run iteratively and thus make up for the lower recall. Rather than attempting to add a lot of words in one pass, our method will add fewer words in each of multiple passes.

When using this method to actually add new words, sometimes it is necessary to create new Paragraphs or SGs. If a POS is identified but no Paragraph, then a new Paragraph will be created. Likewise, if a Paragraph but not an SG can be identified, then the word is placed in a new SG in the selected Paragraph.

The methods were tuned on the same dataset as that used to evaluate the MSR in Section 3. For evaluation, we constructed a test set equal in size to the tuning set. We evaluated all methods on the task of identifying the correct POS to place a target word t. The best method is then applied to the task of placing a word in the appropriate Paragraph and SG.

4.2 *Baseline*

Table 4 shows the results of the baseline experiments, measured for the 1911 and 1987 versions of *Roget's Thesaurus*. The former did not contain all the words for evaluation that the latter did – hence

Table 5: Optimal values for parameters X (the number of nearest neighbours), Y (the minimal relatedness score) and Z (the relative score)

		1987		1911	
Parameter	POS	$X/Y/Z$	W-POS	$X/Y/Z$	W-POS
X	Noun	26	10	10	4
	Verb	22	7	6	3
	Adjective	19	6	8	3
Y	Noun	.08	15	.07	14
	Verb	.09	9	.13	2
	Adjective	.13	3	.10	4
Z	Noun	.82	4	.93	2
	Verb	.89	3	.98	2
	Adjective	.82	3	.91	2

Table 6: Precision, Recall and F0.33-measure when optimising for X, the number of nearest neighbours

Year	POS	Data	Words	P	R	F0.33
1987	Noun	*Tuning*	*1000*	*0.746*	*0.267*	*0.633*
		Test	1000	0.758	0.262	0.637
	Verb	*Tuning*	*600*	*0.565*	*0.285*	*0.514*
		Test	600	0.536	0.252	0.482
	Adjective	*Tuning*	*600*	*0.658*	*0.273*	*0.577*
		Test	600	0.590	0.233	0.512
1911	Noun	*Tuning*	*817*	*0.613*	*0.171*	*0.488*
		Test	840	0.659	0.182	0.522
	Verb	*Tuning*	*542*	*0.484*	*0.131*	*0.381*
		Test	538	0.471	0.097	0.340
	Adjective	*Tuning*	*489*	*0.571*	*0.184*	*0.472*
		Test	497	0.503	0.141	0.400

the differences in word counts. The results show a small advantage of adding words to the 1987 *Thesaurus* over the 1911 version.

4.3 *Tuning parameters for adding new words*

Table 5 shows the parameters, optimised for F0.33, for the three non-baseline methods. Tables 6–8 present the results on the tuning and test data.

When optimising for the X nearest neighbours (Table 6), the results show a large improvement over the baseline (Table 4). The results for nouns were actually better on the test dataset than on tuning data,

Table 7: Precision, Recall and F0.33-measure when optimising for Y, the minimal relatedness score

Year	POS	Data	Words	P	R	F0.33
1987	Noun	*Tuning*	*1000*	*0.596*	*0.182*	*0.486*
		Test	1000	0.507	0.160	0.417
	Verb	*Tuning*	*600*	*0.477*	*0.078*	*0.316*
		Test	600	0.573	0.062	0.313
	Adjective	*Tuning*	*600*	*0.529*	*0.122*	*0.396*
		Test	600	0.421	0.103	0.322
1911	Noun	*Tuning*	*817*	*0.420*	*0.120*	*0.336*
		Test	840	0.367	0.110	0.297
	Verb	*Tuning*	*542*	*0.211*	*0.096*	*0.189*
		Test	538	0.234	0.063	0.184
	Adjective	*Tuning*	*489*	*0.480*	*0.084*	*0.326*
		Test	497	0.274	0.066	0.209

but somewhat worse for verbs and adjectives. As with the baseline, the results were better for the 1987 *Roget's Thesaurus* than the 1911 version. Generally about one third to half of the words found in the top X needed to be present in the same *Roget's grouping* in order to accurately select the correct grouping.

Table 7 shows optimising word placement with scores Y or higher. The optimal scores were noticeably lower than when we optimised for X nearest neighbours (Table 6). The minimum score Y appeared to be lower for nouns than for verbs or adjectives, though more words were required in order to identify the *Roget's grouping* positively. This method is not as successful as simply selecting the X nearest neighbours. For verbs added to the 1911 *Roget's Thesaurus*, there was actually no improvement over the baseline (Table 4). This is the least successful method of the three.

Table 8 reports on optimising for the relative score Z. We found that most neighbouring words had to be within 80–90% of the closest neighbour in terms of score. This improved the results noticeably over a simple selection of a hard score cut-off (Table 7). Nonetheless, we did not improve on simply taking the X nearest neighbours (Table 6). For determining relatedness, it would appear, rank is often a feature more important than score. With this in mind, we applied the nearest-neighbour function using X to find the best parameters for identifying the POS, Paragraph and SG. The parameter W shown in Table 5 was

Table 8: Precision, Recall and F0.33-mesure when optimising for Z, the relative score

Year	POS	Data	Words	P	R	F0.33
1987	Noun	*Tuning*	*1000*	*0.643*	*0.190*	*0.519*
		Test	1000	0.595	0.215	0.506
	Verb	*Tuning*	*600*	*0.468*	*0.147*	*0.384*
		Test	600	0.492	0.163	0.410
	Adjective	*Tuning*	*600*	*0.512*	*0.215*	*0.450*
		Test	600	0.463	0.200	0.409
1911	Noun	*Tuning*	*817*	*0.468*	*0.200*	*0.413*
		Test	840	0.542	0.219	0.473
	Verb	*Tuning*	*542*	*0.438*	*0.118*	*0.344*
		Test	538	0.389	0.091	0.293
	Adjective	*Tuning*	*489*	*0.478*	*0.145*	*0.389*
		Test	497	0.434	0.129	0.351

Table 9: Optimal parameters for X (the number of nearest neighbours) and W (neighbours needed to insert a word into a *Roget's grouping*) at the POS, Paragraph and SG levels

Year	POS	X	W-POS	W-Para	W-SG
1987	Noun	26	10	5	2
	Verb	22	7	4	3
	Adjective	19	6	4	2
1911	Noun	10	4	3	3
	Verb	6	3	2	2
	Adjective	8	3	2	2

for the POS level. We have three versions, W-POS, W-Para and W-SG for the POS, Paragraph and SG respectively.

Table 9 shows the optimal values of X, W-POS, W-Para and W-SG. The same value of X was used for identifying groupings at the POS, Paragraph and SG levels. There is a bit of variance in the measures. The values of W-POS, W-Para and W-SG decrease as the groupings become smaller. To identify the correct SG, only 2 or 3 words were used. For the 1911 *Roget's Thesaurus*, the same number of words were used to identify the Paragraph as the SG. More words could be used to identify the POS for the 1987 *Thesaurus* than for the 1911 version.

Tables 10 and 11 show the precision, recall and F1 measure at the POS, Paragraph and SG level for the 1987 and 1911 *Thesauri*. The results show clearly that the F1 measure is highest when identifying the Paragraph level; this is largely because the POS level is optimised for the F0.33 measure. Once again, the scores for the 1987 version

Table 10: Identifying best POS, Paragraph and SG using optimised values for X, W-POS, W-Para and W-SG, using the F1 measure for evaluation on the **1987** *Roget's Thesaurus*

	Data	RG	P	R	F1
Noun	*Tuning*	*POS*	*306/410 (0.746)*	*267/1000 (0.267)*	*0.393*
	Tuning	*Para*	*225/402 (0.560)*	*189/267 (0.708)*	*0.625*
	Tuning	*SG*	*104/664 (0.157)*	*92/189 (0.487)*	*0.237*
	Test	POS	304/401 (0.758)	262/1000 (0.262)	0.389
	Test	Para	234/416 (0.562)	196/262 (0.748)	0.642
	Test	SG	101/659 (0.153)	93/196 (0.474)	0.232
Verb	*Tuning*	*POS*	*227/402 (0.565)*	*171/600 (0.285)*	*0.379*
	Tuning	*Para*	*186/413 (0.450)*	*137/171 (0.801)*	*0.577*
	Tuning	*SG*	*34/129 (0.264)*	*32/137 (0.234)*	*0.248*
	Test	POS	185/345 (0.536)	151/600 (0.252)	0.343
	Test	Para	148/339 (0.437)	114/151 (0.755)	0.553
	Test	SG	18/103 (0.175)	17/114 (0.149)	0.161
Adj	*Tuning*	*POS*	*227/345 (0.658)*	*164/600 (0.273)*	*0.386*
	Tuning	*Para*	*182/312 (0.583)*	*136/164 (0.829)*	*0.685*
	Tuning	*SG*	*75/381 (0.197)*	*63/136 (0.463)*	*0.276*
	Test	POS	193/327 (0.590)	140/600 (0.233)	0.334
	Test	Para	152/294 (0.517)	116/140 (0.829)	0.637
	Test	SG	59/351 (0.168)	51/116 (0.440)	0.243

tend to be better than those for the 1911 version. Most of the time it is possible to identify the correct POS with at least 40% accuracy. The recall for the 1987 *Thesaurus* was 0.233 or higher at the POS level. This is important, because it indicates how many new word additions to the *Thesaurus* can be expected. For the 1911 *Thesaurus*, the results tend to be much lower, with scores from 0.097 to 0.182 on the test set. The number for verbs is very low; for nouns and adjectives it is better, but still lower than the corresponding results for the 1987 thesaurus.

4.4 *Adding words to the Thesaurus*

We now show how the method described in Section 4.3 adds words to *Roget's Thesaurus*. In practice, a few small modifications were needed. First, we only let a word be placed in a POS if it was not already present in either that POS or in another POS within the same Head Group. This reduced the possibility of entering antonyms, which may be distributionally similar, into the same POS. Within each POS, we let a word be placed only in one Paragraph. We also did not allow

Table 11: Identifying best POS, Paragraph and SG using optimised values for X, W-POS, W-Para and W-SG, using the F1 measure for evaluation on the **1911** *Roget's Thesaurus*

	Data	RG	P	R	F1
Noun	*Tuning*	*POS*	*157/256 (0.613)*	*140/817 (0.171)*	*0.268*
	Tuning	*Para*	*89/163 (0.546)*	*83/140 (0.593)*	*0.568*
	Tuning	*SG*	*31/62 (0.500)*	*29/83 (0.349)*	*0.411*
	Test	POS	162/246 (0.659)	153/840 (0.182)	0.285
	Test	Para	83/155 (0.535)	78/153 (0.510)	0.522
	Test	SG	29/55 (0.527)	28/78 (0.359)	0.427
Verb	*Tuning*	*POS*	*76/157 (0.484)*	*71/542 (0.131)*	*0.206*
	Tuning	*Para*	*55/136 (0.404)*	*53/71 (0.746)*	*0.525*
	Tuning	*SG*	*24/86 (0.279)*	*24/53 (0.453)*	*0.345*
	Test	POS	57/121 (0.471)	52/538 (0.097)	0.160
	Test	Para	39/112 (0.348)	35/52 (0.673)	0.459
	Test	SG	22/76 (0.289)	19/35 (0.543)	0.378
Adj	*Tuning*	*POS*	*109/191 (0.571)*	*90/489 (0.184)*	*0.278*
	Tuning	*Para*	*80/188 (0.426)*	*71/90 (0.789)*	*0.553*
	Tuning	*SG*	*23/107 (0.215)*	*22/71 (0.310)*	*0.254*
	Test	POS	79/157 (0.503)	70/497 (0.141)	0.220
	Test	Para	46/148 (0.311)	42/70 (0.600)	0.409
	Test	SG	14/91 (0.154)	13/42 (0.310)	0.206

adding the same word to multiple SGs within the same Paragraph or indeed to multiple Paragraphs in the same POS.

Once a new word has been added to *Roget's Thesaurus*, it can be used as an anchor to help add subsequent words. We built two updated versions of each *Thesaurus*, one with a single pass to update the *Thesaurus*, another with five updating passes. We considered each word in each matrix, excluding stop words,[10] to be a target and generated a list of the nearest 100 neighbours for each of these words.[11] It was from these lists that we attempted to add new words to the *Thesaurus*.

Several measures are of interest when adding new words to the *Thesaurus*. The first is the number of times a target word has sufficient X and W values to be placed in *Roget's Thesaurus*, regardless of whether it was already present. The second measure is the total num-

[10] We applied a 980-element union of five stop lists first used in Jarmasz (2003): Oracle 8 ConText, SMART, Hyperwave, a list from the University of Kansas and a list from Ohio State University.

[11] Only the top X of those 100 helped identify the best place for a new word.

ber of words added to the *Thesaurus*. The third measure is the number of unique words added. These two are likely to be similar since most often a target word is only added to a single location in the *Thesaurus*. The fourth measure counts new words whose derivational form already exists in the *Thesaurus*. The fifth measure counts new words which have no derivationally related words in the *Thesaurus*. The last measure is the number of Heads where a new word was added. The results for all five passes can be seen in Table 12.

In addition to the five passes of adding new words, we experimented with random addition. All process parameters are the same, up to the point when our system determines a location where it believes a word belongs. Before checking whether that word already appears at this location, it is swapped for a random word. The counts appear in Table 13. Since the random word is selected after a location has been decided, it is very rare for this word already to be in that Head Group. As a result, the number of attempted placements is very close to the total number of words added, much closer than for the counts from Table 12.

Ultimately three updated version each of the 1911 and 1987 versions of the *Thesaurus* were created, those updated with one pass, five passes and one random pass – X1, X5 and R in Table 14. The updated versions are referred to as 1911X1, 1911X5, 1911R, 1987X1, 1987X5 and 1987R. The new thesauri have been evaluated manually (Section 5) and through selected NLP applications (Section 6).

Another statistic to consider is the total number of words, SGs and Paragraphs added to each version of *Roget's Thesaurus*, shown in Table 14. Overall, some 5500 new words were added to 1911X5 and 9600 to 1987X5. In the 1911 *Thesaurus*, approximately two thirds of the new words were placed in a new SG, while about a quarter were added to a new Paragraph. For the 1987 *Thesaurus*, a little under half of the new words were placed in new SGs, while around one fifth were added to new Paragraphs.

5 MANUAL EVALUATION

To determine the quality of the additions reliably, one needs manual evaluation. In the next subsection, we describe several possibilities and explain how we chose our evaluation method.

Table 12: New words added after the 1st, 2nd, 3rd, 4th and 5th pass (P)

P	Year	POS	Matches	Total Words	Unique Words	Derived Words	New Words	Heads Affected
1	1987	Nouns	6755	1510	1414	175	98	206
		Verbs	2870	893	735	52	45	129
		Adj	3053	858	713	15	10	183
	1911	Nouns	3888	1259	1193	148	68	274
		Verbs	1069	407	378	22	19	133
		Adj	1430	539	480	18	16	198
2	1987	Nouns	8388	774	742	37	14	139
		Verbs	4335	747	653	23	16	92
		Adj	4412	612	549	4	4	114
	1911	Nouns	5315	762	719	65	13	164
		Verbs	1530	247	238	14	14	71
		Adj	2083	287	262	6	5	95
3	1987	Nouns	9213	499	478	16	6	88
		Verbs	5303	600	543	16	14	61
		Adj	5275	532	463	7	2	80
	1911	Nouns	6109	549	520	35	11	100
		Verbs	1761	147	142	6	6	36
		Adj	2393	205	191	5	4	57
4	1987	Nouns	9767	384	378	11	2	60
		Verbs	6068	523	496	11	9	49
		Adj	5926	451	404	6	6	55
	1911	Nouns	6652	417	395	20	5	76
		Verbs	1898	106	105	0	0	21
		Adj	2571	139	129	1	0	35
5	1987	Nouns	10210	330	324	12	2	49
		Verbs	6689	464	422	6	3	39
		Adj	6509	424	382	3	1	38
	1911	Nouns	7026	295	288	22	10	54
		Verbs	1979	76	74	0	0	14
		Adj	2710	119	115	1	0	22

Table 13: Random words added after one pass

Year	POS	Matches	Total Words	Unique Words	Derived Words	New Words	Heads Affected
1987	Nouns	6755	6189	5007	3923	3593	306
	Verbs	2870	2238	1366	734	715	186
	Adj	3053	2631	1670	1547	1488	278
1911	Nouns	3888	3718	3203	2736	2554	379
	Verbs	1069	946	759	468	465	195
	Adj	1430	1349	1051	952	926	276

Table 14: New Paragraphs, SGs and words in the updated versions of *Roget's Thesaurus*

Resource	New Paragraphs	New SGs	New Words
1911X1	633	1442	2209
1911X5	1851	3864	5566
1911R	1477	3803	6018
1987X1	653	1356	3261
1987X5	2063	4466	9601
1987R	1672	3731	11058

5.1 *Methods considered*

The first evaluation method would test how well people can identify newly added words. Given a set of Paragraphs from *Roget's Thesaurus*, the annotator would be asked to identify which words she thought were added automatically and which were originally in the *Thesaurus*. The percentage of times the annotator correctly identifies newly added words can be used to evaluate the additions. If a word already in the *Thesaurus* were as likely to be picked as one newly added, then the additions would be indistinguishable – an ideal outcome. We could also perform a "placebo test": the annotator gets a Paragraph where no words have been added, and decides whether to remove any words at all. A drawback is that the annotator may be more likely to select words whose meaning she does not know, especially in the 1911 *Thesaurus*, where there are many outdated words. Even the 1987 version has many words infrequently used today.

The second method of manual evaluation we considered was to ask the annotator to assign a new word to the correct location in the *Thesaurus*. A weighted edit-distance score could then tell how many steps the system's placement is from that location. We would also mea-

Score	*Roget's* Paragraph
(word fits in this SG)	*Head 25: Agreement, noun* fitness, aptness; relevancy; pertinence, pertinencey; sortance; case in point; **aptitude, coaptation, propriety, applicability, admissibility, commensurability,** ***<u>compatibility</u>*****;** cognation.

Figure 3: Example of the annotator task for adding a word to a Paragraph

sure how often the annotator needed to create a new Paragraph or SG for the word, and how many SGs and Paragraphs were automatically created but should not have been. Such a method would be labour-intensive: the annotator would need to read an entire Head before deciding how far a word is from its correct location. Larger Heads, where most new words are added, could contain thousands of words. Identifying whether there is an SG more appropriate for a given word could also take a fair bit of effort. It might not be feasible to annotate enough data to perform a meaningful evaluation.

The strategy we finally adopted combines elements of the two preceding methods. The first step of this evaluation exercise is to decide whether new words added to an existing SG or a new SG in an existing Paragraph are in the correct location. The annotator is given the name of the Head, the part of speech and the text of the Paragraph where the word has been added. The new term is specially highlighted, and other terms in its SG are in bold. The annotator is asked to decide whether the new word is in the correct SG, wrong SG but correct Paragraph, wrong Paragraph but correct Head, or incorrect Head. Figure 3 shows a sample question.

The second evaluation step determines whether a word added to a new Paragraph is in the correct Head. As context, we provide the first word in every Paragraph in the same POS. It is too onerous to determine precisely in which SG or Paragraph a new word would belong, because some POSs are very large. Instead, we only ask whether the word is in the correct Head. A sample question appears in Figure 4.

Score	*Roget's* Paragraph
	Head 25: Agreement, noun
(closely related)	agreement.. / conformity.. / fitness.. / adaption.. / **consent;**

Figure 4: Example of the annotator task for adding a word to a POS

We manually evaluated only the additions to the 1911 *Roget's Thesaurus*. As Paragraph size, we allowed at most 250 characters, thus limiting the number of words the annotators had to look at. The evaluation was completed by the first author and four volunteers. We chose enough samples to guarantee a 5% confidence interval at a 95% confidence level.[12] We also included a high baseline and a low baseline: words already present in the *Thesaurus*[13] and words randomly added to it. There are enough samples from the baselines to guarantee a 5% confidence interval at a 95% confidence level if the samples from all three parts of speech are combined, though individually the confidence interval exceeds 5%.

Every new word in 1911X1 appears in 1911X5,[14] so a percentage of the samples needed to evaluate 1911X5 can be selected from the samples used to evaluate 1911X1. We thus must evaluate only a selection of the words from 1911X5 not present in 1911X1. We randomly selected words from the sample set for 1911X1 to make up the rest of the samples for the 1911X5 evaluation.

Random selection was made from each annotator's dataset: 40 tests for adding words to existing Paragraphs and 40 tests for adding words to new Paragraphs. These data points were added to each annotator's test sets so that there would be an overlap of 200 samples for each experiment, on which to calculate inter-annotator agreement. The positive examples are words already present in *Roget's Thesaurus*. The negative examples are words randomly placed in the *Thesaurus*.

---

[12] `http://www.macorr.com/sample-size-calculator.htm`

[13] They are referred to as "pre-existing" in Tables 15–16, in Figures 5–6 and in the discussion in Section 5.2

[14] We remind the reader that X1 and X5 denote updating with one pass and five passes respectively.

5.2 *Manual annotation results*

Tables 15 and 16 show the combined manual annotation results for new words added to existing Paragraphs and for new Paragraphs. A number of interesting observations can be taken from Table 15. The results are summarised in Figure 5. In the case of pre-existing examples, around 60% of the time the annotators could correctly determine when a word belonged in the SG in which it was found. The annotators agreed on the correct Head approximately 80–90% of the time. One reason why annotators might believe the words belonged in a different grouping was that many of the words were difficult to understand. A high number of words which the annotators could not label fell into the pre-existing category. For the randomly assigned words, 70–80% of the time the annotators correctly stated that those words did not belong in that Head. For nouns there were numerous cases when the annotators could not answer. It would appear that the meaning of words pre-existing in the *Thesaurus*, and of those randomly added, is harder to determine than the meaning of automatically added words.

We now turn to the quality of additions. The distribution of 1911X1 scores in Table 15 is very close to that of the distribution for words pre-existing in *Roget's Thesaurus*. This suggests that after one pass the added words are nearly indistinguishable from those already in the *Thesaurus*. This is very good news: it confirms that our process of updating the lexicon has succeeded. The distribution of 1911X5 scores suggests that those additions were less reliable. The scores are worse than for 1911X1, but still much closer to the pre-existing baseline than the random baseline. Multiple passes increase the error, but not by much.

The results are a bit different when it comes to inserting words into new Paragraphs. These results are summarised in Figure 6. Once again the high and low baselines appeared to be fairly easy for the annotators, who usually got around 80% of the questions right. Also, a solid majority of the unknown words appeared in these two groups. The additions to 1911X1 showed high scores, too, comparable to the high baseline, sometimes even exceeding it slightly. It may be that for this baseline the annotators were unaware of the sense of some words, so they mistakenly labelled those words as incorrect.

Table 15: Manual evaluation results for words added to previously existing Paragraphs

Task	POS	Correct SG	Correct Para	Correct Head	Wrong Head	N/A
Pre-existing Words	Noun	117 (*.600*)	20 (*.103*)	22 (*.113*)	21 (*.108*)	15 (*.077*)
	Verb	59 (*.562*)	14 (*.133*)	10 (*.095*)	16 (*.152*)	6 (*.057*)
	Adj.	55 (*.611*)	16 (*.178*)	6 (*.067*)	7 (*.078*)	6 (*.067*)
Random Words	Noun	6 (*.031*)	2 (*.010*)	20 (*.103*)	144 (*.738*)	23 (*.118*)
	Verb	9 (*.086*)	2 (*.019*)	18 (*.171*)	73 (*.695*)	3 (*.029*)
	Adj.	3 (*.033*)	4 (*.044*)	8 (*.089*)	71 (*.789*)	4 (*.044*)
1911X1	Noun	159 (*.624*)	52 (*.204*)	22 (*.086*)	19 (*.075*)	3 (*.012*)
	Verb	92 (*.511*)	37 (*.206*)	24 (*.133*)	24 (*.133*)	3 (*.017*)
	Adj.	135 (*.628*)	44 (*.205*)	17 (*.079*)	17 (*.079*)	2 (*.009*)
1911X5	Noun	181 (*.576*)	59 (*.188*)	44 (*.140*)	25 (*.080*)	5 (*.016*)
	Verb	107 (*.412*)	45 (*.173*)	53 (*.204*)	52 (*.200*)	3 (*.012*)
	Adj.	147 (*.507*)	52 (*.179*)	32 (*.110*)	56 (*.193*)	3 (*.010*)

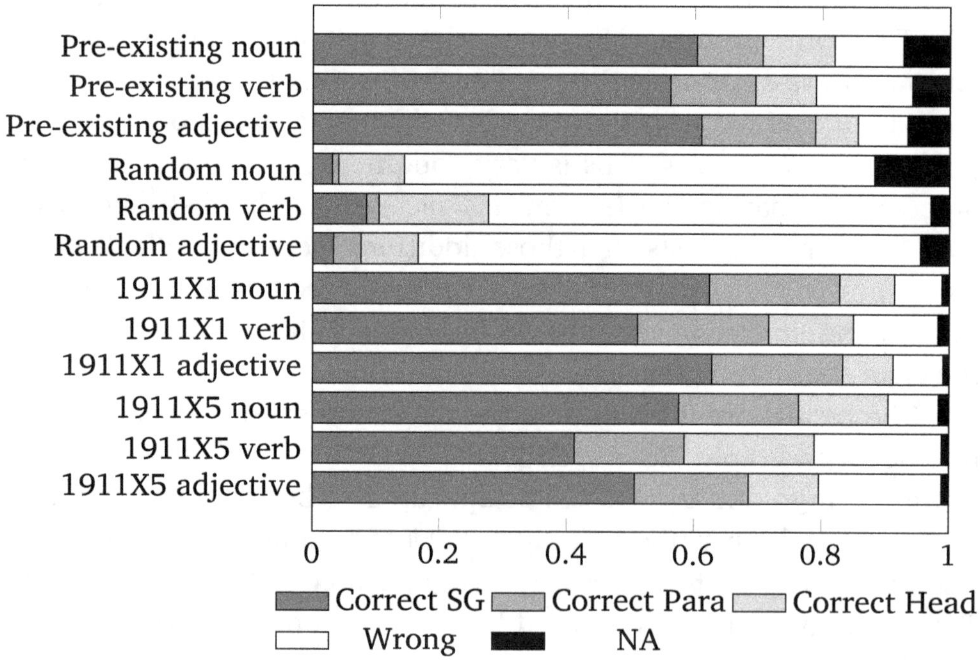

Figure 5: Evaluation on words added to previously existing Paragraphs in the 1911 *Roget's Thesaurus*

Table 16: Manual evaluation results for words added to new Paragraphs

Task	POS	Correct Head	Wrong Head	N/A
Pre-existing Words	Noun	158 (*.810)*	33 (*.169)*	4 (*.021)*
	Verb	87 (*.829)*	17 (*.162)*	1 (*.010)*
	Adj	75 (*.833)*	14 (*.156)*	1 (*.011)*
Random Words	Noun	18 (*.092)*	151 (*.774)*	26 (*.133)*
	Verb	17 (*.162)*	83 (*.790)*	5 (*.048)*
	Adj	13 (*.144)*	74 (*.822)*	3 (*.033)*
1911X1	Noun	189 (*.859)*	27 (*.123)*	4 (*.018)*
	Verb	50 (*.833)*	10 (*.167)*	0 (*.000)*
	Adj	48 (*.873)*	7 (*.127)*	0 (*.000)*
1911X5	Noun	207 (*.674)*	94 (*.306)*	6 (*.020)*
	Verb	64 (*.533)*	55 (*.458)*	1 (*.008)*
	Adj	61 (*.616)*	37 (*.374)*	1 (*.010)*

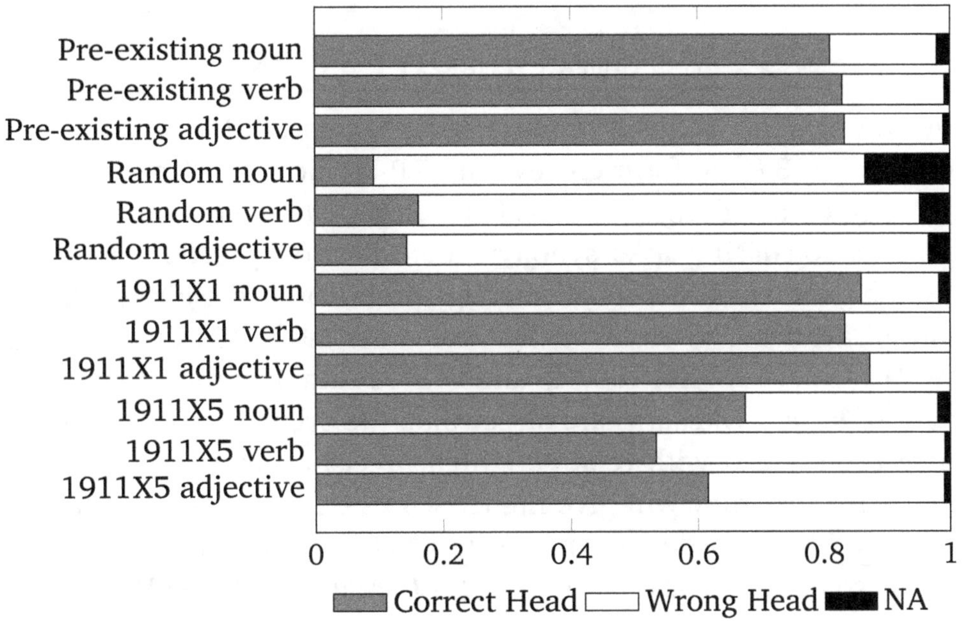

Figure 6: Evaluation on words added to new Paragraphs in the 1911 *Roget's Thesaurus*

The 1911X5 results – multi-pass update – clearly fall a fair distance from the scores for 1911X1. It would appear that multiple passes introduce considerable error into the *Thesaurus*, when words are placed into new Paragraphs. This is in stark contrast to the result of adding words to existing Paragraphs, when the drop in scores between 1911X1 and 1911X5 was relatively small.

5.3 *Inter-annotator agreement*

Each annotator was given 200 examples which reoccurred between the annotations. Inter-annotator agreement was measured on these overlaps, using Krippendorff's α (Krippendorff 2004), a measure designed to work with various kinds of data, including nominal, ordinal and interval annotations. We used ordinal in our experiments. The value of α was calculated for adding words both to existing Paragraphs and to new Paragraphs. When adding words to an existing Paragraph, we obtained a score of $\alpha = 0.340$; when adding words to new Paragraphs, the score was $\alpha = 0.358$. Such scores are often considered a "fair" amount of agreement (Landis and Koch 1977).

6 AUTOMATIC EVALUATION

We now examine how the various versions of *Roget's Thesaurus*, as well as *WordNet* 3.0, perform on several NLP applications. The problems we selected are designed to evaluate *Roget's Thesaurus* on a diverse cross-section of NLP tasks: synonym identification, pseudo-word-sense disambiguation and SAT-style analogy problems. We use *WordNet* 3.0 and all available versions of the *Thesaurus*: 1911, 1911X1, 1911X5, 1911R, 1987, 1987X1, 1987X5 and 1987R. Although the updated versions of *Roget's Thesaurus* are larger than the original, and new words have been added with relatively high precision, there is no *a priori* guarantee that they will give higher scores on any NLP applications. Before we harness these resources into NLP applications, we will very briefly compare the structure of *Roget's Thesaurus* to that of *WordNet*.[15]

A major difference between *WordNet* and *Roget's Thesaurus* is that the former is built around a hypernym hierarchy of arbitrary depth. Words appear at all levels, rather than only at the bottom level, as in

[15] For a detailed presentation of *WordNet*, see (Fellbaum 1998).

Roget's Thesaurus. Words are grouped into synsets. Synsets are similar to SGs in the *Thesaurus*, but are often smaller and contain only close synonyms. Synsets are linked by a variety of explicitly named semantic relations, while in the *Thesaurus* the SGs in a Paragraph are loosely related by a variety of possible implicit relations.

6.1 *Synonym identification*

Synonym identification is a means of evaluating the quality of newly added words in *Roget's Thesaurus*. In this problem one is given a term q and seeks its best synonym s in a set of words C. The system from Jarmasz and Szpakowicz (2003b, 2004) identifies synonyms using the *Thesaurus* as the lexical resource. This method relies on a simple function which counts the number of edges in the *Thesaurus* between q and words in C. In Equation 1, 18 is the highest possible distance in the *Thesaurus*, so the closest words have the highest scores (*edgesBetween* simply counts the edges). We treat a word X as a lexeme: a set of word senses $x \in X$.

$$edgeScore(X, Y) = \max_{x \in X, y \in Y} [18 - edgesBetween(x, y)] \quad (1)$$

The best synonym is selected in two steps. First, we find a set of terms $B \subseteq C$ with the maximum relatedness between q and each word sense $x \in C$ (Equation 2).

$$B = \{x \mid \underset{x \in C}{\operatorname{argmax}}\ edgeScore(x, q)\} \quad (2)$$

Next, we take the set of terms $A \subseteq B$ where each $a \in A$ has the largest number of shortest paths between a and q (Equation 3).

$$A = \{x \mid \underset{x \in B}{\operatorname{argmax}}\ numberOfShortestPaths(x, q)\} \quad (3)$$

The correct synonym s has been selected if $s \in A$ and $|A| = 1$. Often the sets A and B will both contain one item, but if $s \in A$ and $|A| > 1$, there is a tie. If $s \notin A$, the selected synonyms are incorrect. If an n-word phrase $c \in C$ is found, its words $c_1, c_2 ..., c_n$ are considered in turn; the c_i closest to q is chosen to represent c. A sought word can be of any part of speech, though only some *WordNet*-based methods allow for adjectives or adverbs, and none can measure distance between different parts of speech. In these problems, we do not consider a word and its morphological variant to be the same.

We generated synonym selection problems specifically for words newly added to *Roget's Thesaurus*. We took all words which appeared either in 1987X5 or in 1911X5, but were not present in the original 1987 or 1911 versions, and used them as query words q for the new problems. We then found in *WordNet* synsets which contain at least one of q's synonyms found in the original (not updated) version of the *Thesaurus*. We completed the problem by finding in the original *Thesaurus* three detractors from q's co-hyponym synsets. This was done for nouns and for verbs, but not for adjectives, for which *WordNet* does not have a strong hypernym hierarchy.

Four different versions of this problem were generated for the 1911 and 1987 *Roget's Thesauri* using nouns and verbs. The linking structure for adjectives in *WordNet* precludes the creation of a data set in this manner. We present the final scores as precision and recall. The precision excludes questions where q is not in *Roget's Thesaurus*, and recall is the score over the entire data set. Precision is thus the proportion of correct guesses out of the questions attempted, while recall is the proportion of correct guesses out of the maximum number of attempted questions. This method of evaluating such work was proposed by Turney (2006).

Table 17 shows the results for nouns and verbs added to both the 1987 and the 1911 versions of *Roget's Thesaurus*. The results are quite similar for all four data sets. Obviously, a precision and recall of 0 is attained for the original versions of the *Thesaurus*. The randomly updated versions did poorly as well. Versions updated after one pass had recall between 18% and 26%, while the versions updated in 5 passes had 40% or more. The random baseline is 25% if all of the questions can be answered. The thesauri updated in 5 passes significantly beat this baseline.[16] The thesauri updated in one pass tended not to show statistically significant improvement, though many problems were unsolvable (q was absent from 1911X1 or 1987X1).

The recall improvement for *Roget's Thesaurus* updated in 5 passes was significantly better (at $p < 0.05$) than for the *Thesaurus* updated in one pass. In turn, the *Thesaurus* updated in one pass was significantly better than the original *Thesaurus* (again at $p < 0.05$). The exception was the 1911 verb data set, for which the improvement could only

[16] Significance was established with Student's T-test with $p < 0.05$.

Table 17: Evaluation of identifying synonyms from *WordNet*

	Resource	Correct	Wrong	Ties	N/A	Precision	Recall
	1911	0	98	0	98	0	0
1911	1911X1	18	70	10	44	40.13	22.11
Nouns	1911X5	30	45	23	0	39.63	39.63
	1911R	3	93	2	88	39.98	4.08
	1911	0	27	0	27	0	0
1911	1911X1	6	20	1	13	46.42	24.07
Verbs	1911X5	11	14	2	0	44.44	44.44
	1911R	0	27	0	26	0	0
	1987	0	57	0	57	0	0
1987	1987X1	11	38	8	18	38.03	26.02
Nouns	1987X5	18	29	10	0	39.77	39.77
	1987R	0	56	1	52	10.03	0.88
	1987	0	36	0	36	0	0
1987	1987X1	5	27	4	20	41.67	18.52
Verbs	1987X5	12	15	9	0	44.91	44.91
	1987R	1	35	0	29	14.29	2.78

be measured as significant at $p < 0.065$. This is largely because the dataset was fairly small. Another observation is that the randomly updated *Thesaurus* only once had a significant improvement over the original *Thesaurus,* in the case of the 1911 noun data set.

These results suggest that the words newly added to *Roget's Thesaurus* are close to the correct location. The newly added words and their synonyms were closer than the newly added words and their co-hyponyms. Generally the precision measure showed words added to the 1911X1 and 1987X1 thesauri to be approximately as accurate as, if not slightly more accurate than, those added in passes 2–5. The randomly updated *Thesaurus* did not perform as well, usually falling below the 25% baseline on the precision measure. The results for nouns added to the 1911 *Thesaurus* are a noticeable exception. In the other datasets at most one question was answered correctly by the randomly updated *Thesaurus,* but in this case there were three correct answers. It should be noted, however, that the evaluated sample was very small, so this is likely to have been a coincidence.

6.2 *Pseudo-word-sense disambiguation*

Pseudo-word-sense disambiguation (PWSD) is a somewhat contrived task, meant to evaluate the quality of a word-sense disambiguation (WSD) system. The set-up for this task is to take two words and merge them into a *pseudo-word.* A WSD system, then, has the goal of identifying which of the two words actually belongs in a given context in which the whole pseudo-word appears. We have had a chance to create a very large dataset for PWSD. This is an opportunity to consider *WordNet* and the versions of *Roget's Thesaurus* in PWSD, and to compare them not only for accuracy but also for runtime.

We used PWSD instead of real WSD for two main reasons. Firstly, as far as we know, there is no WSD data set annotated with *Roget's* word senses and so one would have to be built from scratch. Worse still, to compare WSD systems built using *Roget's Thesaurus* and *WordNet* we would need a dataset labeled with senses from both. Secondly, PWSD gives us a fast way of building a dataset which can be used to evaluate the WSD systems based on the *Thesaurus* and on *WordNet.*

A common variation on this task is to make triples out of a noun and two verbs, then determine which of the verbs takes the noun as its object. The aim is to create a kind of verb disambiguation system which incorporates the edge count distance between nouns. In theory, this measure can help indicate how well a system identifies contexts (verb object) in which a verb appears. That can be useful in real WSD. Others who have worked on variations of PWSD include Gale *et al.* (1992); Schütze (1998); Lee (1999); Dagan *et al.* (1999); Rooth *et al.* (1999); Clark and Weir (2002); Weeds and Weir (2005); Zhitomirsky-Geffet and Dagan (2009). The methodology we followed was similar to that of Weeds and Weir.

The data set was constructed in four steps.

1. Parse Wikipedia with *MINIPAR* (Lin 1998a).
2. Select all object relations and count the frequency of each noun–verb pair $\langle n, v\rangle$.
3. Separate the noun–verb pairs into a training set (80%) and a test set (20%).
4. For each pair $\langle n, v\rangle$ in the test set find another verb v' with the same frequency as v, such that $\langle n, v'\rangle$ appears neither in the training set nor the test set; replace $\langle n, v\rangle$ with the test triple $\langle n, v, v'\rangle$.

This creates two data sets. One is a training set of noun–verb pairs $\langle n, v \rangle$. The other is a test set made up of noun–verb–verb triples $\langle n, v, v' \rangle$. Examples of such triples are ⟨*task, assign, rock*⟩ and ⟨*data, extract, anticipate*⟩. We selected v' so that its frequency is v's frequency $\pm$ 1. We also ensured that the pair $\langle n, v' \rangle$ does not appear anywhere in the training or test data. To reduce noise and decrease the overall size of the dataset, we removed from both the test and training set all noun–verb object pairs which appeared less than five times. This produced a test set of 3327 triples and a training set of 464,303 pairs. We only used half of Wikipedia to generate this data set, the half not used in constructing the noun matrix.

We employed *edgeScore* (Equation 1) for all versions of *Roget's Thesaurus*. The methods implemented in the *WordNet::Similarity* software package (Pedersen *et al.* 2004) determine how close two words are in *WordNet*. These methods are J&C (Jiang and Conrath 1997), Res (Resnik 1995), Lin (Lin 1998a), W&P (Wu and Palmer 1994), L&C (Leacock and Chodorow 1998), H&SO (Hirst and St-Onge 1998), Path (counts edges between synsets), Lesk (Banerjee and Pedersen 2002), and finally Vector and Vector Pair (Patwardhan *et al.* 2003). The measure most similar to the *edgeScore* method is the Path measure in *WordNet*. J&C, Res, Lin, W&P, L&C and Path can only measure relatedness between nouns and verbs, because they only make use of hypernym links. H&SO uses all available *WordNet* relations in finding a path between two words. The Lesk and Vector methods use glosses and so might be just as easily implemented using a dictionary. They need not take advantage of *WordNet's* hierarchical structure.

To perform the PWSD task for each triple $\langle n, v, v' \rangle$, we found in the training corpus k nouns which were the closest to n. Every such noun m got a vote: the number of occurrences of the pair $\langle m, v \rangle$ minus the number of occurrences of $\langle m, v' \rangle$. Any value of k could potentially be used. This means comparing each noun n in the test data to every noun m in the training set if these nouns share a common verb v or v'. Such a computation is feasible in *Roget's Thesaurus*, but it takes a very long time for any *WordNet*-based measure.[17] To ensure that a fair value is

[17] We ran these experiments on an IBM ThinkCenter with a 3.4 GHz Intel Pentium 4 processor and 1.5GB 400 MHz DDR RAM.

Table 18: Pseudo-word-sense disambiguation error rates and run-time

Method	Error Rate	p-value	Change	Time in seconds
1911	0.257	–	–	58
1911X1	0.252	0.000	+1.9%	59
1911X5	0.246	0.000	+4.3%	60
1911R	0.258	0.202	−0.6%	58
1987	0.252	–	–	135
1987X1	0.250	0.152	+0.8%	135
1987X5	0.246	0.010	+2.3%	134
1987R	0.252	0.997	0.0%	134
J&C	0.253	–	–	23 208
Resnik	0.258	–	–	23 112
Lin	0.251	–	–	19 840
W&P	0.245	–	–	38 721
L&C	0.241	–	–	23 445
H&SO	0.257	–	–	2 452 188
Path	0.241	–	–	22 720
Lesk	0.255	–	–	47 625
Vector	0.263	–	–	32 753
Vct Pair	0.272	–	–	74 803

selected, we divided the test set into 30 sets. We use 29 folds to find the optimal value of k and apply it to the 30th fold.

The score for the PWSD task is typically measured as an error rate where T is the number of test cases (Equation 4).

$$Error\ rate = \frac{1}{T}\left(\#\ incorrect\ choices + \frac{\#\ ties}{2}\right) \tag{4}$$

Table 18 shows the results of this experiment. The improvement on 1911X1 and 1911X5 over the original 1911 version of the *Thesaurus* was statistically significant at $p < 0.05$, according to Student's T-test. The improvement on the updated 1987 version was not statistically significant for 1987X1 with $p \approx 0.15$, but it was significant for 1987X5. The 1911X5 version gave results comparable to the 1987 version. The *Roget's*-based methods were comparable to the best *WordNet*-based methods.

When it comes to the values of k, $k = 1$ was always found to be the optimal value on this dataset. So, the best way to perform PWSD is to select the *nearest* noun taken as the object of either v or v'.

The CPU usage was perhaps the most pronounced difference with *Roget's*-based methods, which ran in a tiny fraction of the time which *WordNet*-based methods required. H&SO took around 28 days to run, so this measure simply is not an option for large-scale semantic relatedness problems. Even Lin, the fastest *WordNet*-based method, took around 5.5 hours, over 340 times longer than than the method based on the 1911 *Thesaurus*.

For all systems, a total of 193192 word pairs must be compared. We also examined the number of necessary comparisons between word senses. If one resource contains a larger number of senses of each word it is measuring distance on, then it will necessarily have to perform many more comparisons. The method based on the 1987 *Thesaurus* required nearly 120 million comparisons. The method based on the 1911 *Thesaurus* needed 14.7 million comparisons. For the *WordNet*-based methods only 3.5 million comparisons were necessary. Clearly the implementation of *Roget's Thesaurus* has a very strong advantage when it comes to runtime.

6.3 *SAT analogies*

The last class of problems to which we applied *Roget's Thesaurus* were analogy problems in the style of Scholastic Aptitude Tests (SAT). In an SAT analogy task, one is given a *target pair* $\langle A, B\rangle$ and then from a list of possible candidates selects the pair $\langle C, D\rangle$ most similar to the target pair. Ideally, the relation between the pair $\langle A, B\rangle$ should be the same as the relation between the pair $\langle C, D\rangle$. For example:

Target pair	*word, language*
Candidates	*paint, portrait*
	poetry, rhythm
	note, music
	tale, story
	week, year

Roget's Thesaurus performs well on problems of selecting synonyms and pseudo-word-sense disambiguation, but it is not clear just

Table 19: Scores in the analogy problem solved by matching kinds of relations (P = precision, R = recall, WN = *WordNet*)

System	Correct	Ties	Incorrect	Filtered	P	R	F1
1911	14	21	39	300	0.307	0.061	0.102
1911X1	15	23	39	297	0.321	0.066	0.110
1911X5	15	27	39	293	0.330	0.072	0.118
1911R	14	21	39	300	0.307	0.061	0.102
1987	18	85	81	190	0.271	0.133	0.179
1987X1	19	85	81	189	0.273	0.135	0.181
1987X5	21	85	81	187	0.278	0.139	0.185
1987R	18	86	80	190	0.271	0.133	0.179
WN 3.0	20	4	12	338	0.600	0.058	0.105

how well it will do on tasks of identifying analogies. That is because relations in the *Thesaurus* are unlabelled. We explore two methods of solving such problems with both the *Thesaurus* and *WordNet*. The first method attempts to identify a few kinds of relations in the *Thesaurus* and then apply them to identifying analogies. The second method uses edge distance between the pairs $\langle A, B\rangle$–$\langle C, D\rangle$ and $\langle A, C\rangle$–$\langle B, D\rangle$ as a heuristic for guessing whether two word pairs contain the same relation.

The dataset contains 374 analogy problems extracted from real SAT tests and practice tests (Turney 2005). A problem contains a *target pair* $\langle A, B\rangle$ and several pairs to choose from: $test_i = \langle X_i, Y_i\rangle$, $i = 1..5$. In evaluation, we consider seven scores: correct, ties, incorrect, filtered out, precision, recall and equal-weighted F-score. We define precision and recall in the same way as in Section 6.1. In the case of an n-way tie, the correct answer counts as $1/n$ towards the precision and recall. We consider recall as the most important measure, because it evaluates each method over the entire data set.

6.3.1 Matching relations

Unlike *WordNet*, *Roget's Thesaurus* contains no explicitly labelled semantic relations, but certain implicit relations can be inferred from its structure. Near-synonyms tend to appear in the same SG. Near-antonyms usually appear in different Heads in the same Head Group. One can also infer a hierarchical relation between two words if (1) they are in the same Paragraph and one of them is in the first SG, or (2) they are in the same POS and one of them is in the first SG of the first Paragraph. So, three relations can be deduced from the *Thesaurus*. Two words can be near-synonymous, near-antonymous or hierarchically related. From *WordNet*, we allow words to be related by any of the explicit semantic relations. We also apply hypernymy/hyponymy transitively.

Using these semantic relations, the analogy problem is solved by identifying a candidate analogy which contains the same relation as the target pair. There will be no solution if no relation can be found for the target pair. This experiment is interesting in that it helps test whether narrower semantic relations in *WordNet* are more useful or less useful than the broader relations in *Roget's Thesaurus*. Table 19 shows the results; "Filtered" shows the number of pairs which were not scored because no relation could be established between the words in the target or candidate pairs.

The *WordNet*-based method has high precision, but recall is low compared to that of the *Roget's*-based versions. Interestingly, the precision and recall both increase as more words are added to the 1911 and 1987 versions of *Roget's*. We consider recall as more important in this evaluation, so it is clear that the most updated versions of *Roget's Thesaurus* outperform *WordNet* by a fair margin. Although the original 1911 version gave a lower F-score than *WordNet*, all other versions performed better. The existence of very specific semantic relations in *WordNet* did give it an edge in precision, but *WordNet* was only able to answer a few questions. This suggests that the relations between pairs in analogy tests are not only of the type encountered in *WordNet*. While the broader relations identified in the *Thesaurus* appear to be less reliable and give lower precision, the recall is much higher.

6.3.2 Edge distance

The second method of solving analogy problems uses edge distance between words as a heuristic. Analogy problems have been solved in this way using Equation 5 proposed by Turney (2006).

$$score(\langle A, B\rangle : \langle X_i, Y_i\rangle) = \frac{1}{2}\left(sim_a(A, X_i) + sim_a(B, Y_i)\right) \tag{5}$$

The highest-scoring pair $\langle X_i, Y_i\rangle$ is guessed as the correct analogy. This method assumes that A and X_i should be closely related and so should B and Y_i. An illustrative example is ⟨*carpenter, wood*⟩ and ⟨*mason, stone*⟩.

In Equation 5, sim_a is the attributional similarity. We replaced it with an edge distance measure r, either *edgeScore* (Equation 1) or one of the measures built on *WordNet*. Because *edgeScore* only returns even numbers between 0 and 18, it tends to give many ties. We used a formula with a tie breaker based on the edge distance between A and B and between X_i and Y_i:[18]

$$score(\langle A,B\rangle,\langle X_i,Y_i\rangle) = r(A,X_i) + r(B,Y_i) + \frac{1}{|r(A,B) - r(X_i,Y_i)| + 1} \tag{6}$$

The last term of the sum in Equation 6 acts as a tie-breaker which favours candidates ⟨X_i, Y_i⟩ with an edge distance similar to the target ⟨A, B⟩. We include another constraint: A and X_i must be in the same part of speech, and so do B and Y_i. Only one sense of each of A, B, X_i and Y_i can be used in the calculation of Equation 6. For example, the same sense of A is used when calculating $r(A, X_i)$ and $r(A, B)$.

We applied Equation 6 to the 374 analogy problems using all versions of *Roget's Thesaurus* and the *WordNet*-based edge distance measures. The results are shown in Table 20. The "Filtered" column shows how many SAT problems could not be solved because at least one of the words needed was absent in either the *Thesaurus* or *WordNet*. Unfortunately, expanding *Roget's Thesaurus* did not reduce the number of filtered results. That said, both precision and recall increased when more words were added to the *Thesaurus*. Overall, we found that in absolute numbers the updated 1987X5 *Roget's Thesaurus* performed better than any other resource examined. Even the updated versions of the 1911 *Thesaurus* performed on par with the best *WordNet*-based systems. We must note, however, that none of the improvements of the 1987X5-based method over any given *WordNet* method are statistically significant.

---

[18] We owe this formula to a personal communication with Dr. Vivi Nastase. It was also used in (Kennedy and Szpakowicz 2007)

Table 20: Scores in the analogy problem solved using semantic distance functions (P = precision, R = recall)

System	Correct	Ties	Misses	Filtered	P	R	F1
1911	98	11	214	51	0.319	0.276	0.296
1911X1	98	17	208	51	0.329	0.284	0.305
1911X5	97	20	206	51	0.330	0.285	0.306
1911R	97	12	218	47	0.313	0.274	0.292
1987	101	35	232	6	0.318	0.313	0.316
1987X1	102	38	228	6	0.324	0.319	0.322
1987X5	102	39	227	6	0.325	0.320	0.323
1987R	103	34	233	4	0.320	0.316	0.318
Path	85	5	166	118	0.342	0.234	0.278
J&C	80	0	176	118	0.312	0.214	0.254
Resnik	91	16	149	118	0.385	0.263	0.313
Lin	82	3	171	118	0.325	0.222	0.264
W&P	90	1	165	118	0.354	0.242	0.287
L&C	91	4	161	118	0.363	0.249	0.295
H&SO	96	39	212	27	0.321	0.298	0.309
Lesk	113	0	234	27	0.326	0.302	0.313
Vector	113	0	234	27	0.326	0.302	0.313
Vector Pair	106	0	241	27	0.305	0.283	0.294

7 CONCLUSION

7.1 *Summary*

We have described a method of automatically updating *Roget's Thesaurus* with new words. The process has two main steps: lists of semantically related words are generated, and next those lists are used to find a place for a new word in the *Thesaurus*. We have enhanced both steps by leveraging the structure of *Roget's Thesaurus*.

When creating lists of related words, we have evaluated a technique for measuring semantic relatedness which enhances distributional methods using lists of known synonyms. We have shown this to have a statistically significant effect on the quality of measures of semantic relatedness.

In the second step, the actual addition of new words to *Roget's Thesaurus*, we generated a list of neighbouring words and used them as anchors to identify where in the *Thesaurus* to place a new word. This process benefits from tuning on the actual *Thesaurus*. The task here is to find words which will be good anchors for determining where to place a new term. We experimented with three methods of finding anchors, using the rank, the relatedness score and a relative relatedness score. We found that rank worked best. The process of adding new words to *Roget's Thesaurus* is hierarchical. First the Part of Speech in the *Thesaurus* is identified, then the Paragraph, then the Semicolon Group. A new Paragraph or Semicolon Group can be created if needed.

A manual evaluation of our methodology found that added words were almost indistinguishable from words already present in the *Thesaurus*. Even after multiple passes the words seemed to find fairly accurate placing in an existing Paragraph. When adding words to a new Paragraph, after one pass the words were highly accurate, but the accuracy fell after additional passes. In total, some 5500 words were added to the 1911 version and some 9600 words to the 1987 version.

We also performed an application-based evaluation to compare the original and updated versions of *Roget's Thesaurus* and, when possible, *WordNet*. The tasks were synonym identification, pseudo-word-sense disambiguation and SAT-style analogy problems. On all tasks the updates to the *Thesaurus* showed a noticeable improvement. In our evaluations, *Roget's Thesaurus* also performed as well as, or better than, *WordNet*. In particular, it could perform calculations many times faster than the *WordNet::Similarity* software package (Pedersen *et al.* 2004).

Most of our experiments show that the 1987 version of *Roget's Thesaurus* outperforms the 1911 version. There are two reasons. First, for our measure of semantic relatedness, the evaluation was conducted on words in the same *Roget's grouping* from the 1987 version. Since the structure of the *Thesaurus* is used to train our MSR, it is natural that scores are higher when training and evaluation are done on the same version. The second reason is simply that the 1987 version is larger. When adding new words to *Roget's Thesaurus*, a larger thesaurus gives more potential anchor words to help find an appropriate placement for a new word. For our task-based evaluation, the applications we chose will naturally benefit from a larger thesaurus as well.

7.2 *Future work*

The supervised measure of semantic relatedness provides an interesting method of re-weighting contexts. Recent work has shown that similar techniques make it possible to find a weighted mapping between the context space in two different languages (Kennedy and Hirst 2012). Methods of this kind could be used to emphasise similarities between words based on sentiment, emotion or formality, rather than simply on synonymy. Using emotionally related words as a source of training data could enable the creation of a measure of semantic relatedness which favours words of the same emotional class over other, nearer, synonyms conveying a different emotion.

Perhaps other more complex methods of adding new words to *Roget's Thesaurus* can be considered. For example, mixing rank and score (maybe using machine learning) might lead to an even more accurate method. Other methods of identifying where in the *Thesaurus* to place a word could also be considered. In particular, Pantel's (2005) method could potentially be modified to work for *Roget's Thesaurus*.

Our method only adds individual words to *Roget's Thesaurus*. It should be possible to expand it into adding multi-word phrases. Many dependency parsers can identify noun phrases and so can be used to create distributional vectors for such phrases. Adding multi-word phrases to verb or adjective *Roget's groupings* may be possible by identifying n-grams which are frequent in a text. Two problems arise. One is determining whether high frequency alone is a good enough reason to add a multi-word phrase. The second is how to represent such multi-word phrases. It could be possible to represent them by vectors of word–relation pairs for syntactically related words in the same sentence, but outside of the phrase being considered. The meaning of a phrase may also be deduced by composing the distributional vectors of its individual words. There is ongoing, and very interesting, research in this area (Mitchell and Lapata 2008; Turney 2012).

A problem which we have not tackled yet is that of adding cross-references: if the same word appears in two places in *Roget's Thesaurus*, then often a cross-reference links the two occurrences. Making use of these cross-references could be a considerable undertaking, because it requires, amongst other things, some form of effective word-sense disambiguation.

The manual annotation has only been conducted on the 1911 version of *Roget's Thesaurus*, because it is the only version which can be released to the public, and because the annotation experiment has been very time-consuming. In the interest of completeness, the updates to the 1987 version could be evaluated similarly. We expect that those updates should actually be more accurate, because the 1911 version is both older and smaller. This would be in line with the automatic evaluation from Section 4, but it is yet to be confirmed manually.

It should be possible to adapt our methods of placing words in *Roget's Thesaurus* to work for *WordNet*. Instead of identifying words in the same POS, then Paragraph, then SG, word groupings could be created from *WordNet*'s hypernym hierarchy. We envisage two ways of doing this. The first would be to pick a relatively high level within the hierarchy and classify each word into one or more of the synsets at that level, much as we did with the POS level. A synset could be represented by all the words in the transitive closure of its hyponym synsets. Next, the word would be propagated down the hierarchy – as we do with Paragraphs and SGs – until it can go no further, and then added to the synset there.

This method could not (yet) be applied to adjectives, and would only take one kind of relation into account when placing a word in *WordNet*. Another option is to create a neighbourhood of words for each synset, based on a variety of relations. A word could then be placed in a larger grouping of multiple synsets before the particular synset it belongs to is determined. If no synset can be picked, then a new synset can be created with some sort of ambiguous link joining it to the other synsets in its neighbourhood. A hybrid of these two methods is also possible. Our first method could be enhanced by using not only a synset's terms, but also its close neighbours. This would expand the set of anchor words at the cost of introducing words common to multiple synsets.

It should also be possible to port our method to thesauri and wordnets in other languages. The main problem might be our method's reliance on a dependency parser. Such parsers are not available yet for many languages. Nonetheless, it could be possible to replicate much of the relevant functionality of a dependency parser using a part-of-speech tagger – and taggers are quite widely available. For example, one may assume that a noun can only be modified by other nouns or adjectives in its vicinity, and so only use those terms in constructing a distributional vector.

Another direction which this kind of research could take would be to test the methods on adding words in a particular domain. Most of the words in *Roget's Thesaurus* are from everyday English, as opposed to, say, medical terms. The nearest synonyms of such technical words will be other technical words. This could make it more difficult to actually add domain-specific terms to *Roget's Thesaurus*. That said, the trainable measure of semantic relatedness from Kennedy and Szpakowicz (2011, 2012) could be built using words of a particular domain. If domain-specific and everyday words could be grouped as near-synonyms, then an MSR could be trained for adding domain-specific terms to *Roget's Thesaurus*.

Similar to adding domain-specific words is the challenge of adding brand new coinage to *Roget's Thesaurus*. Very new words may not have close synonyms in the *Thesaurus*, which is why we add words in multiple passes. It would be interesting to investigate how many passes are required before, say, the word "iPhone" is added to the *Thesaurus*. Closely related phrases like "mobile phone" or "smart phone" would need to already be present. Other terms, such as "cellular network", "texting" or "Apple", could also be useful in choosing where to place a word like "iPhone".

Finally, note that we have only applied *Roget's Thesaurus* to three NLP tasks, to demonstrate value in both its structure and language coverage. Many other applications of the *Thesaurus* are possible. Some obvious ones include real word-sense disambiguation and lexical substitution. *Roget's Thesaurus* has already been used in the construction of lexical chains (Morris and Hirst 1991; Jarmasz and Szpakowicz 2003a). Lexical chains might be applied to summarisation or text segmentation. Since the *Thesaurus* contains a large number of opposing concepts, it may be possible to apply it to lexical entailment as well.

NLP researchers are always on the hunt for newer and larger data sets on which to train and evaluate their experiments. Many of these experiments will require measuring semantic distance among huge sets of words. In the coming years, the trend towards analyzing big data will drive the need for fast semantic relatedness calculation. *Roget's Thesaurus* is uniquely suited for that.

REFERENCES

Satanjeev BANERJEE and Ted PEDERSEN (2002), An Adapted Lesk Algorithm for Word Sense Disambiguation Using WordNet, in *Proceedings of the 3rd International Conference on Intelligent Text Processing and Computational Linguistics – CICLing 2002*, pp. 136–145, Mexico City, Mexico.

Patrick J. CASSIDY (2000), An Investigation of the Semantic Relations in the Roget's Thesaurus: Preliminary Results, in *Proceedings of the Conference on Intelligent Text Processing and Computational Linguistics – CICLing 2000*, pp. 181–204, Mexico City, Mexico.

Stephen CLARK and David WEIR (2002), Class-based Probability Estimation Using a Semantic Hierarchy, *Computational Linguistics*, 28(2):187–206.

Carolyn J. CROUCH (1988), A Cluster-based Approach to Thesaurus Construction, in *Proceedings of the 11th Annual International ACM SIGIR Conference on Research and Development in Information Retrieval – SIGIR 1988*, pp. 309–320, Grenoble, France.

Carolyn J. CROUCH and Bokyung YANG (1992), Experiments in Automatic Statistical Thesaurus Construction, in *Proceedings of the 15th Annual International ACM SIGIR Conference on Research and Development in Information Retrieval – SIGIR 1992*, pp. 77–88, Copenhagen, Denmark.

DAGAN, IDO, Lillian LEE, and Fernando PEREIRA (1999), Similarity-based Models of Word Co-occurrence Probabilities, *Machine Learning*, 34(1-3):43–69.

Andrea ESULI and Fabrizio SEBASTIANI (2006), SentiWordNet: A Publicly Available Lexical Resource for Opinion Mining, in *Proceedings of the 5th Conference on Language Resources and Evaluation – LREC 2006*, pp. 417–422, Genoa, Italy.

Christiane FELLBAUM, editor (1998), *WordNet: an Electronic Lexical Database*, MIT Press, Cambridge, MA, USA.

William A. GALE, Kenneth W. CHURCH, and David YAROWSKY (1992), A Method for Disambiguating Word Senses in a Large Corpus, *Computers and the Humanities*, 26:415–439.

Roxana GIRJU, Adriana BADULESCU, and Dan MOLDOVAN (2003), Learning Semantic Constraints for the Automatic Discovery of Part–Whole Relations, in *Proceedings of the 2003 Human Language Technology Conference of the North American Chapter of the Association for Computational Linguistics – HLT-NAACL 2003*, pp. 1–8, Edmonton, Canada.

Roxana GIRJU, Adriana BADULESCU, and Dan MOLDOVAN (2006), Automatic Discovery of Part–Whole Relations, *Computational Linguistics*, 32(1):83–136.

Marti A. HEARST (1992), Automatic Acquisition of Hyponyms from Large Text Corpora, in *Proceedings of the 14th International Conference on Computational Linguistics – COLING 1992*, pp. 539–545, Nantes, France.

Graeme HIRST and David ST-ONGE (1998), Lexical Chains as Representation of Context for the Detection and Correction of Malapropisms, in Christiane FELLBAUM, editor, *WordNet: An Electronic Lexical Database*, pp. 305–322, MIT Press, Cambridge, MA, USA.

Mario JARMASZ (2003), *Roget's Thesaurus as a Lexical Resource for Natural Language Processing*, Master's thesis, University of Ottawa, Canada.

Mario JARMASZ and Stan SZPAKOWICZ (2003a), Not as Easy As It Seems: Automating the Construction of Lexical Chains Using Roget's Thesaurus, in *16th Conference of the Canadian Society for Computational Studies of Intelligence – AI 2003, Halifax, Canada*, number 2671 in Lecture Notes in Computer Science, pp. 544–549, Springer, Berlin/Heidelberg, Germany.

Mario JARMASZ and Stan SZPAKOWICZ (2003b), Roget's Thesaurus and Semantic Similarity, in *Proceedings of the Conference on Recent Advances in Natural Language Processing – RANLP 2003*, pp. 212–219, Borovets, Bulgaria.

Mario JARMASZ and Stan SZPAKOWICZ (2004), Roget's Thesaurus and Semantic Similarity, in N. NICOLOV, K. BONTCHEVA, G. ANGELOVA, and R. MITKOV, editors, *Recent Advances in Natural Language Processing III: Selected Papers from RANLP 2003*, volume 260 of *Current Issues in Linguistic Theory*, pp. 111–120, John Benjamins, Amsterdam, The Netherlands/Philadelphia, PA, USA.

Jay J. JIANG and David W. CONRATH (1997), Semantic Similarity Based on Corpus Statistics and Lexical Taxonomy, in *Proceedings of the 10th International Conference on Research on Computational Linguistics – ROCLING X*, pp. 19–33, Taipei, Taiwan.

Joshua C. KENDALL (2008), *The Man Who Made Lists : Love, Death, Madness, and the Creation of Roget's Thesaurus*, G.P.Putnam's Sons, New York, NY, USA.

Alistair KENNEDY and Graeme HIRST (2012), Measuring Semantic Relatedness Across Languages, in *xLiTe: Cross-Lingual Technologies, workshop collocated with the Conference on Neural Information Processing Systems – NIPS 2012*, Lake Tahoe, NV, USA.

Alistair KENNEDY and Stan SZPAKOWICZ (2007), Disambiguating Hypernym Relations for Roget's Thesaurus, in *Proceedings of the 10th International Conference on Text, Speech and Dialogue – TSD 2007, Pilsen, Czech Republic*, number 4629 in Lecture Notes in Artificial Intelligence, pp. 66–75, Springer, Berlin/Heidelberg, Germany.

Alistair KENNEDY and Stan SZPAKOWICZ (2011), A Supervised Method of Feature Weighting for Measuring Semantic Relatedness, in *Proceedings of the Canadian Conference on Artificial Intelligence – AI 2011, St. John's, Canada*, number 6657 in Lecture Notes in Artificial Intelligence, pp. 222–233, Springer, Berlin/Heidelberg, Germany.

Alistair KENNEDY and Stan SZPAKOWICZ (2012), Supervised Distributional Semantic Relatedness, in *Proceedings of the 15th International Conference on Text, Speech and Dialogue – TSD 2012, Brno, Czech Republic*, number 7499 in Lecture Notes in Artificial Intelligence, pp. 207–214, Springer, Berlin/Heidelberg, Germany.

Betty KIRKPATRICK, editor (1987), *Roget's Thesaurus of English Words and Phrases*, Longman, Harlow, UK.

Klaus KRIPPENDORFF (2004), *Content Analysis: An Introduction to Its Methodology*, Sage Publications Inc., Los Angeles, CA, USA, 2nd edition.

Oi Yee KWONG (1998a), Aligning WordNet with Additional Lexical Resources, in *Proceedings of the COLING/ACL Workshop on Usage of WordNet in Natural Language Processing Systems*, pp. 73–79, Montréal, Canada.

Oi Yee KWONG (1998b), Bridging the Gap Between Dictionary and Thesaurus, in *Proceedings of the 36th Annual Meeting of the Association for Computational Linguistics – ACL 1998*, pp. 1487–1489, Montréal, Canada.

Robin J. LANDIS and G. G. KOCH (1977), The Measurement of Observer Agreement for Categorical Data, *Biometrics*, 33:159–174.

Claudia LEACOCK and Martin CHODOROW (1998), Combining Local Context and WordNet Sense Similarity for Word Sense Disambiguation, in Christiane FELLBAUM, editor, *WordNet: An Electronic Lexical Database*, pp. 265–284, MIT Press, Cambridge, MA, USA.

Lillian LEE (1999), Measures of Distributional Similarity, in *Proceedings of the 37th Annual Meeting of the Association for Computational Linguistics – ACL 1999*, pp. 25–32, College Park, MD, USA.

Lothar LEMNITZER, Holger WUNSCH, and Piklu GUPTA (2008), Enriching GermaNet with Verb–Noun Relations – a Case Study of Lexical Acquisition, in *Proceedings of the 6th International Conference on Language Resources and Evaluation – LREC 2008*, Marrakech, Morocco.

Dekang LIN (1998a), Automatic Retrieval and Clustering of Similar Words, in *Proceedings of the 17th International Conference on Computational Linguistics – COLING 1998*, pp. 768–774, Montréal, Canada.

Dekang LIN (1998b), Dependency-Based Evaluation of MINIPAR, in *Proceedings of the Workshop on the Evaluation of Parsing Systems at the 1st International Conference on Language Resources and Evaluation – LREC 1998*, Granada, Spain.

Bernardo MAGNINI and Gabriela CAVAGLIÁ (2000), Integrating Subject Field Codes into WordNet, in *Proceedings of the 2nd International Conference on Language Resources and Evaluation – LREC 2000*, pp. 1413–1418, Athens, Greece.

Jeff MITCHELL and Mirella LAPATA (2008), Vector-based models of semantic composition, in *Proceedings of the 46th Annual Meeting of the Association for Computational Linguistics: Human Language Technologies – ACL 2008: HLT*, pp. 236–244, Columbus, OH, USA.

Emmanuel MORIN and Christian JACQUEMIN (1999), Projecting Corpus-Based Semantic Links on a Thesaurus, in *Proceedings of the 37th Annual Meeting of the Association for Computational Linguistics – ACL 1999*, pp. 389–396, College Park, MD, USA.

Jane MORRIS and Graeme HIRST (1991), Lexical Cohesion Computed by Thesaural Relations as an Indicator of the Structure of Text, *Computational Linguistics*, 17(1):21–48.

Vivi NASTASE and Stan SZPAKOWICZ (2001), Word Sense Disambiguation in Roget's Thesaurus Using WordNet, in *Proceedings of the NAACL Workshop on WordNet and Other Lexical Resources*, pp. 12–22, Pittsburgh, PA, USA.

Patrick PANTEL (2003), *Clustering by Committee*, Ph.D. thesis, University of Alberta, Canada.

Patrick PANTEL (2005), Inducing Ontological Co-occurrence Vectors, in *Proceedings of the 43rd Annual Meeting of the Association for Computational Linguistics – ACL 2005*, pp. 125–132, Ann Arbor, MI, USA.

Siddharth PATWARDHAN, Satanjeev BANERJEE, and Ted PEDERSEN (2003), Using Measures of Semantic Relatedness for Word Sense Disambiguation, in *Proceedings of the 4th International Conference on Intelligent Text Processing and Computational Linguistics – CICLing-2003*, pp. 241–257, Mexico City, Mexico.

Ted PEDERSEN, Siddhart PATWARDHAN, and Jason MICHELIZZI (2004), Wordnet::Similarity - Measuring the Relatedness of Concepts, in *Proceedings of the 19th National Conference on Artificial Intelligence – AAAI 2004*, pp. 1024–1025, San Jose, CA, USA.

Maciej PIASECKI, Bartosz BRODA, Michał MARCIŃCZUK, and Stan SZPAKOWICZ (2009), The WordNet Weaver: Multi-criteria Voting for Semi-automatic Extension of a Wordnet, in *Proceedings of the 22nd Canadian Conference on Artificial Intelligence – AI 2009, Kelowna, Canada*, number 5549 in Lecture Notes in Artificial Intelligence, pp. 237–240, Springer, Berlin/Heidelberg, Germany.

Paul PROCTER (1978), *Longman Dictionary of Contemporary English*, Longman Group Ltd., Essex, UK.

Philip RESNIK (1995), Using Information Content to Evaluate Semantic Similarity, in *Proceedings of the 14th International Joint Conference on Artificial Intelligence – IJCAI 1995*, pp. 448–453, Montréal, Canada.

Mats ROOTH, Stefan RIEZLER, Detlef PRESCHER, Glenn CARROLL, and Franz BEIL (1999), Inducing a Semantically Annotated Lexicon via EM-based Clustering, in *Proceedings of the 37th Annual Meeting of the Association for Computational Linguistics – ACL 1999*, pp. 104–111, College Park, MD, USA.

Sara RYDIN (2002), Building a Hyponymy Lexicon with Hierarchical Structure, in *Proceedings of the ACL-02/SIGLEX Workshop on Unsupervised Lexical Acquisition – ULA 2002*, pp. 26–33, Philadelphia, PA, USA.

Benoît SAGOT and Darja FIŠER (2011), Extending wordnets by learning from multiple resources, in *Proceedings of the 5th Language and Technology Conference – LTC 2011*, pp. 526–530, Poznań, Poland.

Erik Tjong Kim SANG (2007), Extracting Hypernym Pairs from the Web, in *Proceedings of the 45th Annual Meeting of the Association for Computational Linguistics – ACL 2007 (Interactive Poster and Demonstration Sessions)*, pp. 165–168, Prague, Czech Republic.

Hinrich SCHÜTZE (1998), Automatic Word Sense Discrimination, *Computational Linguistics*, 24(1):97–123.

Keiji SHINZATO and Kentaro TORISAWA (2004), Acquiring Hyponymy Relations from Web Documents, in *Proceedings of the Human Language Technology Conference of the North American Chapter of the Association for Computational Linguistics – HLT-NAACL 2004*, pp. 73–80, Boston, MA, USA.

Rion SNOW, Daniel JURAFSKY, and Andrew Y. NG (2005), Learning Syntactic Patterns for Automatic Hypernym Discovery, in Lawrence K. SAUL, Yair WEISS, and Léon BOTTOU, editors, *Advances in Neural Information Processing Systems 17*, pp. 1297–1304, MIT Press, Cambridge, MA, USA.

Rion SNOW, Daniel JURAFSKY, and Andrew Y. NG (2006), Semantic Taxonomy Induction from Heterogenous Evidence, in *Proceedings of the 21st International Conference on Computational Linguistics and 44th Annual Meeting of the Association for Computational Linguistics – COLING/ACL 2006*, Sydney, Australia.

Ratanachai SOMBATSRISOMBOON, Yutaka MATSUO, and Mitsuru ISHIZUKA (2003), Acquisition of Hypernyms and Hyponyms from the WWW, in *Procedings of the 2nd International Workshop on Active Mining – AM 2003 (in Conjunction with the International Symposium on Methodologies for Intelligent Systems)*, pp. 7–13, Maebashi City, Japan.

Carlo STRAPPARAVA and Alessandro VALITUTTI (2004), WordNet-Affect: an Affective Extension of WordNet, in *Proceedings of the 4th International Conference on Language Resources and Evaluation – LREC 2004*, pp. 1083–1086, Lisbon, Portugal.

Hiroaki TSURUMARU, Toru HITAKA, and Sho YOSHIDA (1986), An Attempt to Automatic Thesaurus Construction from an Ordinary Japanese Language Dictionary, in *Proceedings of the 11th Conference on Computational Linguistics – COLING 1986*, pp. 445–447, Bonn, Germany.

Peter TURNEY (2005), Measuring Semantic Similarity by Latent Relational Analysis, in *Proceedings of the 19th International Joint Conference on Artificial Intelligence – IJCAI-05*, pp. 1136–1141, Edinburgh, Scotland.

Peter TURNEY (2006), Similarity of Semantic Relations, *Computational Linguistics*, 32(3):379–416.

Peter TURNEY (2012), Domain and Function: A Dual-Space Model of Semantic Relations and Compositions, *Journal of Artificial Intelligence Research*, 44:533–585.

Piek VOSSEN, editor (1998), *EuroWordNet: a Multilingual Database with Lexical Semantic Networks*, Kluwer Academic Publishers, Norwell, MA, USA.

Julie WEEDS and David WEIR (2005), Co-occurrence Retrieval: A Flexible Framework for Lexical Distributional Similarity, *Computational Linguistics*, 31(4):439–475.

Zhibiao WU and Martha PALMER (1994), Verb Semantics and Lexical Selection, in *Proceedings of the 32nd Annual Meeting of the Association for Computational Linguistics – ACL 1994*, pp. 133–138, Las Cruces, NM, USA.

Hao ZHENG, Xian WU, and Yong YU (2008), Enriching WordNet with Folksonomies, in *Proceedings of the Pacific-Asia Conference on Knowledge Discovery and Data Mining – PAKDD 2008*, number 5012 in Lecture Notes in Artificial Intelligence, pp. 1075–1080, Springer, Berlin/Heidelberg, Germany.

Maayan ZHITOMIRSKY-GEFFET and Ido DAGAN (2009), Bootstrapping distributional feature vector quality, *Computational Linguistics*, 35(3):435–461.

2

Combining logical and distributional methods in type-logical grammars

Richard Moot
LIRMM, Montpellier University, CNRS

Keywords: type-logical grammar, Lambek calculus, theorem proving

ABSTRACT

We propose a low-level way of combining distributional and logical ideas into a single formal system. This will be an instantiation of a more general system, adding weights to proof rules. These weights will not measure some sort of "confidence the proof is valid", but rather act as a way to *prefer* some proofs over others, where preference can mean "easier to process (for humans)" or "more coherent (combining words that make sense together)". The resulting system of weighted theorem proving can be implemented either as a best-first proof search strategy or as a polynomial-time approximation of proof search for NP-complete parsing problems.

1 INTRODUCTION

Type-logical grammars (and formal semantics in general) are agnostic about the meaning of atomic terms, such as those corresponding to nouns and verbs (though not about the meaning corresponding to words with logical content such as "not", "and", "all", "which"). Another way to see this is that in standard formal semantics, entailment only holds under strict identity of predicates. As a consequence, practical use of the output of a system computing such formal semantics depends to a large extent on the available world knowledge (Bos and Markert 2005), possibly stated in the form of additional axioms or meaning postulates, stating that "pub" and "bar" (in one meaning of the word) are synonyms, and that "good" and "bad" are antonyms, i.e. "bad" entails "not good" and inversely.

In contrast to formal semantics in the tradition of Montague, distributional or vector-based semantics take semantic similarity, as measured by word cooccurrences, as their basic notion. Systems using only semantic similarity are agnostic about argument structure and agnostic about the meaning of words with logical content. Given a vector of a sequence of words, it is not a priori clear how to combine these into the meaning of a phrase. In other words, vector space models are not compositional by nature, although many ways of computing vector space semantics for texts exist, and even the simplest models (adding or averaging all vectors for the words in a larger text) can perform well on a number of tasks (see Mitchell and Lapata 2010; Pham 2016, for discussion).

Whereas compositional formal semantics, unless augmented by specific lexical meanings or meaning postulates, concludes that "good" and "bad" are unrelated unary predicates, vector semantics concludes that "good" and "bad" are very similar. Other semantically similar words are "animal" and "veterinarian", and "sweater" and "warm". The absence of argument structure (who does what to whom) from the vectors makes "animal" and "veterinarian" similar: even though many sentences contain both words, these tend to be sentences where the veterinarian treats or examines the animal, or where the owner takes an animal to the veterinarian.

There appears to be some complementarity to these two approaches: formal semantics takes compositionality as its basic principle but has little to say about the meaning of individual predicates; vector semantics takes the similarity of predicates as its basic concept but then has little to say about compositionality and the words with logical content.

In this paper, we will look at a low-level way of combining distributional and logical ideas into a single formal system. This will be an instantiation of a more general system, adding weights to proof rules. These weights will not measure some sort of "confidence the proof is valid", but rather act as a way to *prefer* some proofs over others, where preference can mean "easier to process (for humans)" or "more coherent (combining words that make sense together)". The resulting system of weighted theorem proving can be implemented either as a best-first proof search strategy or as a polynomial-time approximation of proof search for NP-complete parsing problems.

2 TYPE-LOGICAL GRAMMAR AND FORMAL SEMANTICS

Definition 2.1 (Type-logical grammar) *Given a logic $\mathscr{L}$ with formulas $\mathscr{F}$, a type-logical grammar over $\mathscr{L}$ is a tuple $\langle \Sigma, Lex, goal, yield, h \rangle$, where*

1. *Σ is a set of words (the vocabulary of the language),*
2. *the lexicon* Lex, *is a function from $w \in \Sigma$ to a (non-empty) subset of $\mathscr{F}$,*
3. *goal, the set of goal formulas is a (non-empty) subset of $\mathscr{F}$,*
4. *yield is a function from antecedents of $\mathscr{L}$ to sequences of formulas,*
5. *h is a homomorphism from proofs in $\mathscr{L}$ to proofs in multiplicative intuitionistic linear logic representing their "deep structure".*

Informally, a sentence is grammatical whenever the lexicon assigns each word in the sentence a formula, and these formulas produce a derivable statement in the logic. More formally, we say a sentence $w_1, \ldots, w_n$ is *grammatical* if for all i, $w_i \in \Sigma$ (each word is in the vocabulary) and there is an $A_i \in Lex(w_i)$ (we choose, for each word, one of the formulas assigned to it by the lexicon), there is a structure Γ with $yield(\Gamma) = A_1, \ldots, A_n$, and there is a $C \in goal$ such that the statement $\Gamma \vdash C$ is a theorem of the logic $\mathscr{L}$. A sentence is *ungrammatical* otherwise.

Many authors choose the set $\{s\}$ for *goal* (that is, the only valid goal category is s, for *sentence*). However, for more elaborate grammars, we may be interested not only in declarative sentences, but also in yes-no questions, *wh* questions, imperatives, etc., and it seems reasonable to allow such sentences to have a different type of meaning from declarative sentences.

For the Lambek calculus (Lambek 1958), the logic is **L**, the yield function is the identity function (since antecedents Γ of **L** are already sequences of formulas), and h translates the Lambek calculus slashes "/" and "\" to the multiplicative linear logic implication "$\multimap$" (and the product "$\bullet$" to multiplicative conjunction "$\otimes$").

For multimodal type-logical grammars (Moortgat 1997), sequents are of the form $\Gamma \vdash C$ where the antecedent Γ is a labelled tree with unary and binary branches and with formulas as its leaves. The yield

$$\frac{A/B : M^{U \to T} \quad B : N^{U}}{A : (MN)^{T}} /E \qquad \frac{B : N^{U} \quad B\backslash A : M^{U \to T}}{A : (MN)^{T}} \backslash E$$

$$\frac{\begin{array}{c} \ldots [B : x^{U}]_i \\ \vdots \\ A : M^{T} \end{array}}{A/B : (\lambda x.M)^{U \to T}} /I_i \qquad \frac{\begin{array}{c} [B : x^{U}]_i \ldots \\ \vdots \\ A : M^{T} \end{array}}{B\backslash A : (\lambda x.M)^{U \to T}} \backslash I_i$$

Figure 1: Proof rules and corresponding lambda term operations

function is simply the left-to-right sequence of formulas occurring as its leaves (i.e. we use the standard definition of the yield of a tree).

2.1 *The Lambek calculus*

To makes this more concrete, we'll instantiate the general type-logical grammar framework to Lambek's Syntactic Calculus, **L** (Lambek 1958). Formulas of the Lambek calculus are inductively defined from a set of atomic formulas, including *np* (noun phrase), *n* (common noun), *s* (sentence) and *pp* (prepositional phrase). A formula in the Lambek calculus is:

- an atomic formula,
- if A and B are formulas, then A/B (pronounced "A over B", it looks for a B formula to its right to produce an A), $B\backslash A$ (pronounced "B under A", it looks for a B formula to its left to produce an A) are formulas.[1]

Figure 1 shows the natural deduction proof rules for the Lambek calculus (and the associated lambda term assignments).

The elimination rule for "/", labeled "$/E$" states that if we have a proof with conclusion A/B which is assigned term M (of type $U \to T$) and a proof with conclusion B which is assigned term N (of type U), then we can combine these two proofs to form a proof of A which is assigned lambda-term $(M\ N)$. The order of the premisses is important: B must occur adjacent to and to the right of A/B. The elimination rule for \ is left-right symmetric, with B occurring to the immediate left of $B\backslash A$.

[1] To keep the discussion simple, we do not present the natural deduction proof rules for the product $A \bullet B$, representing the concatenation of A and B.

The introduction rule, labeled "$/I$", states that if we have a proof of A with lambda-term M of some type T, which we have derived while using a hypothesis B, which is assigned a variable x of type U and which is the rightmost undischarged hypotheses of this proof, then we can discharge this B hypothesis to derive A/B of type $U \to T$ with term $\lambda x.M$. The discharged hypothesis is co-indexed with the rule, using an index i unique to the proof (for the Lambek calculus without product, this index is strictly speaking superfluous, since the leftmost and rightmost undischarged hypotheses are uniquely determined for each subproof). The introduction rule for $\backslash I$ is again left-right symmetric, requiring B to be the leftmost undischarged hypothesis.

We will write $A_1,\ldots,A_n \vdash C$ for a proof with undischarged hypotheses $A_1,\ldots,A_n$ (in the given order) and conclusion C.

As an example, the following Lambek calculus proof shows that "moons which Galileo discovered" is a noun n. To make the proof more readable, the lexical entries have been indicated as the conclusions of a rule *Lex* with the word occurring above it and the corresponding formula assigned by the lexicon below it (we will add the lambda terms later).

$$\dfrac{\dfrac{\text{moons}}{n}\,Lex \quad \dfrac{\dfrac{\text{which}}{(n\backslash n)/(s/np)}\,Lex \quad \dfrac{\dfrac{\dfrac{\text{Galileo}}{np}\,Lex \quad \dfrac{\dfrac{\text{discovered}}{(np\backslash s)/np}\,Lex \quad [np]_1}{np\backslash s}\,/E}{s}\,\backslash E}{s/np}\,/I_1}{n\backslash n}\,/E}{n}\,\backslash E$$

We can read off the lexical assignments from the undischarged leaves of the proof above. So "discovered" is a transitive verb, looking for a noun phrase (np, its object) to its right, then for a noun phrase (its subject) to its left to form a sentence s. The relativiser "which" looks for a complex formula s/np (that is a sentence missing a noun phrase in its rightmost position) to its right and for a noun to its left. The hypothetical np corresponds to a trace in mainstream syntactic theory. A weakness of the Lambek calculus is that this analysis does not extend to only slightly more complicated examples such as "moons which Galileo discovered in 1610", where the hypothetical noun phrase no longer occurs in a peripheral position. Many variants and extensions of the Lambek calculus have been developed with the goal of solving this and other problems (see, for example Moortgat 1997; Morrill 2011).

Given the lexicon, the phrase "moons which Galileo discovered" is a noun n iff the following holds.

$$n, (n\backslash n)/(s/np), np, (np\backslash s)/np \vdash n$$

The proof above shows this statement holds. Even though it is easy to verify this proof is correct by inspecting each rule application, it may not be immediately obvious how to find natural deduction proofs. In the next section, we will present a proof search procedure for the implicational fragment of Lambek calculus natural deduction.

2.2 *Proof search in natural deduction*

For our proof search procedure, the notion of *result* is useful.

Definition 2.2 *Given a formula F, its result is the atomic subformula of F defined as follows.*

$$\begin{aligned} \mathit{result}(A) &= A \qquad \text{if } A \text{ atomic} \\ \mathit{result}(A/B) &= \mathit{result}(A) \\ \mathit{result}(B\backslash A) &= \mathit{result}(A) \end{aligned}$$

Essentially, the result is the atomic formula we obtain once we have combined a formula with all its arguments. So the result of $(np\backslash s)/np$ is s and the result of $(n\backslash n)/(s/np)$ is n. Proof search for a sequent $A_1,\ldots,A_n \vdash C$ in natural deduction works as follows (a more precise description can be found in Moot and Retoré 2012).

1. If C is a complex formula, apply the appropriate introduction rules until we obtain an atomic formula p (this may add formulas to the left of A_1 and to the right of A_n).
2. Select an active hypothesis H of the proof such that $\mathit{result}(H) = p$ (that is, select a formula which eventually produces the current atomic goal formula).
3. Our current sequent is of form $A_1,\ldots,A_{i-1},H,A_{i+1},\ldots,A_n \vdash p$ and we need to subdivide the formulas to the left of H $(A_1,\ldots,A_{i-1})$ into m subsequences $\Gamma_1,\ldots,\Gamma_m$, where m is the number of arguments H takes to its left, and we need to subdivide the formulas to the right of H $(A_{i+1},\ldots,A_n)$ into k subsequences $\Delta_1,\ldots,\Delta_k$

where k is the number of arguments H takes to its right (this fails if H selects no arguments to its left and $A_1,\ldots,A_{i-1}$ is not empty, and similarly if H has no arguments to its right and $A_{i+1},\ldots,A_n$ is not empty). We apply all elimination rules to H until we arrive at atomic formula p, then recursively find the proofs from step 1 for each of the arguments: proofs $\Gamma_q \vdash B_q$ for arguments to the left and proofs $\Delta_r \vdash D_r$ for arguments to the right. In the simplest case with a single argument on the right and a single argument on the left, $H = (B\backslash p)/D$; there is no need for splitting the A_i further and we simply try to find proofs for $A_1,\ldots A_{i-1} \vdash B$ and for $A_{i+1},\ldots,A_n \vdash D$. Succeed if all recursive steps succeed. If not, try other subdivisions of the hypotheses. Fail when there is no way to divide the hypotheses such that all subproofs succeed.

The algorithm above has non-determinism in two places. The first step is deterministic, but in the second step there may be several choices for the atomic goal formula and in the third step there may be several ways to split up the sequence of formulas (we need multiple arguments either to the right or to the left for this).

As an example, the sequent $n, (n\backslash n)/(s/np), np, (np\backslash s)/np \vdash n$ has an atomic conclusion, so nothing needs to be done for the first step. For the second step, there is the choice of two formulas: either n (corresponding to "moons") or $(n\backslash n)/(s/np)$ (corresponding to "which"). The first choice fails immediately since there are still formulas to the right which are not arguments of the formula producing the result (as it is atomic). The second choice provides a formula looking for an s/np to its right and an n to its left. Simply writing out the required elimination rules and separating the hypotheses produces the following.

$$\dfrac{\dfrac{\dfrac{\text{moons}}{n}\,Lex \quad \vdots\;\delta_1}{n} \qquad \dfrac{\dfrac{\text{which}}{(n\backslash n)/(s/np)}\,Lex \qquad \dfrac{\dfrac{\text{Galileo}}{np}\,Lex \quad \dfrac{\text{discovered}}{(np\backslash s)/np}\,Lex \quad \vdots\;\delta_2}{s/np}}{n\backslash n}\,/E}{n}\,\backslash E$$

We now need to complete the procedure recursively to find the proofs δ_1 and δ_2. The first subproof is trivial: we are looking for a noun and there is one, so δ_1 is empty and the n premiss and the n conclusion of δ_1 become the same formula occurrence. The second subproof has a complex goal, so according to step 1 we apply the introduction rule for "/" which produces the following.

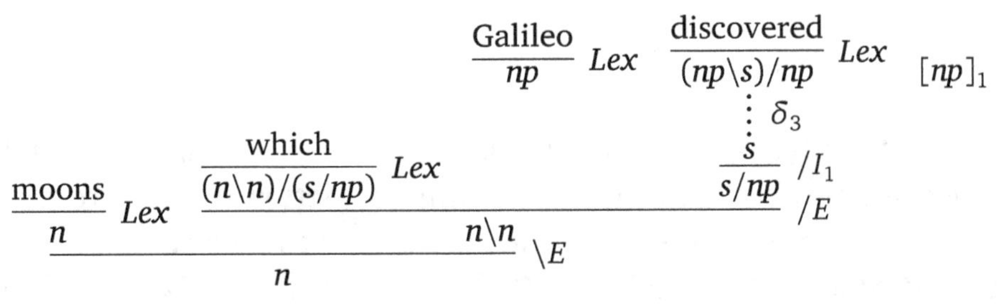

Our subproof δ_3 requires us to prove $np, (np\backslash s)/np, np \vdash s$. Since s is atomic and only the transitive verb has s as its goal, this produces the following.

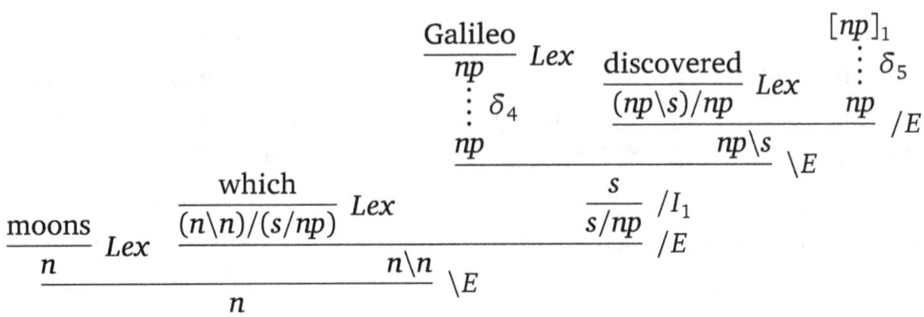

We can complete the proof by identifying the atomic noun phrases in δ_4 and in δ_5. The given proof procedure is top-down and enumerates eta-long beta-normal form proofs. In addition, different proofs correspond to different meanings, that is, different proofs will have different lambda terms assigned to them using the term assignment of Figure 1. This correspondence between natural deduction proofs and lambda-terms is the well-known Curry-Howard correspondence. It is not an isomorphism for the Lambek calculus, since not all intuitionistic proofs have a corresponding Lambek calculus proof. Even stronger, not all multiplicative intuitionistic linear logic proofs have a corresponding Lambek calculus proof: the Lambek calculus is a logic without contraction and weakening, like linear logic, but also without the exchange rule.

Adding the term assignment of Figure 1 produces the following proof.

$$\cfrac{\cfrac{\text{moons}}{n:m}\,Lex \quad \cfrac{\cfrac{\text{which}}{(n\backslash n)/(s/np):w}\,Lex \quad \cfrac{\cfrac{\cfrac{\text{Galileo}}{np:g}\,Lex \quad \cfrac{\cfrac{\text{discovered}}{(np\backslash s)/np:d}\,Lex \quad [np:x]_1}{np\backslash s:(d\,x)}\,/E}{s:((d\,x)\,g)}\,\backslash E}{s/np:\lambda x.((d\,x)\,g)}\,/I_1}{n\backslash n:(w\,(\lambda x.((d\,x)\,g)))}\,/E}{n:((w\,(\lambda x.((d\,x)\,g)))\,m)}\,\backslash E$$

Each lexical assumption of the proof is assigned a unique variable (in the example above, this variable is the first letter of the corresponding word for the convenience of the reader) and these have exactly one free occurrence in the final term (these are linear lambda terms, since each abstraction binds exactly one variable as well). The lexicon assigns both a formula and a corresponding lambda term to each lexical entry. Computing the formal semantics corresponds to replacing each word by its lexical semantics. In the current case, ignoring complications such as tense and the plural, many words have a trivial meaning assignment, so we replace m by the constant $moon^{e\to t}$ (or, if we prefer, by its eta expansion $\lambda x^e.moon(x)$), d by the constant $discover^{e\to(e\to t)}$, g by the constant $Galileo^e$. The crucial case is the lexical assignment for "which", for which we replace w by $\lambda Q^{e\to t}\lambda P^{e\to t}\lambda y^e.(P\,y)\wedge(Q\,y)$. Making all lexical substitutions in our original term $((w\,(\lambda x.((d\,x)\,g)))\,m)$ produces the following term.

$$((\lambda Q\lambda P\lambda y.((P\,y)\wedge(Q\,y)))\,(\lambda x.((discover\,x)\,Galileo)))\,moon$$

We apply beta-reduction by substituting $\lambda x.((discover\,x)\,Galileo)$ for Q, which produces the following.

$$(\lambda P\lambda y.((P\,y)\wedge((\lambda x.((discover\,x)\,Galileo))\,y)))\,moon$$

A second beta-reduction replaces x by y as follows.

$$(\lambda P\lambda y.((P\,y)\wedge((discover\,y)\,Galileo)))\,moon$$

The final beta-reduction replaces P by $moon$ to produce the following normal form.

$$\lambda y.((moon\,y)\wedge((discover\,y)\,Galileo))$$

According to the standard notational conventions of Montague semantics (Gamut 1991), this corresponds to the following more natural term.

$$\lambda y.(moon(y) \wedge discover(Galileo, y))$$

That is, the y such that they are moons and were discovered by Galileo.

2.3 *Proof nets*

Type-logical grammars generally have multiple proof systems which are provably equivalent (in the sense that they derive the same theorems). Having multiple proof systems available is a great benefit, because meta-theoretical properties are often easier to prove in one system than in another.

Even though natural deduction is a nice proof system producing proofs which are fairly easy to read and which have a direct connection to the semantics, we will introduce a second proof system, *proof nets*, which makes some aspects of proof combinatorics easier to see[2].

Proof nets are a proof system introduced for linear logic by Girard (1987). Proof nets represent proofs as (hyper)graphs, where the vertices are (polarized) formulas and the hyperlinks represent a connection between the main formula of a rule and its immediate subformulas. The links for the Lambek calculus are shown in Table 1. The formulas above a link are its premisses whereas the formulas below it are its conclusions. The axiom link, on the top left of Table 1 has no premisses and two conclusions (the order between them is irrelevant), whereas the cut link, on the top right, has two premisses (in any order) and no conclusions). The cut link is presented only for completeness, since the Lambek calculus satisfies cut elimination, we never need to use a cut link when using proof nets for proof search.

The links for the negative implications correspond to the natural deduction elimination rules, though the complex formula is the conclusion of the link and the main premiss of the elimination rule. The links for the positive implications correspond to the introduction rules, with the withdrawn hypothesis as the negative premiss of the rule.

Positive and negative formulas correspond essentially to unnegated and negated formulas (as in the classical equivalences be-

[2] Another advantage of proof nets is that, unlike natural deduction, adding the product rules to the proof net calculus presents no complications.

Table 1: Links for Lambek calculus proof structures

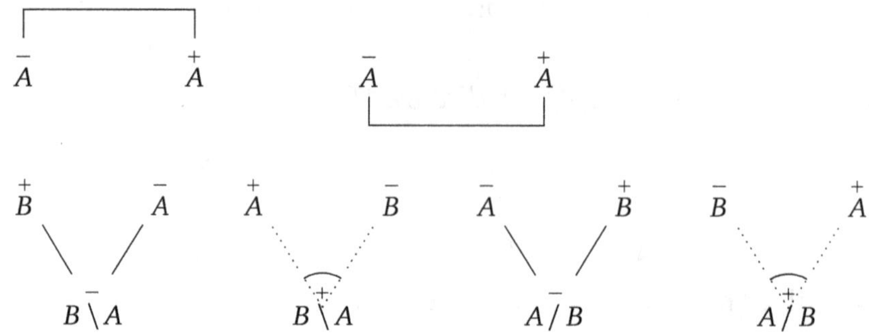

tween $B \rightarrow A \equiv \neg B \vee A$ and $\neg(B \rightarrow A) \equiv B \wedge \neg A$). In the context of linear logic, polarities function as a restriction on classical formulas to ensure the intuitionistic restriction to a single conclusion. The distinction between solid and dotted links corresponds to the distinction between a logical conjunction (solid) and a logical disjunction (dotted). This distinction plays a key role in deciding the correctness of proof structures below.

Given a statement $A_1, \ldots, A_n \vdash C$, we obtain a proof frame by unfolding the formulas according to the logical links on the bottom row of Table 1, using the negative unfolding for the A_i and the positive unfolding for C, until we reach the atomic formulas. We then connect the atomic formulas by means of the axiom link shown on the top left of Table 1. We need to respect the linear order of the premisses for the logical links (and the linear order of the formulas in the sequent), but the axiom link can connect a positive and a negative atom in either order.

Figure 2 shows the formula unfolding corresponding to "moons which Galileo discovered". The occurrences of the atomic formulas have been numbered to allow easy reference to them; these numbers are not a formal part of the proof structure. We saw the natural deduction proof for this noun in Section 2.1. When all axioms of a formula unfolding have been linked we call the resulting structure a *proof structure*. Not all proof structures correspond to proofs. The proof structures which do are *proof nets*. As we will see, we can distinguish proof nets from other proof structures just by looking at properties of the graph.

For the formula unfolding, it is immediately clear what the search space for potential proofs is: we need to find a 1-1 matching between positive and negative occurrences of the same atomic formula. So for Figure 2, we need to match the positive s_1 to the negative s_2 (there

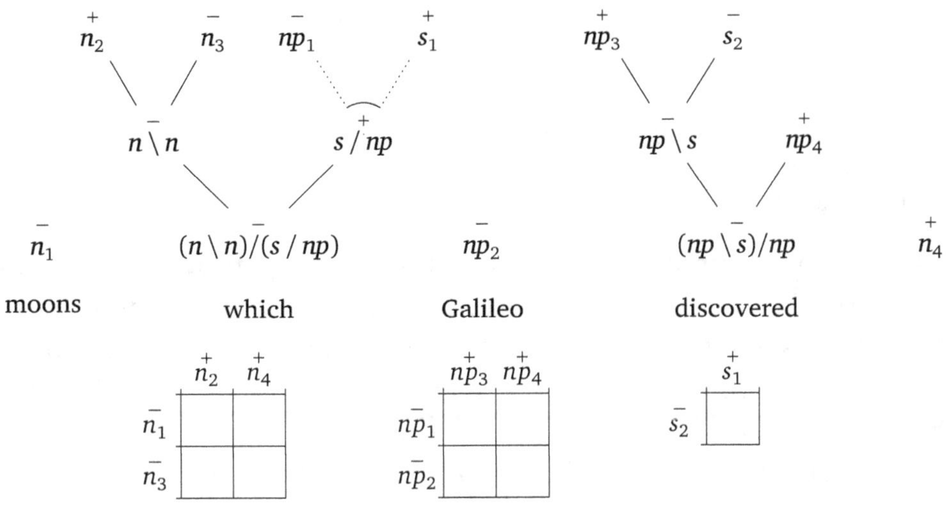

Figure 2: Formula unfolding for "moons which Galileo discovered"

is only one possible solution here), the two positive *n*'s to the two negative ones, and the two positive *np*'s to the two negative ones. The squares at the bottom of Figure 2 summarise the possibilities.

For Lambek calculus proof nets, the matching of atomic formulas must be planar. Planarity corresponds to non-commutativity of the logic and it therefore holds for the Lambek calculus but not for its extensions. Given that there is only one possibility for *s*, planarity constrains the possible axiom connections for the *np* formulas: when the two *s* formulas have been connected, the negative np_2 corresponding to "Galileo" can only be connected to the leftmost (subject) noun phrase np_3 of "discovered" since connecting it to the rightmost (object) noun phrase would force the link to cross the *s* axiom link. Similarly, the negative np_1 of "which" can only be linked to the object np_4 of "discovered" when we require a planar connection.

Finally, there are two planar matchings possible between the two positive and the two negative nouns: we either connect the negative n_1 of "moons" to the positive n_2 of "which" and the negative n_3 of "which" to the positive goal n_4, or vice versa (we had the same choice for natural deduction proof search in Section 2.2).

However, only one of these two possibilities produces a proof net. There are many graph-theoretical ways to characterise the proof nets among other proof structures. One simple way, due to Danos (1990), uses the graph contractions shown in Figure 3.

We first remove all formula information from a proof structure, replacing formula occurrence by unique vertex indices v_0, v_1, …, then

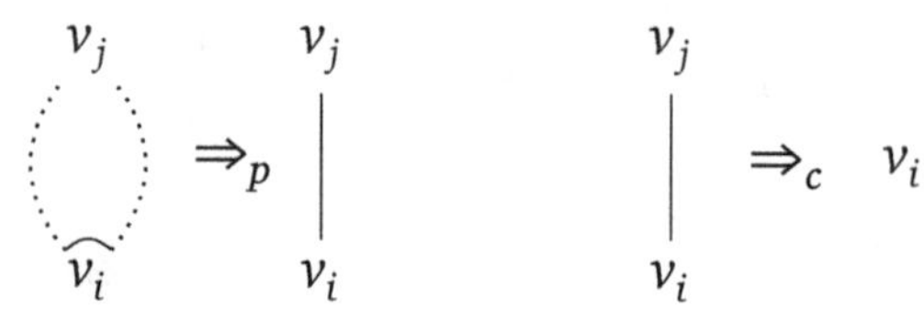

Figure 3: Contractions for proof nets

applying the contractions. A proof structure is a proof net iff it contracts to a single vertex using these contractions. The condition on the rightmost contraction is that the two vertices are distinct. In other words, if the proof structure has a cycle containing only solid links, then we can use this contraction to reduce this cycle to a self-loop, but we can never eliminate it. Similarly, the contractions only shorten paths, but do not create new ones. Therefore, if a proof structure is disconnected, it will never contract to a single point. The leftmost reduction corresponds to the dotted links for the positive implications and it essentially requires us to "join" the two premisses of the link. As the previous discussion suggests, the contraction criterion is quite close to the more well-known acyclicity and connectedness condition (Danos and Regnier 1989). However, the contraction condition has the advantage of allowing a compact representation of intermediate structures in proof search, and is therefore more suitable for proof search (Moot 2017).

With this in mind, it is clear that of the two possible connections between the *n* formulas, connecting the two *n* formulas of "which" together produces a cycle of solid links, and therefore a structure which doesn't contract to a point. In addition, connecting the noun "moons" to the goal formula produces an axiom link disconnected from the rest of the structure. Therefore, the structure shown in Figure 4 is the only proof net given this sequence of formulas. It is easy to verify it contracts to a point given the contractions of Figure 3. One way of proceeding is eliminating all "dangling" links (that is, links connecting a single vertex to the rest of the structure). When such links have been recursively removed, we end up with the pair of dotted links and a solid path between the positive *s* and the negative *np* of this dotted link. We can contract this path to a single vertex, producing the correct configuration for contracting the pair of dotted links and apply the final contraction to the resulting solid link to produce a single vertex.

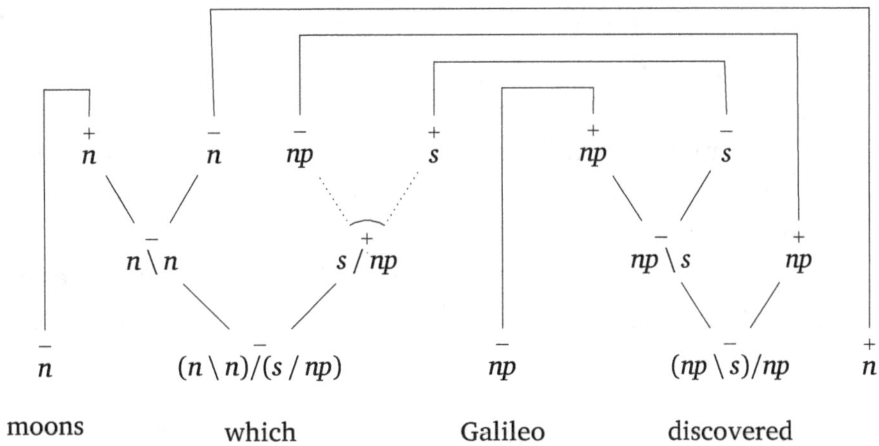

Figure 4: Proof net for "moons which Galileo discovered"

3 COMBINATORICS AND COMPLEXITY

Using type-logical grammars for computing the meaning of sentences and using the resulting meaning for different tasks (entailment, question answering, etc.) has the following bottlenecks.

1. Lexical lookup. For wide-coverage grammars, the number of formulas that the lexicon assigns to many common words is rather large.
2. Proof combinatorics. Finding a proof (or the best proof for some numerical definition of best) is NP-complete for most type-logical grammars.
3. Meaning computation. Computing the meaning of a sentence is done by substituting lexical lambda terms and then normalising the resulting simply typed lambda term. Normalising simply typed lambda terms is known to be of non-elementary complexity.
4. Meaning use. Questions of logical entailment between sentences are undecidable, even in the first-order case.

The focus of the rest of this article will be on Item 2, proof combinatorics, but I will offer some brief remarks on the other items.

A probabilistic lexicon The number of lexical formulas per word is a major problem for real-world applications. However, when we fix a set of possible formulas and have enough examples of sentences with the correct formula assignment, we can define a probability model over words, together with a limited amount of context (typically the two preceding and succeeding words). This general approach is called supertagging (Bangalore and Joshi 2011) and it has been applied successfully to many formalisms including type-logical grammars (Moot 2010, 2014b, presents supertaggers for multimodal type-logical grammars for Dutch and for French).

Since the topic of supertagging has been discussed at length elsewhere and provides good, practical solutions to the problem of lexical ambiguity we will not elaborate on it here.

Meaning computation Schwichtenberg (1982) shows that normalising simply typed lambda terms has non-elementary worst-case complexity. This complexity result essentially exploits recursive copying. However, there are many implementations of the simply typed lambda calculus for computational linguistics which perform rather efficiently, and this in spite of the fact that, in general, little effort is spent on optimising the implementation of the normalisation component. We claim that the meaning recipes necessary for the lexicon are all terms of soft linear logic, and hence can be reduced in polynomial time (Lafont 2004; Baillot and Mogbil 2004). This accounts for the observed fact that lambda term normalisation is not a real bottleneck in practice (Moot and Retoré 2016).

Logical entailment Given that logical entailment is undecidable in general, there are two basic strategies:

1. We can use an off-the-shelf theorem prover (generally using some time limit) and simply see whether it finds a proof. Bos and Markert (2005) use this approach (as well as some more approximative measures).
2. We can use an incomplete but decidable logical fragment for computing entailment. Abzianidze (2017) uses this approach.

In both cases, the result is a high-precision but low-recall system (that is, when the system produces an answer, it is usually right, but there are many correct answers for which no proofs are found). The main bottleneck to improving recall is adding a logical formalisation of a sufficient amount of world knowledge (without reducing prover performance), a classic problem in artificial intelligence.

4 WEIGHTED PROOF SYSTEMS

Given a sequent $\Gamma \vdash C$, the formula unfolding into a proof frame gives a compact representation of the proof combinatorics for the given sequent. We can combine positive and negative occurrences of the same atomic formulas until we obtain a proof structure. An atomic formula a with n positive and n negative occurrences (the number of positive and negative occurrences for each atomic formula must be equal if the sequent is derivable; this is called the *count check*) corresponds to an $n \times n$ matrix, and a potential reading for this sequent, that is a proof structure, is a perfect matching between positive and negative occurrences.

When we fill the matrix with weights (we will discuss some different ways of computing these weights below), it becomes possible to compute the best proof structure according to these weights. We can either use best-first search, connecting the "best" axiom links first for each local choice, or use a k-best proof structure computation, computing the k total links which are the best globally. Given that computing the k-best proof structures this way can be done in polynomial time (Kuhn 1955), there is no guarantee that the best proof structure is actually a proof net (unless P = NP). However, we can use a polynomial k-best system as an incomplete approximation of proof search.

Given two atomic formulas a_1 and a_2 of the same type (n, np, s) but of opposite polarity there are different ways of assigning a weight to the possible axiom link between them.

1. We can use the distance between words as weight, using distance 0 when the two atomic formulas are subformulas of the same formula occurrence, distance 1 between adjacent words, etc.
2. We can use a probability-like measure, estimated from proof nets in a large corpus.
3. We can use the word similarity measure between w_1 and w_2.

We will discuss each of these alternative measures in turn in the next sections.

4.1 *Word distance*

One simple metric to use is word distance, preferring axiom connections between closer words. This gives a strong preference to linking atomic subformulas of the same formula, followed by linking atomic subformulas of adjacent formulas.

Given a proof net with k axiom links, when processing this proof net left-to-right performing axiom links as soon as possible, this will mean each link of distance of n will cause the leftmost corresponding atom to be open/unlinked for n steps. Measuring the number of open axioms after each word has been proposed as a straightforward model of human sentence processing which, in spite of its simplicity, makes a number of correct predictions about processing (Johnson 1998; Morrill 1998, 2011).

We illustrate this by examining the contrast between Dutch and German verb clusters. Verb clusters in both Dutch and German can have a sequence of verb arguments followed by a sequence of verbs selecting these arguments. The difference between German and Dutch is that German verbs select these arguments right-to-left (that is, the leftmost verb selects the rightmost argument) and the Dutch verb select these arguments left-to-right (that is, the leftmost verb selects the leftmost argument). This is illustrated by the following contrast.

(1) Wolfgang hat die Lehrerin die Murmeln aufräumen helfen
Wolfgang has the teacher the marbles collect help
Wolfgang helped the teacher collect the marbles

(2) Jantje heeft de lerares de knikkers helpen opruimen
Jantje has the teacher the marbles help collect
Jantje helped the teacher collect the marbles

Bach *et al.* (1986) find that, in an experimental setting, German sentences like the one above are harder for German native speakers than the Dutch sentences are for Dutch native speaker: although the difference is not very large, the German sentences are not only judged as harder by the German speakers, but the German test subjects also make more comprehension errors.

Figure 5 shows the proof net corresponding to sentence (1). The noun phrases "die Lehrerin" and "die Murmeln" have been not been treated as a combination of np/n and n but as a simple np to reduce the size of the proof net. This will not affect the comparison with the Dutch example.[3]

[3] Some other simplifications have been made: neither the German auxiliary "hat" nor the Dutch auxiliary "heeft" can select a simple infinitive argument (i.e.

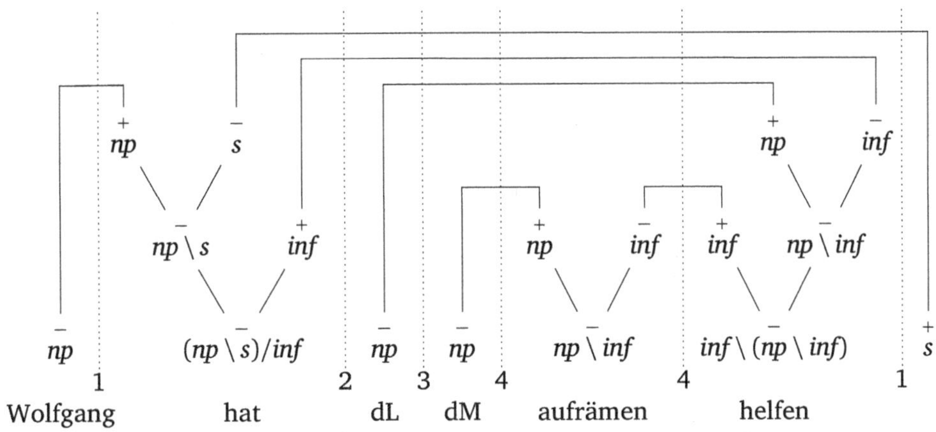

Figure 5: Proof net for "Wolfgang hat die Lehrerin die Murmeln aufräumen helfen"

Computing the processing complexity using a proof net such as the one shown in Figure 5 requires us to make some choices. We can assume that the hearer knows to expect a sentence (and therefore put the goal formula initially). Morrill (2011) chooses this option. We can also keep the goal formula at the end, as done here.

There are some other potential complexity issues to take into account: some choices of lexical formulas and of axiom links lead to failure and it is possible that this affects processing complexity (at least it does so for a computer implementation). The *size* of the partial proof net constructed so far may also play a role (the size of the contracted partial proof net according to the contractions of Figure 3 seems a good candidate for such a size measure).

Morrill and Johnson use the simplest solution here, measuring complexity by the successful proof nets when processed left to right, counting the number of unlinked axioms at each step.

Figure 5 shows a dotted column after each word, together with a count of the number of axioms it crosses. In the example, after the first word, "Wolfgang", there is a single unlinked *np*, therefore the count is 1. After "hat", the *np* of "Wolfgang" becomes linked but an unlinked *s* and an unlinked *inf* are added, leaving a total of 2 unlinked atoms.

we have "Die Lehrerin hat die Murmeln aufgeräumt", with a past participle rather than an infinitive); they only take an infinitive argument when this infinitive itself selects for another infinitive. This can be solved either by adding features or by distinguishing the atomic types. Bach *et al.* (1986) note that for German (but not for Dutch) both grammar textbooks and speakers disagree over whether the final verb should be an infinitive or a past participle.

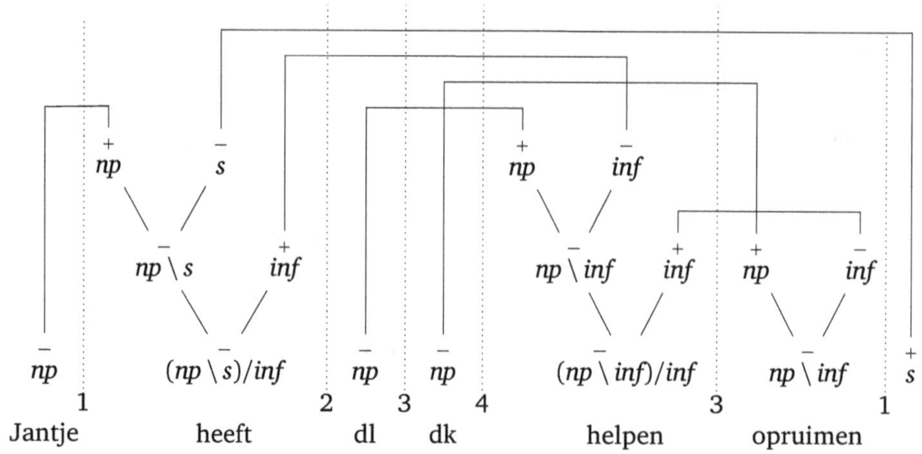

Figure 6: Proof net for "Jantje heeft de lerares de knikkers helpen opruimen"

In general, the complexity profile of verb clusters in German (and in Dutch) rises when the arguments of the verbs in the cluster are encountered (the noun phrases "die Lehrerin" and "die Murmeln"), then descends when the verbs start selecting their arguments. This provides an explanation for why these sentences quickly become unacceptable with multiple levels of embedding.

The complexity profile of Figure 5 has a maximum complexity of 4 and a total complexity of 15.

To provide a proof net for the Dutch example (2), we need somewhat more complex proof net machinery, since the crossed dependencies of Dutch cannot be handled by planar structures. Since these more complicated proof nets do not affect our chosen complexity measure, we will simply look at the complexity profile for the non-planar proof net in Figure 6: this is not a Lambek calculus proof net, and we assume a proof net calculus which allows only this structure for the example sentence.

The complexity profiles of the two sentences are the same until the first infinitive, but then the Dutch sentence has a slight advantage: its maximum complexity, like the German example, is 4; but its total complexity is 14, compared to 15 for the German example. This advantage becomes somewhat more pronounced when we add a third and a fourth verb.

These examples are interesting because many known psycholinguistic facts, even some fairly subtle ones like shown here, are a direct consequence of rather minimal assumptions about a model of processing. Morrill (2011) presents many other examples.

4.2 *Corpus estimation*

Given a sequent, it is not hard to define a probability distribution over its proof structures: to obtain such a probability distribution we simply need to fill the $n \times n$ matrix for each atomic formula in such a way that all rows and all columns sum to 1. In other words, each atomic formula is assigned a probability distribution over the atomic formulas of opposite polarity. For example, looking to Figure 6, for a full proof search the negative np corresponding to 'Jantje' can be linked to the positive np of 'heeft', the positive np of 'helpen' and the positive np of 'opruimen' and the sum of these probabilities must be 1. Similarly, the positive np of 'heeft' can be linked to the negative np of 'Jantje', the negative np of 'de lerares' and the negative np of 'de knikkers'.

Mathematically, it is much harder to define a probability distribution over proof *nets*. When we define a probability distribution over proof structures, we assign a non-zero probability to structures which do not correspond to proofs. Even though it makes sense a priori to want non-proofs to have zero probability, this entails that an underivable sequent should fail to be assigned a probability distribution at all, since no axiom link can contribute to a proof. However, this means assigning probabilities becomes an NP-hard problem, since we would be able to decide derivability of a sequent from the success or failure of computing a probability distribution.

Accepting the assignment of non-zero probability to axiom links which are not part of any proof is comparable to probabilistic context-free grammar parsers assigning non-zero probability to constituents which cannot be part of a derivation of the complete string.

The question for probability assignment is how likely is the nth atomic formula of word w_1 to combine with the kth atomic formula of w_2 (with some form of backoff, for example to the two part-of-speech tags). In general, we can use well-known statistical methods (Berger *et al.* 1996) to compute a probability function from any combination of properties from formulas, words and context. This possibility has so far been little explored in the context of type-logical grammars.

In terms of assigning weights to atomic formulas, this is not fundamentally different from the other weighted approaches discussed here. It has the advantage over the other methods that it can distinguish between different arguments of the same formula (neither the distance measure nor the vector similarity measure does this). However, it has the disadvantage that it requires a large amount of annotated data to estimate the probabilities.

4.3 *Vector similarity*

An advantage of using vector similarity rather than a large corpus of parsed text is that it is much easier to obtain the former than it is to obtain the latter: a high-quality parsed corpus of sufficiently large size requires an enormous effort in times of person-hours; on the other hand, computing word vectors can be done automatically and, using the enormous amount of text available on the internet, on a scale unrealistic for any manual method. Computing word vectors from the web still requires an important effort in crawling, cleaning, duplicate detection, etc., but nowhere near the person-hours needed to manually annotate a similar size corpus, something especially relevant for under-resourced languages: as discussed by Kilgarriff and Grefenstette (2003), even 'smaller' languages such as Icelandic, Basque, Latin and Esperanto have over 50 million words of text available according to conservative estimates. For many of the most-used languages on the internet, cleaned-up and (automatically) annotated versions of this content are freely available and can be used to extract word vectors (Baroni *et al.* 2009).

Weighting axiom links according to the similarity of the words given by distributional semantics means preferring connections between words with related meanings (this appears to be close to the notion of *discourse coherence* as used by Asher and Lascarides 2003, only in a more shallow, syntactic context).

Even though this basic idea is easily stated, implementing it requires making some choices. While distributional semantic similarity is easily defined for two words, defining it for two complex expressions is essentially the compositionality problem for vector space semantics.

A simple solution would be to choose the vector sum for composition, and this already performs surprisingly well on several similarity tasks. However, the vector sum approach is ill-adapted to preferences in type-logical proofs: given that we need to match the atomic subformulas of all words in a sentence in any case, and given that the vector sum operation is associative and commutative, this would not allow us to distinguish between different word groupings (or even between different word orders).

We therefore need a slightly more sophisticated method for combining vector similarity with proof rules. We adapt the basic idea of lexicalised parsing with context-free grammars and use a *head word* for each expression — the verb for a verb phrase, the noun for a noun phrase, etc. In the context of type-logical grammar, we therefore specify the following general principles, as sort of type-logical equivalences to the head percolation principles of Magerman (1994):

1. the head of a lexical hypothesis is the word itself,
2. the head of the combination of A/A with A and of A with $A\backslash A$ is the head of A
3. the head of np/n with n (resp. pp/np with np) is the head of the noun n (resp. the head of the noun phrase np)
4. the head of other formulas A/B and $B\backslash A$, with $A \neq B$, is the head of A.

Moreover, for the semantic assignments in a type-logical lexicon, we can distinguish between the lexical entries whose semantic content is purely logical (using only the logical constants like "$\neg$" "$\wedge$", "$\forall$", and a few other predicates whose meaning is invariant across models, like "="and "<") and those whose semantic content is not (these typically contain predicates like "*love*" and "*book*" corresponding to the lexical entry itself).[4]

The basic elements in our formal setup are now triples containing a *formula*, a *head word*, and *vector distance weight*, with each lexical entry starting with the word lemma as its head and distance zero. For each elimination rule, the new head word is defined by the propagation rules above (it is the head of the argument when the functor is a modifier, a determiner or a preposition, and the head of the functor otherwise) and the weight is updated by adding the weights of the two premisses and additionally adding the distance of the two head words according to the vector model. The rule be-

[4] This contrast is unfortunately not as sharp as we would like it to be: while it is simple to see "all" and "some" as purely logical, it is much less easy to see how other words such as "few" and "many" can be interpreted in terms of purely logical operators.

low presents a general elimination rule operating on triples (with "$\multimap$" generalising over both "/" and "\") according to this description.

$$\frac{\langle w_1, h_1, A \multimap B\rangle \quad \langle w_2, h_2, A\rangle}{\langle w_1 + w_2 + d(h_1, h_2), h, B\rangle} \multimap E$$

From a purely logical point of view (that is, looking only at the third element of the triple), this rule operates just like a normal elimination rule. The head h of the conclusion will be either h_1 or h_2 depending on the head propagation rules described above. The weight computation uses a distance measure d computing the distance between the two head words and simple addition. Nothing in particular hinges on the use of "+" here; any function monotone in both its arguments can be used here. Many choices are also possible for the distance measure d, but in the examples below we use the simple cosine measure which is the most commonly used for distributional similarity. The cosine measure produces 1 when the vectors point in the exact same direction, 0 when the vectors are orthogonal.[5] This ensures the highest-weight proof combines the nearest vectors.

For the introduction rules, it is somewhat more difficult to define the proper elements for the discharged hypothesis of the rule. We can simply choose zero for its weight, but it is unclear what the proper head word for a hypothesised constituent is. One simple solution is to assign the empty word ϵ to such hypotheses and stipulate that the empty word has distance zero to all other words (i.e. for all w, $d(\epsilon, w) = d(w, \epsilon) = 0$). This would give the following introduction rule.

$$\frac{\begin{array}{c}\langle 0, \epsilon, B\rangle \\ \vdots \\ \langle w, h, A\rangle\end{array}}{\langle w, h, B \multimap A\rangle} \multimap I$$

We can also use a somewhat more sophisticated rule for subproofs of the following form.

[5] In principle, we can have -1 when the vectors point in the exact opposite direction, although many methods are guaranteed to obtain positive vectors only.

$$\dfrac{\begin{array}{c}\vdots \\ \langle w_1, h_1, (B \multimap A) \multimap C\rangle\end{array} \quad \dfrac{\begin{array}{c}[\langle 0, h_1, B\rangle]^k \\ \vdots \\ \langle w_2, h_2, A\rangle\end{array}}{\langle w_2, h_2, B \multimap A\rangle} \multimap I_k}{\langle w_1 + w_2, h_1, C\rangle} \multimap E$$

Where for relative pronouns $A = s$, $B = np$ and $C = n\backslash n$, and for generalised quantifiers $A = s$, $B = np$ and $C = s$. Essentially, h_1 is propagated from the left premiss of the elimination rule to the hypothesis of the introduction rule. This works well since the head word of a determiner phrase (of type $(np \multimap s) \multimap s$) is its noun, and similarly, the noun argument of the relative pronoun is semantically identical to the extracted noun phrase $B = np$.

As a concrete example, a French fragment like "concert de piano gratuit", like its English translation "free piano concert", has two possible readings, one where there is a piano concert which is free and one where a free piano is used to give a concert. This type of ambiguity, although somewhat reduced by noun/adjective agreement, is quite common in the French Treebank (Abeillé *et al.* 2003) and apparently a difficult construction both for journalists and annotators. Treating this example according the the method described above provides the following (to reduce horizontal space, we have used w_1, w_2 and w_3 for the weight terms to be discussed later).[6]

$$\dfrac{\dfrac{\dfrac{\text{concert}}{\langle 0, \mathit{concert}, n\rangle} Lex \quad \dfrac{\dfrac{\text{de}}{\langle 0, \mathit{de}, (n\backslash n)/n\rangle} Lex \quad \dfrac{\text{piano}}{\langle 0, \mathit{piano}, n\rangle} Lex}{\langle w_1, \mathit{piano}, n\backslash n\rangle} /E}{\langle w_2, \mathit{concert}, n\rangle} \backslash E \quad \dfrac{\text{gratuit}}{\langle 0, \mathit{gratuit}, n\backslash n\rangle} Lex}{\langle w_3, \mathit{concert}, n\rangle} \backslash E$$

The weight w_1 of the proof showing "de piano" is of type $n\backslash n$ is equal to the weight of its to premisses (both zero) plus the distance between the heads of the two premisses of the rule, "de" and "piano" in our case, which have a distance of 0.0740, so we conclude w_1 is 0.0740. We can now compute the weight of the proof showing "concert de piano" to be of type n by combining the weight 0 of "concert" with

[6] Here and elsewhere, all weights are computed used the models provided by Fauconnier (2016) at `http://fauconnier.github.io/#software`

the weight 0.0740 of “de piano” and adding the distance between the two head words “concert” and “piano’, which is 0.4398 (that is, these words are fairly close) to arrive at $w_2 = 0.5138$. Finally, we combine this n with the adjective “gratuit” to compute the final weight w_3 by adding the previously computed w_2 to 0 (the weight of “gratuit”) and adding the distance between “concert” and “gratuit”, which is 0.1921. This gives us a total weight w_3 of 0.7059 for this reading (note that this number is not a probability and meaningful only in comparison to similarly computed numbers).

The second proof looks as follows.

$$\dfrac{\dfrac{\text{concert}}{\langle 0, \mathit{concert}, n\rangle}\,\mathit{Lex} \qquad \dfrac{\dfrac{\text{de}}{\langle 0, \mathit{de}, (n\backslash n)/n\rangle}\,\mathit{Lex} \qquad \dfrac{\dfrac{\text{piano}}{\langle 0, \mathit{piano}, n\rangle}\,\mathit{Lex} \qquad \dfrac{\text{gratuit}}{\langle 0, \mathit{gratuit}, n\backslash n\rangle}\,\mathit{Lex}}{\langle w_1, \mathit{piano}, n\rangle}\,\backslash E}{\langle w_2, \mathit{piano}, n\backslash n\rangle}\,/E}{\langle w_3, \mathit{concert}, n\rangle}\,\backslash E$$

Even though the second reading uses the exact same words, it combines them in a different way, and this affects the weight calculations. We now combine “piano’ and “gratuit” first, to obtain $w_1 = 0+0+d(\mathit{piano}, \mathit{gratuit}) = 0.0695$. We then combine this result with “de” and calculate $w_2 = 0 + w_1 + d(\mathit{de}, \mathit{piano}) = 0.0695 + 0.0740 = 0.1435$. Finally, we combine the previous result with “concert” and calculate $w_3 = 0 + w_2 + d(\mathit{concert}, \mathit{piano}) = 0.1435 + 0.4398 = 0.5833$.

These calculations show a preference for the first reading, where the concert is free rather than the piano. The key difference between the two readings is that $d(\mathit{concert}, \mathit{gratuit}) > d(\mathit{piano}, \mathit{gratuit})$, whereas the other computed terms are equal.

We can use the same method to compute “voir la fille avec les lunettes” (to see the girl with the glasses), since $d(\mathit{voir}, \mathit{lunettes}) > d(\mathit{fille}, \mathit{lunettes})$, which gives a preference for “voir ... avec les lunettes” over “fille avec les lunettes”.

Using semantic relatedness like this is, of course, not without its defects. For example, the verb phrase “saw the star with the telescope” is structurally identical to the example above, but has only one plausible reading, where “with the telescope” is a verb phrase modifier. However, “star” and “telescope” are closer semantically than “girl” and “telescope” are. The problem here is essentially that semantic vector similarity as we are using it here doesn’t give us any information about argument structure.

This suggests the need for more sophisticated ways to combine vector semantics, such as used by Baroni and Lenci (2010). In the context of a real-world system, the lexicon is a probability distribution over a finite set of formulas and therefore the highest-weight proof for a sentence must be a combination of the probability over the formulas with the weight over the axioms. The right way of combining the weights of the supertagger (a probability distribution over formulas) with the vector weights needs to be determined empirically, of course. Two simple possibilities are:

1. taking the best supertagger sequence for which a proof is found, then finding the maximum weight proof for this sequence;
2. combine the supertagger probabilities with the weight of the proof into a single weighted sum; that is, we treat finding the relative importance of the two weights as a standard machine learning objective to be determined empirically.

In the case of "voir l'étoile avec le téléscope" (*see the star with the telescope*), the supertagger (Moot 2014b) strongly prefers adverbial use of "with" over adjectival use (26.4% against 0.9%), a very strong preference in favour of the preferred reading. Therefore, in a real-world system this problem disappears unless the weighted sum gives a very strong priority to the vector weight component.

4.4 *Vector similarity and proof nets*

We can adapt the above strategy with minor modifications to a proof net parser. This is done by replacing atomic formulas by binary predicates, where the first argument represents the head and the second argument the weight. For weights, we use the real numbers with the usual function "$+$" and the $d(w_1, w_2)$ function computing the distance between two words w_1 and w_2. Instead of having extra-logical head percolation and weight computation principles, these now form a part of the lexical entries (although these extra-logical principles would explain many common patterns occurring in the lexical entries and would make it possible to create an automatic compilation step adding the head and weight arguments to a 'standard' lexicon). Using first-order arguments has many applications, including as a solution for the Dutch verb clusters we've seen in Section 4.1 (Moot 2014a). As we use them here, these arguments are extra-grammatical and serve

Table 2: Lexical assignments with head word and weight computation information

$$\begin{aligned}
lex(\text{book}) &= n(book, 0)\\
lex(\text{the}) &= np(X, w)/np(X, w)\\
lex(\text{interesting}) &= n(X, w + d(interesting, X))/n(X, w)\\
lex(\text{read}) &= (np(X, w_1)\backslash s(read, w_1+w_2+d(w_1, read)+d(w_2, read))/np(Y, w_2)\\
lex(\text{which}) &= (n(X, w_1)\backslash n(X, w_1 + w_2))/(s(Y, w_2)/np(X, 0)\\
lex(\text{every}) &= (s(Y, w_1 + w_2)/(np(X, 0)\backslash s(Y, w_2)))/n(X, w_1)
\end{aligned}$$

only as a way to compute preferences among different proofs using the same formulas.

As before, atomic content words, like the noun "book" are assigned the entry $n(book, 0)$. That is, the head constituent of the noun is "book" itself and the weight assigned to this expression is zero. Table 2 lists some other lexical entries in the current context.

As shown in the table, the determiner "the" is assigned an entry simply copying both the head word and the weight, following the principles of a purely logical word in the previous section.

An adjective such as "interesting" on the other hand copies the head word, but adds the distance between the head word to the previous weight.[7]

Similarly, the transitive verb "read" adds both the distance between the verb and its subject and the distance between the verb and its object to the weight of its two arguments.

The weighted entry for "which" requires some explanation. First of all, the head word X of the resulting noun is the same as the head of the argument noun (this behaviour is consistent with a noun modifier, and it makes, for example, "book which ..." behave the same as "book" in this respect). Second, the extracted *np*, being a hypothetical element, starts at weight 0 and shares the head with the noun argument. This approach therefore expects the long-distance dependency

[7] Modifiers of modifiers (e.g. adverbs like "very") cannot be handled in the same way as in the natural deduction based account of the previous section. Since they modify the adjective or adverb they select, and since these no longer contain this adjective or adverb as their head word, we can no longer compute the distance between e.g. "very" and "interesting", and between "very" and "quickly" since both "interesting" and "quickly" are not arguments of any of their atomic subformulas. The natural deduction approach of the previous section assigns heads to formulas with no requirement that these be atomic, and this provides a potential benefit for these cases.

between a noun and a relative clause to occur most likely between the head noun and the verb which is semantically closest to it.

Compared to the standard proof net matching algorithm using minimisation (or maximisation) of weight, we have now added computation of weights to the matching process. This presents something of a complication. However, since we need to do only simple computations (addition, vector cosine) in each cell of the matrices representing the search space, this doesn't make a big difference computationally.

4.5 *Limitations*

The current method doesn't distinguish between object and subject arguments and this is an important weakness.[8] This limitation is essentially a consequence of the division of labour between the distributional and type-logical approaches: the type-logical component of the system is solely responsible for word order while the distributional component only tests for similarity between a verb and its argument, taking neither grammatical nor structural considerations into account. We therefore need either a more subtle similarity measure or another way of distinguishing the likely relations between a verb and its different arguments.

5 CONCLUSIONS AND FUTURE WORK

We have given an overview of several methods of adding weights to proof search in type-logical grammars. With the exception of Bonfante and de Groote (2001), this possibility has been seldom discussed in the type-logical grammar literature, to our surprise. We have given applications of weighted proof search to modelling human processing, to finding parses most similar to those found in a given corpus, and to finding parses which prefer grouping similar words together. These methods still need to be thoroughly evaluated beyond the manually calculated examples shown here. Fortunately, for many current type-logical grammars and their theorem provers, the groundwork for incorporating weighted proof search has already been laid down. Given

[8] As discussed in Section 4.2, we can incorporate this when estimating probabilities from a corpus, but not for the other methods discussed here, i.e. vector similarity and word distance.

the many potential applications of weighted proof search, we look forward to testing these methods against available data for parsing and human processing.

REFERENCES

Anne ABEILLÉ, Lionel CLÉMENT, and François TOUSSENEL (2003), Building a Treebank for French, in Anne ABEILLÉ, editor, *Treebanks*, volume 20 of *Text, Speech and Language Technology*, pp. 165–187, Springer.

Lasha ABZIANIDZE (2017), *A natural proof system for natural language*, Ph.D. thesis, Tilburg University.

Nicolas ASHER and Alex LASCARIDES (2003), *Logics of Conversation*, Cambridge University Press.

Emmon BACH, Colin BROWN, and William MARSLEN-WILSON (1986), Crossed and Nested Dependencies in German and Dutch: A Psycholinguistic Study, *Language and Cognitive Processes*, 1(4):249–262.

Patrick BAILLOT and Virgile MOGBIL (2004), Soft Lambda-calculus: A Language for Polynomial Time Computation, in *Foundations of software science and computation structures*, pp. 27–41, Springer.

Srinivas BANGALORE and Aravind JOSHI (2011), *Supertagging: Using Complex Lexical Descriptions in Natural Language Processing*, MIT Press, Cambridge, Massachusetts.

Marco BARONI, Silvia BERNARDINI, Adriano FERRARESI, and Eros ZANCHETTA (2009), The WaCky Wide Web: A Collection of Very Large Linguistically Processed Web-Crawled Corpora, *Language Resources and Evaluation*, 43(3):209–226.

Marco BARONI and Alessandro LENCI (2010), Distributional Memory: A General Framework for Corpus-based Semantics, *Computational Linguistics*, 36(4):673–721.

Adam BERGER, Stephen DELLA PIETRA, and Vincent DELLA PIETRA (1996), A Maximum Entropy Approach to Natural Language Processing, *Computational Linguistics*, 22(1):39–71.

Guillaume BONFANTE and Philippe DE GROOTE (2001), Stochastic Lambek Categorial Grammars, in Geert-Jan KRUIJFF, Larry MOSS, and Richard T. OEHRLE, editors, *Proceedings of FGMOL 2001*, volume 53 of *Electronic Notes in Theoretical Computer Science*, Elsevier.

Johan BOS and Katja MARKERT (2005), Recognising Textual Entailment with Logical Inference, in *Proceedings of the 2005 Conference on Empirical Methods in Natural Language Processing (EMNLP 2005)*, pp. 628–635.

Vincent DANOS (1990), *La logique linéaire appliquée à l'étude de divers processus de normalisation (principalement du λ-calcul)* [Linear logic applied to the study of various normalisation processes (mainly of the lambda calculus)], Ph.D. thesis, University of Paris VII.

Vincent DANOS and Laurent REGNIER (1989), The Structure of Multiplicatives, *Archive for Mathematical Logic*, 28:181–203.

Jean-Philippe FAUCONNIER (2016), *Acquisition de liens sémantiques à partir d'éléments de mise en forme des textes : exploitation des structures énumératives* [Acquisition of semantic relations from text layout elements: exploitation of enumerative structures], Ph.D. thesis, Université de Toulouse.

L. T. F. GAMUT (1991), *Logic, Language and Meaning*, volume 2, The University of Chicago Press.

Jean-Yves GIRARD (1987), Linear Logic, *Theoretical Computer Science*, 50:1–102.

Mark JOHNSON (1998), Proof Nets and the Complexity of Processing Center-Embedded Constructions, *Journal of Logic, Language and Information*, 7(4):443–447.

Adam KILGARRIFF and Gregory GREFENSTETTE (2003), Introduction to the Special Issue on the Web as Corpus, *Computational Linguistics*, 29:333–347.

Harold W. KUHN (1955), The Hungarian Method for the Assignment Problem, *Naval Research Logistics Quarterly*, 2:83–97.

Yves LAFONT (2004), Soft Linear Logic and Polynomial Time, *Theoretical Computer Science*, 318(1):163–180.

Joachim LAMBEK (1958), The Mathematics of Sentence Structure, *American Mathematical Monthly*, 65:154–170.

David M. MAGERMAN (1994), *Natural language parsing as statistical pattern recognition*, Ph.D. thesis, University of Pennsylvania.

Jeff MITCHELL and Mirella LAPATA (2010), Composition in Distributional Models of Semantics, *Cognitive Science*, 34:1388–1429.

Michael MOORTGAT (1997), Categorial Type Logics, in Johan VAN BENTHEM and Alice TER MEULEN, editors, *Handbook of Logic and Language*, chapter 2, pp. 93–177, Elsevier/MIT Press.

Richard MOOT (2010), Automated Extraction of Type-logical Supertags from the Spoken Dutch Corpus, in Srinivas BANGALORE and Aravind JOSHI, editors, *Complexity of Lexical Descriptions and its Relevance to Natural Language Processing: A Supertagging Approach*, chapter 12, pp. 291–312, MIT Press, Cambridge, Massachusetts.

Richard MOOT (2014a), Extended Lambek Calculi and First-order Linear Logic, in Claudia CASADIO, Bob COECKE, Michael MOORTGAT, and Philip SCOTT, editors, *Categories and Types in Logic, Language, and Physics: Essays dedicated to*

Jim Lambek on the Occasion of this 90th Birthday, number 8222 in Lecture Notes in Artificial Intelligence, pp. 297–330, Springer, Heidelberg.

Richard MOOT (2014b), A Type-logical Treebank for French, *Journal of Language Modelling*, 2(2).

Richard MOOT (2017), The Grail Theorem Prover: Type Theory for Syntax and Semantics, in Zhaohui LUO and Stergios CHATZIKYRIAKIDIS, editors, *Modern Perspectives in Type Theoretical Semantics*, Springer.

Richard MOOT and Christian RETORÉ (2012), *The Logic of Categorial Grammars: A Deductive Account of Natural Language Syntax and Semantics*, number 6850 in Lecture Notes in Artificial Intelligence, Springer, Heidelberg.

Richard MOOT and Christian RETORÉ (2016), Natural Language Semantics and Computability, Technical report, LIRMM.

Glyn MORRILL (1998), Incremental Processing and Acceptability, Technical Report LSI–98–46–R, Departament de Llenguatges i Sistemes Informàtics, Universitat Politècnica de Catalunya.

Glyn MORRILL (2011), *Categorial Grammar: Logical Syntax, Semantics, and Processing*, Oxford University Press, Oxford.

The Nghia PHAM (2016), *Sentential Representations in Distributional Semantics*, Ph.D. thesis, University of Trento.

Helmut SCHWICHTENBERG (1982), Complexity of Normalization in the Pure Typed Lambda-Calculus, in *The L. E. J. Brouwer Centenary Symposium*, pp. 453–457, North-Holland.

3

Chomsky-Schützenberger parsing for weighted multiple context-free languages

Tobias Denkinger
Faculty of Computer Science
Technische Universität Dresden
Germany

Keywords: Chomsky-Schützenberger, parsing, multiple context-free grammars, linear context-free rewriting systems

ABSTRACT

We prove a Chomsky-Schützenberger representation theorem for multiple context-free languages weighted over complete commutative strong bimonoids. Using this representation we devise a parsing algorithm for a restricted form of those devices.[1]

1 INTRODUCTION

Mildly context-sensitive languages receive much attention in the natural language processing community since they are able to express non-projective constituents (Maier and Søgaard 2008) and non-projective dependencies (Kuhlmann and Satta 2009). Figure 1 shows an example of a non-projective constituency tree. Figure 2 shows an example of a non-projective dependency tree. Non-projectivity is evident from crossings of edges, highlighted by circles. The phenomenon of non-projectivity occurs frequently in natural language corpora, e.g. about 28 percent of all sentences in both the NeGra corpus[2] and the TIGER corpus (Brants *et al.* 2004) contain non-projective constituents

[1] The CS parser for weighted MCFL (Sections 5 and 6) is original to this work. Sections 2 to 4 are a substantially revised version of Denkinger (2015).

[2] `http://www.coli.uni-saarland.de/projects/sfb378/negra-corpus/`

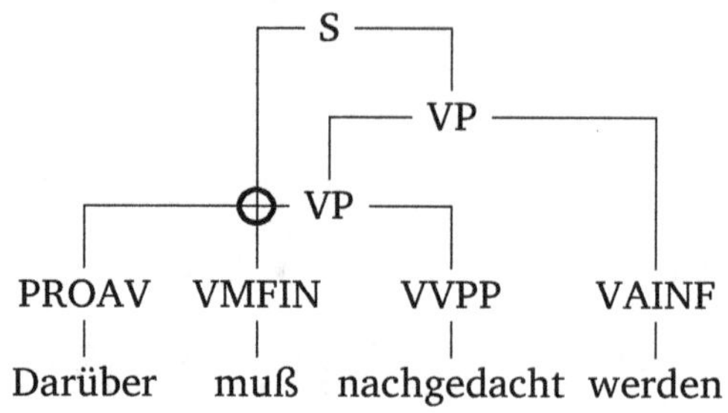

Figure 1: A non-projective constituency tree (taken from Maier and Søgaard 2008, Figure 3)

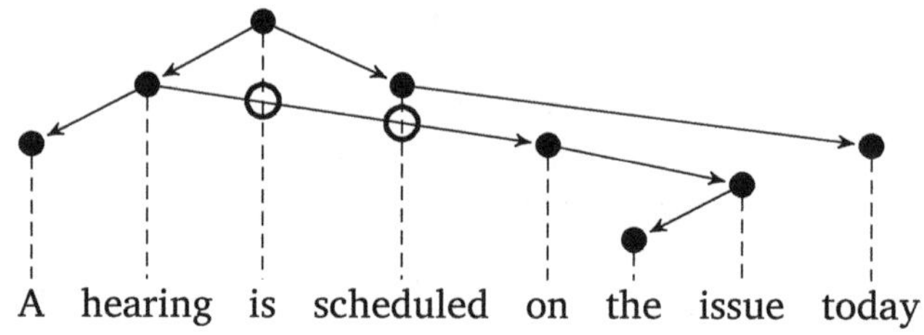

Figure 2: A non-projective dependency tree (taken from Kuhlmann and Satta 2009, Figure 2)

(Maier and Søgaard 2008, Table 6) and about 23 percent of all sentences in the Prague Dependency Treebank[3] contain non-projective dependencies (Kuhlmann and Satta 2009, Section 1).

Multiple context-free grammars describe the language classes induced by many mildly context-sensitive grammar formalisms, e.g. head grammars (Seki *et al.* 1991), linear context-free rewriting systems (Seki *et al.* 1991), combinatory categorial grammars (Vijay-Shanker *et al.* 1986; Weir and Joshi 1988), linear indexed grammars (Vijay-Shanker 1988), minimalist grammars (Michaelis 2001b,a), and finite-copying lexical functional grammars (Seki *et al.* 1993).

Parsing, i.e. the annotation of a sentence with syntactic structure, is one of the main concerns of natural language processing. Many parsing approaches are known for multiple context-free grammars, e.g.

- Cocke-Younger-Kasami-style parsing (Seki *et al.* 1991, Procedure MEMBER; and Burden and Ljunglöf 2005, Section 3),
- guided parsing (Barthélemy *et al.* 2001; Burden and Ljunglöf 2005, Section 4; and van Cranenburgh 2012),
- active parsing (Burden and Ljunglöf 2005, Section 5),
- incremental parsing (Villemonte de la Clergerie 2002; Burden and Ljunglöf 2005, Section 6; and Angelov 2009), and
- LR-style parsing (Kallmeyer and Maier 2015).

[3] `https://ufal.mff.cuni.cz/pdt/Corpora/PDT_1.0/`

The Chomsky-Schützenberger (CS) representation for context-free languages (Chomsky and Schützenberger 1963, Proposition 2) has been generalised to a variety of unweighted and weighted settings, e.g. context-free languages weighted with commutative semirings (Salomaa and Soittola 1978, Theorem 4.5), tree adjoining languages (Weir 1988, Lemma 3.5.2), multiple context-free languages (Yoshinaka *et al.* 2010, Theorem 3), context-free languages weighted with unital valuation monoids (Droste and Vogler 2013, Theorem 2), yields of simple context-free tree languages (Kanazawa 2014, Theorem 8.3), indexed languages (Duske *et al.* 1979, Theorems 1 and 2; Fratani and Voundy 2015, Theorem 4; and Fratani and Voundy 2016, Theorem 18), and automata with storage weighted with unital valuation monoids (Herrmann and Vogler 2015, Theorem 11).

We give a generalisation to the case of multiple context-free languages weighted with a complete commutative strong bimonoid and apply it to devise a parsing algorithm. Sections 3 to 5 contain the main contributions of this article.

- In Section 3 we provide a CS representation for weighted multiple context-free languages by means of a modular proof that first separates the weights from the given grammar and then employs the result for the unweighted case (using the same overall idea as in Droste and Vogler 2013).
- In Section 4 we give a more algebraic variant of multiple Dyck languages using congruence relations together with a decision algorithm for membership that is strongly related to those congruence relations. Also we show that congruence multiple Dyck languages can be used to develop a CS representation of weighted MCFLs.
- Using the CS representation based on congruence multiple Dyck languages and given a partial order on the weights, we derive a parsing algorithm (Section 5) similar to the one described by Hulden (2011). It employs a regular language and a weight function to generate output that is then filtered by an acceptor for a specific congruence multiple Dyck language in order to obtain the best derivations with respect to the partial order.
- The idea behind the Chomsky-Schützenberger parser presented in Section 5 is similar to already established approaches. Section 6 relates the known approaches to the one presented in this article.

Since our proofs do not require distributivity, we can be slightly more general than complete commutative semirings: We consider complete commutative strong bimonoids.

2 PRELIMINARIES

In this section we recall formalisms used in this article and fix some notation: We denote by $\mathbb{N}$ the set of natural numbers (including zero), and by $\mathbb{N}_+$ the set $\mathbb{N} \setminus \{0\}$. For every $n \in \mathbb{N}$ we abbreviate $\{1, \ldots, n\}$ by $[n]$. Let A be a set. The *power set of* A is denoted by $\mathscr{P}(A)$. Let B be a finite set. A *partition of* B is a set $\mathfrak{P} \subseteq \mathscr{P}(B)$ where the elements of $\mathfrak{P}$ (called *cells*) are non-empty, pairwise disjoint, and $\bigcup_{\mathfrak{p} \in \mathfrak{P}} \mathfrak{p} = B$.

Let A and B be sets and $A' \subseteq A$. The *set of functions from A to B* is denoted by $A \to B$, we still write $f : A \to B$ rather then $f \in A \to B$. Let f be a function. The *domain and codomain of* f are denoted by $\mathrm{dom}(f)$ and $\mathrm{codom}(f)$, respectively. The *restriction of* f *to* A', denoted by $f|_{A'}$, is a function from A' to B such that $f|_{A'}(a') = f(a')$ for every $a' \in A'$. Let g be a function such that $\mathrm{codom}(f) \subseteq \mathrm{dom}(g)$. We denote the function obtained by applying g *after* f by $g \circ f$. Let F be a set of functions and $B \subseteq \bigcap_{f \in F} \mathrm{dom}(f)$. The set $\{f(B) \mid f \in F\} \subseteq \mathscr{P}(\bigcup_{f \in F} \mathrm{codom}(f))$ is denoted by $F(B)$. Let G and H be sets of functions such that $\bigcap_{g \in G} \mathrm{codom}(g) \subseteq \bigcap_{h \in H} \mathrm{dom}(h)$. The set $\{h \circ g \mid h \in H, g \in G\}$ of functions is denoted by $H \circ G$.

Let A be a set and $\approx \subseteq A \times A$ a binary relation on A. We call $\approx$ an *equivalence relation (on A)* if it is reflexive, symmetric, and transitive. Let $a \in A$ and $\approx$ be an equivalence relation. The *equivalence class of* a *in* $\approx$, denoted by $[a]_\approx$, is $\{b \in A \mid a \approx b\}$. Let $f : A^k \to A$ be a function. We say that $\approx$ *respects* f if for every $(a_1, b_1), \ldots, (a_k, b_k) \in \approx$ holds $f(a_1, \ldots, a_k) \approx f(b_1, \ldots, b_k)$. Now let $\mathscr{A}$ be an algebra with domain A. We call $\approx$ a *congruence relation (on* $\mathscr{A}$*)* if $\approx$ is an equivalence relation on A and respects every operation of $\mathscr{A}$.

Let $\trianglelefteq \subseteq A \times A$ be a binary relation on A. We call $\trianglelefteq$ a *partial order (on A)* if it is reflexive, antisymmetric, and transitive.

2.1 *Sorts*

We will use the concept of sorts to formalise restrictions on building terms (or trees), e.g. derivation trees or terms over functions. One can think of sorts as data types in a programming language: Every concrete value has a sort (type) and every function requires its arguments to be of fixed sorts (types) and returns a value of some fixed sort (type).

Let S be a countable set (of *sorts*) and $s \in S$. An *S-sorted set* is a tuple (B, sort) where B is a set and sort is a function from B to S. We denote the preimage of s under sort by B_s and abbreviate (B, sort) by B; sort will always be clear from the context. Let A be an $(S^* \times S)$-sorted set. The *set of terms over A*, denoted by T_A, is the smallest S-sorted set T where $\xi = a(\xi_1, \ldots, \xi_k) \in T_s$ if there are $s_1, \ldots, s_k, s \in S$ such that $a \in A_{(s_1 \cdots s_k, s)}$ and $\xi_i \in T_{s_i}$ for every $i \in [k]$. Let $\xi = a(\xi_1, \ldots, \xi_k) \in T_A$. The *set of positions in ξ* is defined as $\mathrm{pos}(\xi) = \{\varepsilon\} \cup \{iu \mid i \in [k], u \in \mathrm{pos}(\xi_i)\}$ and for every $\pi \in \mathrm{pos}(\xi)$ the *symbol in ξ at position π* is defined as $\xi(\pi) = a$ if $\pi = \varepsilon$ and as $\xi(\pi) = \xi_i(u)$ if $\pi = iu$ for some $i \in [k]$ and $u \in \mathrm{pos}(\xi_i)$.

2.2 *Weight algebras*

A *monoid* is an algebra $(\mathcal{A}, \cdot, 1)$ where $\cdot$ is associative and 1 is neutral with respect to $\cdot$. A *bimonoid* is an algebra $(\mathcal{A}, +, \cdot, 0, 1)$ where $(\mathcal{A}, +, 0)$ and $(\mathcal{A}, \cdot, 1)$ are monoids. We call a bimonoid *strong* if $(\mathcal{A}, +, 0)$ is commutative and for every $a \in \mathcal{A}$ we have $0 \cdot a = 0 = a \cdot 0$. Intuitively, a strong bimonoid is a semiring without distributivity. A strong bimonoid is called *commutative* if $(\mathcal{A}, \cdot, 1)$ is commutative. A commutative strong bimonoid is *complete* if there is an infinitary sum operation $\sum$ that maps every indexed family of elements of $\mathcal{A}$ to $\mathcal{A}$, extends $+$, and satisfies infinitary associativity and commutativity laws (cf. Droste and Vogler 2013, Section 2), i.e. for every countable set I and every I-indexed family $a\colon I \to \mathcal{A}$ it holds that:

(i) $\sum_{i \in \emptyset} a(i) = 0$;
(ii) for every $j \in I$: $\sum_{i \in \{j\}} a(i) = a(j)$;
(iii) for every $j, k \in I$ with $j \neq k$: $\sum_{i \in \{j,k\}} a(i) = a(j) + a(k)$; and
(iv) for every countable set J and family $\mathcal{I}\colon J \to \mathcal{P}(I)$ with $I = \bigcup_{j \in J} \mathcal{I}(j)$ and for every $j, j' \in J$ with $j \neq j' \implies \mathcal{I}(j) \cap \mathcal{I}(j') = \emptyset$, we have $\sum_{j \in J} \sum_{i \in \mathcal{I}(j)} a(i) = \sum_{i \in I} a(i)$.

For the rest of this article let $(\mathcal{A}, +, \cdot, 0, 1)$, abbreviated by $\mathcal{A}$, be a complete commutative strong bimonoid.

Example 2.1. We provide a list of complete commutative strong bimonoids (cf. Droste *et al.* 2010, Example 1) some of which are relevant for natural language processing:

- any complete commutative semiring, e.g.
  - the *Boolean semiring* $\mathbb{B} = (\{0,1\}, \vee, \wedge, 0, 1)$,
  - the *probability semiring* $\mathrm{Pr} = (\mathbb{R}_{\geq 0}, +, \cdot, 0, 1)$,
  - the *Viterbi semiring* $([0,1], \max, \cdot, 0, 1)$,
  - the *tropical semiring* $(\mathbb{R} \cup \{\infty\}, \min, +, \infty, 0)$,
  - the *arctic semiring* $(\mathbb{R} \cup \{-\infty\}, \max, +, -\infty, 0)$,
- any complete lattice, e.g.
  - any non-empty finite lattice $(L, \vee, \wedge, 0, 1)$ where L is a non-empty finite set,
  - the lattice $(\mathscr{P}(A), \cup, \cap, \emptyset, A)$ where A is an arbitrary set,
  - the lattice $(\mathbb{N}, \mathrm{lcm}, \mathrm{gcd}, 1, 0)$,
- the *tropical bimonoid* $(\mathbb{R}_{\geq 0} \cup \{\infty\}, +, \min, 0, \infty)$,
- the *arctic bimonoid* $(\mathbb{R}_{\geq 0} \cup \{-\infty\}, +, \max, 0, -\infty)$, and
- the algebras $\mathrm{Pr}_1 = ([0,1], \oplus_1, \cdot, 0, 1)$ and $\mathrm{Pr}_2 = ([0,1], \oplus_2, \cdot, 0, 1)$ where $a \oplus_1 b = a + b - a \cdot b$ and $a \oplus_2 b = \min\{a + b, 1\}$ for every $a, b \in [0,1]$.

where $\mathbb{R}$ and $\mathbb{R}_{\geq 0}$ denote the set of reals and the set of non-negative reals, respectively; $+$, $\cdot$, max, min denote the usual operations; $\vee$, $\wedge$ denote disjunction and conjunction, respectively, for the boolean semiring and join and meet, respectively, for any non-empty finite lattice; and lcm and gcd are binary functions that calculate the least common multiple and the greatest common divisor, respectively.

Also, there are some bimonoids that are interesting for natural language processing but are *not* complete commutative strong bimonoids. E.g.

- the *semiring of formal languages* $(\mathscr{P}(\Sigma^*), \cup, \cdot, \emptyset, \{\varepsilon\})$ where Σ is an alphabet and $\cdot$ is language concatenation, i.e. $L_1 \cdot L_2 = \{uv \mid u \in L_1, v \in L_2\}$ for every $L_1, L_2 \subseteq \Sigma^*$; and
- the semiring $(\Sigma^* \cup \{\infty\}, \wedge, \cdot, \infty, \varepsilon)$ where Σ is an alphabet, $\cdot$ is concatenation, $\wedge$ calculates the longest common prefix of its arguments, and ∞ is a new element that is neutral with respect to $\wedge$ and annihilating with respect to $\cdot$ (cf. Mohri 2000).

None of the two examples is commutative. □

An $\mathscr{A}$*-weighted language (over* Δ*)* is a function $L\colon \Delta^* \to \mathscr{A}$. The *support of* L, denoted by $\mathrm{supp}(L)$, is $\{w \in \Delta^* \mid L(w) \neq 0\}$. If $|\mathrm{supp}(L)| \leq 1$, we call L a *monomial*. We write $\mu.w$ for L if $L(w) = \mu$ and for every $w' \in \Delta^* \setminus \{w\}$ we have $L(w') = 0$.

2.3 *Recognisable languages*

For the many known results concerning finite state automata and regular languages, we will rely on Hopcroft and Ullman (1969) and Hopcroft and Ullman (1979). We nevertheless recall the basic definitions:

Definition 2.2. A *finite state automaton*, for short: FSA, is a tuple $\mathscr{M} = (Q, \Delta, q_0, F, T)$ where Δ is an alphabet (*terminals*), Q is a finite set (*states*) disjoint from Δ, $q_0 \in Q$ (*initial state*), $F \subseteq Q$ (*final states*), and $T \subseteq Q \times \Delta^* \times Q$ is a finite set (*transitions*). □

A *run in* $\mathscr{M}$ is a string $\kappa \in (Q \cup \Delta)^*$ where for every substring of κ of the form quq' (for some $q, q' \in Q$ and $u \in \Delta^*$) we have that $(q, u, q') \in T$, the first symbol of κ is q_0, and the last symbol of κ is in F. If a run κ contains a substring of the form quq' (for some $q, q' \in Q$ and $u \in \Delta^*$), we say that the transition (q, u, q') *occurs in* κ. The *word corresponding to* κ is obtained by removing the elements of Q from κ. The *language of* $\mathscr{M}$ is denoted by $L(\mathscr{M})$. The *set of recognisable languages*, denoted by REC, is the set of languages L for which there is an FSA $\mathscr{M}$ with $L = L(\mathscr{M})$.

2.4 *Weighted string homomorphisms*

Let Δ and Γ be alphabets and $g\colon \Delta \to (\Gamma^* \to \mathscr{A})$ (i.e. a function that takes an element of Δ and returns a function that takes an element of Γ^* and returns an element of $\mathscr{A}$) such that $g(\delta)$ is a monomial for every $\delta \in \Delta$. We define $\widehat{g}\colon \Delta^* \to (\Gamma^* \to \mathscr{A})$ where for every $k \in \mathbb{N}$, $\delta_1, \ldots, \delta_k \in \Delta$, and $v \in \Gamma^*$ we have

$$\widehat{g}(\delta_1 \cdots \delta_k)(v) = \sum_{\substack{v_1, \ldots, v_k \in \Gamma^* \\ v = v_1 \cdots v_k}} g(\delta_1)(v_1) \cdot \ldots \cdot g(\delta_k)(v_k).$$

We call $\widehat{g}$ an $\mathscr{A}$*-weighted (string) homomorphism*. Since $g(\delta_1), \ldots, g(\delta_k)$ are monomials for each $\delta_1, \ldots, \delta_k \in \Delta$, there is at most one tuple $(v_1, \ldots, v_k) \in (\Gamma^*)^k$ such that $g(\delta_i)(v_i) \neq 0$ for every $i \in [k]$. Hence, there is at most one $v \in \Gamma^*$ with $\widehat{g}(\delta_1 \cdots \delta_k)(v) \neq 0$ (namely $v = v_1 \cdots v_k$). Therefore, $\widehat{g}(u)$ is a monomial for every $u \in \Delta^*$. We call $\widehat{g}$

alphabetic if there is a function $h\colon \Delta \to (\Gamma \cup \{\varepsilon\} \to \mathcal{A})$ with $\widehat{g} = \widehat{h}$. If $\widehat{g}(u) = \mu.w$ (recall the end of Section 2.2) for $u \in \Delta^*$, then we will sometimes say "$\widehat{g}$ maps u to w" (leaving out the weight μ) or "$\widehat{g}$ weights u with μ" (leaving out the word w). Now assume that $\mathcal{A} = \mathbb{B}$ and we have $|\text{supp}(g(\delta))| = 1$ for every $\delta \in \Delta$. Then g can be construed as a function from Δ to Γ^* and $\widehat{g}$ can be construed as a function from Δ^* to Γ^*. In this case we call $\widehat{g}$ a *(string) homomorphism*. The sets of all $\mathcal{A}$-weighted homomorphisms, $\mathcal{A}$-weighted alphabetic homomorphisms, homomorphisms, and alphabetic homomorphisms are denoted by HOM($\mathcal{A}$), αHOM($\mathcal{A}$), HOM, and αHOM, respectively.

2.5 *Weighted multiple context-free languages*

We fix a set $X = \{x_i^j \mid i, j \in \mathbb{N}_+\}$ of *variables*. Let Δ be an alphabet. The set of *composition representations over* Δ is the $(\mathbb{N}^* \times \mathbb{N})$-sorted set RF_Δ where for every $s_1, \ldots, s_\ell, s \in \mathbb{N}$ we define $X_{(s_1\cdots s_\ell, s)} = \{x_i^j \mid i \in [\ell], j \in [s_i]\} \subseteq X$ and $(\text{RF}_\Delta)_{(s_1\cdots s_\ell, s)}$ as the set that contains $[u_1, \ldots, u_s]_{(s_1\cdots s_\ell, s)}$ for every $u_1, \ldots, u_s \in (\Delta \cup X_{(s_1\cdots s_\ell, s)})^*$. We will often write X_f instead of $X_{(s_1\cdots s_\ell, s)}$. Let $f = [u_1, \ldots, u_s]_{(s_1\cdots s_\ell, s)} \in \text{RF}_\Delta$. The *string function of* f, also denoted by f, is the function from $(\Delta^*)^{s_1} \times \cdots \times (\Delta^*)^{s_\ell}$ to $(\Delta^*)^s$ such that $f((w_1^1, \ldots, w_1^{s_1}), \ldots, (w_\ell^1, \ldots, w_\ell^{s_\ell})) = (u_1', \ldots, u_s')$ where $(u_1', \ldots, u_s')$ is obtained from $(u_1, \ldots, u_s)$ by replacing each occurrence of x_i^j by w_i^j for every $i \in [\ell]$ and $j \in [s_\ell]$. The set of all string functions for some composition representation over Δ is denoted by F_Δ. From here on we no longer distinguish between composition representations and string functions. We define the *rank of* f, denoted by rank(f), and the *fan-out of* f, denoted by fan-out(f), as ℓ and s, respectively. Also, we will denote s_i by fan-out$_i$(f) for every $i \in [\ell]$. The string function f is called *linear* if in $u_1 \cdots u_s$ every element of X_f occurs at most once, f is called *non-deleting* if in $u_1 \cdots u_s$ every element of X_f occurs at least once, and f is called *terminal-free* if $u_1, \ldots, u_s \in X_f^*$. The subscript is dropped from the string function if its sort is clear from the context.

Note that for every $s' \in \mathbb{N}^* \times \mathbb{N}$, the set of linear terminal-free string functions of sort s' is finite.

Definition 2.3. A *multiple context-free grammar (over* Δ*)*, for short: MCFG, is a tuple (N, Δ, S, P) where N is a finite $\mathbb{N}$-sorted set (*non-terminals*), $S \in N_1$ (*initial non-terminal*), and $P \subseteq_{\text{fin}} \{(A, f, A_1 \cdots A_\ell) \in N \times \text{F}_\Delta \times N^\ell \mid \text{sort}(f) = (\text{sort}(A_1) \cdots \text{sort}(A_\ell), \text{sort}(A)), f \text{ is linear}, \ell \in \mathbb{N}\}$

(*productions*). We construe P as an $(N^* \times N)$-sorted set where for every $\rho = (A, f, A_1 \cdots A_\ell) \in P$ we have $\text{sort}(\rho) = (A_1 \cdots A_\ell, A)$. □

Let $G = (N, \Delta, S, P)$ be an MCFG and $w \in \Delta^*$. A production $(A, f, A_1 \cdots A_\ell) \in P$ is usually written as $A \to f(A_1, \ldots, A_\ell)$; it inherits its rank, fan-out, and $\text{fan-out}_1, \ldots, \text{fan-out}_\ell$ from f. Also, $\text{rank}(G) = \max_{\rho \in P} \text{rank}(\rho)$ and $\text{fan-out}(G) = \max_{\rho \in P} \text{fan-out}(\rho)$. MCFGs of fan-out at most k and rank at most r are called *(k, r)-MCFGs*.

The function $\text{yield}\colon T_P \to \bigcup_{s=0}^{\max_{\rho \in P} \text{fan-out}(\rho)} (\Delta^*)^s$ assigns to every tree $d \in T_P$ the tuple obtained by projecting every production in d to the contained function (i.e. the second component) and then evaluating the resulting term over F_Δ.

Let $A \in N$. The *set of subderivations in G from A*, denoted by $D_G(A)$, is the set of all terms over P with sort A, i.e. $D_G(A) = (T_P)_A$. The *set of derivations in G* is $D_G = D_G(S)$. Let $w \in \Delta^*$. The *set of derivations of w in G* is $D_G(w) = \{d \in D_G \mid \text{yield}(d) = w\}$.[4]

The *language of G* is $L(G) = \{w \in \Delta^* \mid D_G(w) \neq \emptyset\}$. A language L is called *multiple context-free* if there is an MCFG G with $L = L(G)$. The *set of multiple context-free languages (for which a (k, r)-MCFG exists)* is denoted by MCFL ((k, r)-MCFL, respectively).

The language class (k, r)-MCFL is a substitution-closed full abstract family of languages (Seki *et al.* 1991, Theorem 3.9). Thus (k, r)-MCFL is closed under homomorphisms and under intersection with regular languages.

Definition 2.4. An *$\mathscr{A}$-weighted MCFG (over Δ)* is a tuple (N, Δ, S, P, μ) where (N, Δ, S, P) is an MCFG and $\mu\colon P \to \mathscr{A} \setminus \{0\}$ (*weight assignment*). □

Let $G = (N, \Delta, S, P, \mu)$ be an $\mathscr{A}$-weighted MCFG and $w \in \Delta^*$. The *set of derivations of w in G* is the set of derivations of w in (N, Δ, S, P). G inherits fan-out and rank from (N, Δ, S, P); $\mathscr{A}$-weighted MCFGs of fan-out at most k and rank at most r are called *$\mathscr{A}$-weighted (k, r)-MCFGs*. We define a function $\widehat{\mu}\colon D_G \to \mathscr{A}$ that applies μ at every position of a given derivation and then multiplies the resulting values (in any order, since $\cdot$ is commutative). The *$\mathscr{A}$-weighted language induced by G* is the function $[\![G]\!]\colon \Delta^* \to \mathscr{A}$ where for every $w \in \Delta^*$ we have $[\![G]\!](w) = \sum_{d \in D_G(w)} \widehat{\mu}(d)$.

[4] We identify the 1-tuple containing a word $w \in \Delta^*$ with the word w itself.

Two ($\mathscr{A}$-weighted) MCFGs are *equivalent* if they induce the same ($\mathscr{A}$-weighted) language. An $\mathscr{A}$-weighted language L is called *multiple context-free* if there is an $\mathscr{A}$-weighted MCFG G such that $L = [\![G]\!]$; (k,r)-MCFL($\mathscr{A}$) denotes the set of languages induced by multiple context-free $\mathscr{A}$-weighted grammars of fan-out at most k and rank at most r.

Example 2.5. Consider the Pr_2-weighted MCFG $G = (N, \Delta, S, P, \mu)$ where $N_1 = \{S\}$, $N_2 = \{A, B\}$, $N = N_1 \cup N_2$, $\Delta = \{a, b, c, d\}$, and P and μ are given by

$$
\begin{aligned}
P\colon\ & \rho_1 = S \to [x_1^1 x_2^1 x_1^2 x_2^2](A,B) & \mu\colon\ & \mu(\rho_1) = 1\\
& \rho_2 = A \to [a x_1^1, c x_1^2](A) & & \mu(\rho_2) = 1/2\\
& \rho_3 = B \to [b x_1^1, d x_1^2](B) & & \mu(\rho_3) = 1/3\\
& \rho_4 = A \to [\varepsilon, \varepsilon]() & & \mu(\rho_4) = 1/2\\
& \rho_5 = B \to [\varepsilon, \varepsilon]() & & \mu(\rho_5) = 2/3\,.
\end{aligned}
$$

Note that G has fan-out 2 and rank 2. We observe that $\mathrm{supp}([\![G]\!]) = \{a^m b^n c^m d^n \mid m, n \in \mathbb{N}\}$ and for every $m, n \in \mathbb{N}$ we have

$$
\begin{aligned}
[\![G]\!](a^m b^n c^m d^n) &= \mu(\rho_1) \cdot \big(\mu(\rho_2)\big)^m \cdot \mu(\rho_4) \cdot \big(\mu(\rho_3)\big)^m \cdot \mu(\rho_5)\\
&= 1/(2^m \cdot 3^{n+1}).
\end{aligned}
$$

The derivation d of $w = ac$ and the derivation $\bar{d}$ of $\bar{w} = aabccd$ in G are shown in Figure 3, their weights are $1/(2^1 \cdot 3^{0+1}) = 1/6$ and $1/(2^2 \cdot 3^{1+1}) = 1/36$, respectively. Since d and $\bar{d}$ are unique derivations for w and $\bar{w}$, we have $[\![G]\!](w) = 1/6$ and $[\![G]\!](\bar{w}) = 1/36$. □

A non-terminal is called *productive in an ($\mathscr{A}$-weighted) MCFG* if there is at least one subderivation starting from this non-terminal. It is obvious that every ($\mathscr{A}$-weighted) (k,r)-MCFL can be recognised by an ($\mathscr{A}$-weighted) (k,r)-MCFG that only has productive non-terminals.

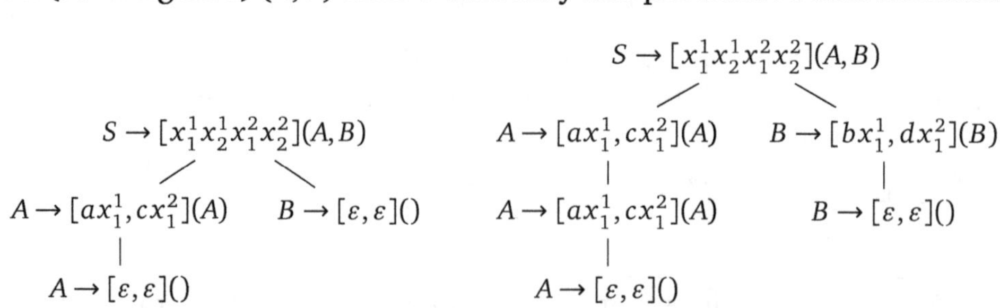

Figure 3: Derivation d of ac (left) and derivation d of $aabccd$ (right) in G (Example 2.5)

Non-deleting normal form

An ($\mathcal{A}$-weighted) MCFG is called *non-deleting* if the string function in every production is linear and non-deleting. Non-deleting MCFGs are also called linear context-free rewriting systems (Vijay-Shanker *et al.* 1987) in the literature. Seki *et al.* (1991, Lemma 2.2) proved that for every (k,r)-MCFG there is an equivalent non-deleting (k,r)-MCFG. We generalise this to $\mathcal{A}$-weighted MCFGs.

Lemma 2.6. For every $\mathcal{A}$-weighted (k,r)-MCFG there is an equivalent non-deleting $\mathcal{A}$-weighted (k,r)-MCFG.

Proof idea. We modify the construction for the unweighted case (Seki *et al.* 1991, Lemma 2.2) such that it preserves the structure of derivations. Then a weight assignment can be defined in an obvious manner.

Proof. Let $G = (N, \Delta, S, P, \mu)$ be an $\mathcal{A}$-weighted (k,r)-MCFG. We construct the (k,r)-MCFG $G' = (N', \Delta, S\langle\varnothing\rangle, P')$ where $N' = \{A\langle\Psi\rangle \mid A \in N, \Psi \subseteq [\mathrm{sort}(A)]\}$, $P' = \{\rho_\Psi \mid \rho \in P, \Psi \subseteq [\text{fan-out}(\rho)]\}$, and $\rho_\Psi = A\langle\Psi\rangle \to [u_{j_1}, \ldots, u_{j_\ell}](A_1\langle\Psi_1\rangle, \ldots, A_k\langle\Psi_k\rangle)$ for every $\rho = A \to [u_1, \ldots, u_m](A_1, \ldots, A_k) \in P$ and $\Psi \subseteq [\mathrm{sort}(A)]$ such that

(i) $\{j_1, \ldots, j_\ell\} = [\mathrm{sort}(A)] \setminus \Psi$ with $j_1 < \cdots < j_\ell$ and
(ii) $\Psi_i = \{j \subseteq [\mathrm{sort}(A_i)] \mid x_i^j$ does not occur in $u_{j_1} \cdots u_{j_\ell}\}$ for each $i \in [k]$.

The construction of G' here is a slight modification of the original construction (Lemma 2.2 in Seki *et al.* 1991, step 2 of Procedure 1) where we dropped the restrictions that $\Psi \neq [\mathrm{sort}(A)]$ and $\Psi \neq [\text{fan-out}(\rho)]$ in the definitions of N' and P', respectively.[5] Note that for each ρ and Ψ, the sets $\Psi_1, \ldots, \Psi_k$ are uniquely defined. Let $g: P' \to P$ such that $g(\rho_\Psi) = \rho$ and $\widehat{g}: D_{G'} \to D_G$ be the function obtained by applying g point-wise. We show the following hypothesis by induction on the structure of subderivations:
Induction hypothesis: For every $A \in N$ and $\Psi \subseteq [\mathrm{sort}(A)]$: $\widehat{g}$ is a bijection between $D_{G'}(A\langle\Psi\rangle)$ and $D_G(A)$.
Induction step: Let $d \in D_G(A)$ and $\Psi \subseteq [\mathrm{sort}(A)]$ with $d = \rho(d_1, \ldots, d_k)$ for some production $\rho \in P$ and derivations $d_1 \in D_G(A_1)$, …, $d_k \in D_G(A_k)$. By construction, $\Psi_1 \subseteq [\mathrm{sort}(A_1)]$, …, $\Psi_k \subseteq [\mathrm{sort}(A_k)]$ and therefore

[5] This construction may therefore create productions of fan-out 0.

ρ_Ψ are uniquely defined for every ρ and Ψ. By the induction hypothesis, we know that there are derivations $d'_1, \ldots, d'_k$ which are unique for $(d_1, \Psi_1), \ldots, (d_k, \Psi_k)$, respectively. Therefore, $d' = \rho(d'_1, \ldots, d'_k)$ is unique for d and Ψ. Hence for every Ψ, $\widehat{g}$ is a bijection between $D_{G'}(A\langle\Psi\rangle)$ and $D_G(A)$.

By construction, the new start symbol is $S\langle\varnothing\rangle$; hence for the elements of $D_{G'}$, we set $\Psi = \varnothing$ and by induction hypothesis we obtain that $\widehat{g}$ is bijective. Since $\widehat{g}$ preserves the structure of derivations and is a bijection, we obtain $\widehat{\mu \circ g} = \widehat{\mu} \circ \widehat{g}$. Hence $[\![(N', \Delta, S\langle\varnothing\rangle, P', \mu \circ g)]\!] = [\![G]\!]$. Fan-out and rank are not increased by this construction. ∎

3 CS CHARACTERISATION FOR WEIGHTED MCFLS

In this section we generalise the CS characterisation of (unweighted) MCFLs (Yoshinaka *et al.* 2010, Theorem 3) to the weighted case. We prove that an $\mathscr{A}$-weighted MCFL L can be decomposed into an $\mathscr{A}$-weighted alphabetic homomorphism h, a regular language R and a multiple Dyck language mD such that $L = h(R \cap mD)$.

To show this, we use the proof idea from Droste and Vogler (2013): We separate the weight from our grammar formalism and then use the unweighted CS representation on the unweighted part. The outline of our proof is as follows:

(i) We separate the weights from L (Lemma 3.3), obtaining an MCFL L' and a weighted alphabetic homomorphism.

(ii) We use a corollary of the CS representation of (unweighted) MCFLs (Corollary 3.8) to obtain a CS representation of L'.

(iii) Using the two previous items and Lemma 3.10 for the composition of weighted and unweighted alphabetic homomorphisms, we obtain a CS representation of L (Theorem 3.12).

Figure 4 outlines the proof of Theorem 3.12. The boxes represent sub-diagrams for which the corresponding lemmas prove existence of the arrows and that the sub-diagram commutes.

3.1 *Separating the weights*

We split a given weighted MCFG G into an unweighted MCFG $G_{\mathbb{B}}$ and a weighted alphabetic homomorphism $\mathrm{weights}_G$ such that $[\![G]\!](w) = \sum_{u \in L(G_{\mathbb{B}})} \mathrm{weights}_G(u)(w)$ for every $w \in \Delta^*$.

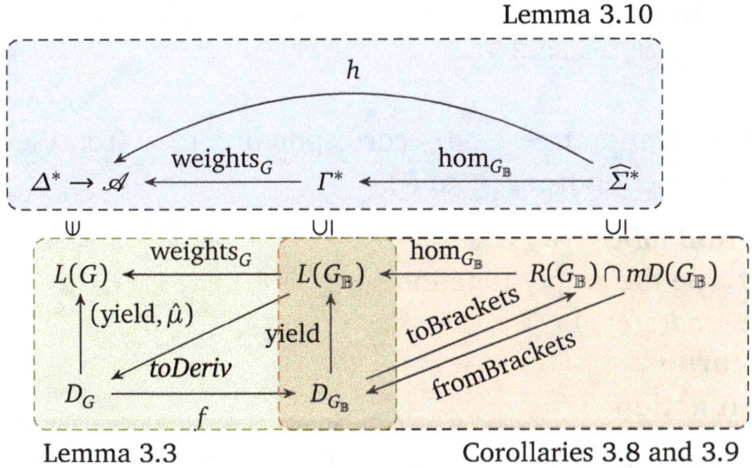

Figure 4: Outline of the proof of Theorem 3.12

Definition 3.1. Let $G = (N, \Delta, S, P, \mu)$ be a non-deleting $\mathscr{A}$-weighted k-MCFG. The *unweighted MCFG for* G is the non-deleting k-MCFG $G_\mathbb{B} = (N, \Gamma, S, P_\mathbb{B})$ where $\Gamma = \Delta \cup \{\rho^i \mid \rho \in P, i \in [\text{fan-out}(\rho)]\}$ and $P_\mathbb{B}$ is the smallest set P' such that for every production $\rho = A \to [u_1, \ldots, u_s](A_1, \ldots, A_m) \in P$ there is a production

$$A \to [\rho^1 u_1, \ldots, \rho^s u_s](A_1, \ldots, A_m) \in P'. \qquad \square$$

Definition 3.2. Let $G = (N, \Delta, S, P, \mu)$ be a non-deleting $\mathscr{A}$-weighted MCFG. The *weight homomorphism for* G is the $\mathscr{A}$-weighted alphabetic homomorphism $\text{weights}_G \colon \Gamma^* \to (\Delta^* \to \mathscr{A})$ where $\text{weights}_G(\delta) = 1.\delta$, $\text{weights}_G(\rho^1) = \mu(\rho).\varepsilon$, and $\text{weights}_G(\rho^i) = 1.\varepsilon$ for every $\delta \in \Delta$, $\rho \in P$ and $i \in \{2, \ldots, \text{fan-out}(\rho)\}$. $\square$

$L(G_\mathbb{B})$ stands in bijection to D_G via the function *toDeriv* given in Algorithm 1.

Lemma 3.3. $(k, r)\text{-MCFL}(\mathscr{A}) = \alpha\text{HOM}(\mathscr{A})\big((k, r)\text{-MCFL}\big)$

Proof. ($\subseteq$) Let $L \in (k, r)\text{-MCFL}(\mathscr{A})$. By Lemma 2.6 there is a non-deleting $\mathscr{A}$-weighted (k, r)-MCFG $G = (N, \Delta, S, P, \mu)$ such that $[\![G]\!] = L$. Let $f : P \to P_\mathbb{B}$ where for every $\rho = A \to [u_1, \ldots, u_s](A_1, \ldots, A_m) \in P$ we have $f(\rho) = A \to [\rho^1 u_1, \ldots, \rho^s u_s](A_1, \ldots, A_m)$, in other words f represents the construction of rules in $P_\mathbb{B}$ from the corresponding rules in P (see Definition 3.1). We extend f to $\widehat{f} \colon D_G \to D_{G_\mathbb{B}}$ by position-wise application, i.e. $\widehat{f}(d) = (f(\rho))(\widehat{f}(d_1), \ldots, \widehat{f}(d_k))$ for every subderivation $d = \rho(d_1, \ldots, d_k)$ in G; and we write f instead of $\widehat{f}$. For every

Algorithm 1: Function *toDeriv* to calculate for every word in $L(G_{\mathbb{B}})$ the corresponding derivation in D_G, cf. Lemma 3.3

Input: $w \in L(G_{\mathbb{B}})$
Output: derivation tree $t \in D_G$ corresponding to w (represented as a partial function from $\mathbb{N}^*$ to P)

```
function toDeriv(w)
    let t be the empty function
    descend(t, ε, 1)
    return t
end function

procedure descend(t: ℕ* → P, π ∈ ℕ*, j ∈ ℕ)
    let ρ = A → [u_1, ..., u_s](A_1, ..., A_k) ∈ P and u such that ρ^j u = w
    add the assignment π ↦ ρ to t
    remove ρ^j from the beginning of w
    for every symbol δ' in u_j do
        if δ' ∈ Δ then
            remove δ' from the beginning of w
        else
            let i, j' such that x_i^{j'} = δ'
            descend(t, πi, j')
        end if
    end for
end procedure
```

$w \in L(G_{\mathbb{B}})$ we can calculate the corresponding derivation t in G (as a function with domain $\mathrm{dom}(t)$ and labelling function t) using *toDeriv* (Algorithm 1), hence $\mathrm{yield} \circ f$ is bijective. We derive for every $w \in \Delta^*$:

$$\begin{aligned}
L(w) &= [\![G]\!](w) \\
&= \textstyle\sum_{d \in D_G(w)} \mu(d) \\
&= \textstyle\sum_{d \in D_G} (\mathrm{weights}_G \circ \mathrm{yield} \circ f)(d)(w) && (\text{by } \dagger) \\
&= \textstyle\sum_{\substack{d \in D_G, u \in L(G_{\mathbb{B}}) \\ u = (\mathrm{yield} \circ f)(d)}} \mathrm{weights}_G(u)(w) \\
&= \textstyle\sum_{u \in L(G_{\mathbb{B}})} \mathrm{weights}_G(u)(w) && (L(G_{\mathbb{B}}) \text{ and } D_G \text{ are in bijection}) \\
&= \mathrm{weights}_G(L(G_{\mathbb{B}}))(w)
\end{aligned}$$

For †, one can immediately see from the definitions of f, yield, and $\mathrm{weights}_G$ that for every $w \in \Delta^*$ we have $(\mathrm{weights}_G \circ \mathrm{yield} \circ f)(d)(w) =$

$\mu(d)$ if $d \in D_G(w)$ and $(\mathrm{weights}_G \circ \mathrm{yield} \circ f)(d)(w) = 0$ otherwise. Hence $L = \mathrm{weights}_G(L(G_{\mathbb{B}}))$.

($\supseteq$) Let $L \in (k,r)$-MCFL and $h\colon \Gamma^* \to (\Delta^* \to \mathscr{A})$ be an $\mathscr{A}$-weighted alphabetic homomorphism. By Seki *et al.* (1991, Lemma 2.2) there is a non-deleting (k,r)-MCFG $G = (N, \Gamma, S, P)$ such that $L(G) = L$. We construct the $\mathscr{A}$-weighted (k,r)-MCFG $G' = (N, \Delta, S, P', \mu)$ as follows: We extend h to $h'\colon (\Gamma \cup X)^* \to ((\Delta \cup X)^* \to \mathscr{A})$ where $h'(x) = 1.x$ for every $x \in X$ and $h'(\gamma) = h(\gamma)$ for every $\gamma \in \Gamma$. We define P' as the smallest set such that for every $\rho = A \to [u_1, \ldots, u_s](A_1, \ldots, A_m) \in P_{(s_1 \cdots s_m, s)}$ and $(u'_1, \ldots, u'_s) \in \mathrm{supp}(h'(u_1)) \times \ldots \times \mathrm{supp}(h'(u_s))$ we have that P' contains the production $\rho' = A \to [u'_1, \ldots, u'_s](A_1, \ldots, A_m)$ and $\mu(\rho') = h'(u_1)(u'_1) \cdot \ldots \cdot h'(u_s)(u'_s)$. Since $\cdot$ is commutative and G is non-deleting, we obtain $[\![G']\!] = h(L(G))$. ∎

By setting $k = 1$ in the above lemma we reobtain the equivalence of 1 and 3 in Theorem 2 of Droste and Vogler (2013) for the case of complete commutative strong bimonoids.

Example 3.4. Recall the Pr_2-weighted MCFG G from Example 2.5. The set of productions and the weight assignment of G are:

$$
\begin{aligned}
P\colon\ & \rho_1 = S \to [x_1^1 x_2^1 x_1^2 x_2^2](A,B) & \mu\colon\ & \mu(\rho_1) = 1\\
& \rho_2 = A \to [a x_1^1, c x_1^2](A) & & \mu(\rho_2) = 1/2\\
& \rho_3 = B \to [b x_1^1, d x_1^2](B) & & \mu(\rho_3) = 1/3\\
& \rho_4 = A \to [\varepsilon, \varepsilon]() & & \mu(\rho_4) = 1/2\\
& \rho_5 = B \to [\varepsilon, \varepsilon]() & & \mu(\rho_5) = 2/3\,.
\end{aligned}
$$

By Definitions 3.1 and 3.2 we obtain the MCFG $G_{\mathbb{B}} = (N, \Gamma, S, P')$ where $\Gamma = \{a, b, c, d, \rho_1^1, \rho_2^1, \rho_2^2, \rho_3^1, \rho_3^2, \rho_4^1, \rho_4^2, \rho_5^1, \rho_5^2\}$ and P' is given by

$$
\begin{aligned}
P'\colon\ & \rho'_1 = S \to [\rho_1^1 x_1^1 x_2^1 x_1^2 x_2^2](A,B)\\
& \rho'_2 = A \to [\rho_2^1 a x_1^1, \rho_2^2 c x_1^2](A) & & \rho'_4 = A \to [\rho_4^1, \rho_4^2]()\\
& \rho'_3 = B \to [\rho_3^1 b x_1^1, \rho_3^2 d x_1^2](B) & & \rho'_5 = B \to [\rho_5^1, \rho_5^2](),
\end{aligned}
$$

and the $\mathscr{A}$-weighted alphabetic homomorphism $\mathrm{weights}_G\colon \Gamma^* \to (\Delta^* \to \mathscr{A})$ where $\mathrm{weights}_G$ is given for every $\gamma \in \Gamma$ and $\omega \in \Delta \cup \{\varepsilon\}$ by

$$\text{weights}_G(\gamma)(\omega) = \begin{cases} \mu(\rho_i) & \text{if } \gamma = \rho_i^1 \text{ and } \omega = \varepsilon \text{ for } 1 \le i \le 5 \\ 1 & \text{if } \gamma = \rho_i^2 \text{ and } \omega = \varepsilon \text{ for } 2 \le i \le 5 \\ 1 & \text{if } \gamma \in \Delta \text{ and } \omega = \gamma \\ 0 & \text{otherwise,} \end{cases}$$

Now recall the derivation $d = \rho_1\big(\rho_2(\rho_4), \rho_5\big)$ of $w = ac$. Then

$$\begin{aligned} f(d) &= \rho_1'\big(\rho_2'(\rho_4'), \rho_5'\big) && =: d', \\ g(d') &= \rho_1^1\, \rho_2^1\, a\, \rho_4^1\, \rho_5^1\, \rho_2^2\, c\, \rho_4^2\, \rho_5^2 && =: w', \text{ and} \\ \text{weights}_G(w') &= (1 \cdot 1/2 \cdot 1 \cdot 1/2 \cdot 2/3 \cdot 1 \cdot 1 \cdot 1 \cdot 1).w && = (1/6).w\,. \quad \square \end{aligned}$$

3.2 *The unweighted CS characterisation*

We recall the definition of multiple Dyck languages (Yoshinaka *et al.* 2010, Definition 1):

Definition 3.5. Let Δ be a finite $\mathbb{N}$-sorted set,[6] $\overline{(\cdot)}$ be a bijection between Δ and some alphabet $\overline{\Delta}$, $k = \max_{\delta \in \Delta} \text{sort}(\delta)$, and $r \ge k$. The *multiple Dyck grammar with respect to* Δ *and* r is the (k, r)-MCFG $G_\Delta^r = \big(\{A_1, \ldots, A_k\}, \widehat{\Delta}, A_1, P\big)$ where $\widehat{\Delta} = \{\delta^{[i]}, \bar{\delta}^{[i]} \mid \delta \in \Delta, i \in [\text{sort}(\delta)]\}$, $\text{sort}(A_i) = i$ for every $i \in [k]$, and P is the smallest set such that

(i) for every linear non-deleting[7] terminal-free string function $f \in (F_\Delta)_{(s_1 \cdots s_\ell, s)}$ with $\ell \in [r]$ and $s_1, \ldots, s_\ell, s \in [k]$ we have

$$A_s \to f(A_{s_1}, \ldots, A_{s_\ell}) \in P\,,$$

(ii) for every $\delta \in \Delta$ with sort s we have

$$A_s \to \big[\delta^{[1]} x_1^1 \bar{\delta}^{[1]}, \ldots, \delta^{[s]} x_1^s \bar{\delta}^{[s]}\big](A_s) \in P\,, \text{ and}$$

(iii) for every $s \in [k]$ we have

$$A_s \to [u_1, \ldots, u_s](A_s) \in P$$

where $u_i \in \big\{x_i,\ x_i\delta^{[1]}\bar{\delta}^{[1]},\ \delta^{[1]}\bar{\delta}^{[1]}x_i \mid \delta \in \Delta_1\big\}$ for every $i \in [s]$.

---

[6] In Yoshinaka *et al.* (2010), $\mathbb{N}$-sorted sets are called indexed sets and sort is denoted as dim.

[7] We add the restriction "non-deleting" in comparison to the original definition since the proof of Lemma 1 in Yoshinaka *et al.* (2010) only uses non-deleting rules.

The *multiple Dyck language with respect to* Δ *and* r, denoted by $mD(\Delta, r)$, is $L(G^r_\Delta)$. We call $\max_{\delta \in \Delta} \mathrm{sort}(\delta)$ the *dimension* and r the *rank* of $mD(\Delta, r)$. The *set of multiple Dyck languages of dimension at most* k *and rank at most* r is denoted by (k, r)-mDYCK. □

Yoshinaka *et al.* (2010) define (in Section 3.2) a sorted alphabet Δ, a right-linear regular grammar R, and a homomorphism h for some given non-deleting MCFG G that has no rule with two or more identical non-terminals on the right-hand side (this form of G can be assumed without loss of generality). We recall their construction. To fit our notation and highlight the connection to G, we will conceive R as an FSA and call it $\mathcal{M}(G)$; also, h will be called hom_G.

Definition 3.6. Let $G = (N, \Gamma, S, P)$ be an MCFG. The *generator set with respect to* G is the $\mathbb{N}$-sorted alphabet

$$\Sigma = \{[\![_\gamma \mid \gamma \in \Gamma\} \cup \{[\![_\rho \mid \rho \in P\} \cup \{[\![_{\rho,i} \mid \rho \in P, i \in [\mathrm{rank}(\rho)]\}$$

where $\mathrm{sort}([\![_\gamma) = 1$, $\mathrm{sort}([\![_\rho) = \text{fan-out}(\rho)$, and $\mathrm{sort}([\![_{\rho,i}) = \text{fan-out}_i(\rho)$ for every $\gamma \in \Gamma$, $\rho \in P$, and $i \in \mathrm{rank}(\rho)$. The *generator alphabet with respect to* G is

$$\widehat{\Sigma} = \{[\![^{[i]}_u,]\!]^{[i]}_u \mid [\![_u \in \Sigma, i \in [\mathrm{sort}(\sigma)]\}.$$

For each $u = \gamma_1 \cdots \gamma_m \in \Gamma^*$ (with $\gamma_1, \ldots, \gamma_m \in \Gamma$), we will abbreviate $[\![^{[1]}_{\gamma_1}]\!]^{[1]}_{\gamma_1} \cdots [\![^{[1]}_{\gamma_m}]\!]^{[1]}_{\gamma_m}$ by $\tilde{u}$. The *generator automaton with respect to* G is the FSA $\mathcal{M}(G) = (Q, \widehat{\Delta}, S^{[1]}, \{T\}, \tau)$ where $Q = \{A^{[k]} \mid A \in N, k \in [\mathrm{sort}(A)]\} \cup \{T\}$ and τ is the smallest set that contains for every production $\rho = A \to [v_1, \ldots, v_s](B_1, \ldots, B_m) \in P$ and each $k \in [s]$ (where v_k is of the form $u_{k,0} x^{j(j,1)}_{i(k,1)} u_{k,1} \cdots x^{j(k,p_k)}_{i(k,p_k)} u_{k,p_k}$ with $u_{k,0}, \ldots, u_{k,p_k} \in \Gamma^*$), the transitions

$$\begin{aligned}
&(A^{[k]}, [\![^{[k]}_\rho \tilde{u}_{k,0}]\!]^{[k]}_\rho, T) && \text{if } p_k = 0,\\
&(A^{[k]}, [\![^{[k]}_\rho \tilde{u}_{k,0} [\![^{[j(k,1)]}_{\rho,i(k,1)}, B^{[j(k,1)]}_{i(k,1)}) && \text{if } p_k > 0,\\
&(T,]\!]^{[j(k,\ell-1)]}_{\rho,i(k,\ell-1)} \tilde{u}_{k,\ell-1} [\![^{[j(k,\ell)]}_{\rho,i(k,\ell)}, B^{[j(k,\ell)]}_{i(k,\ell)}) && \text{if } p_k > 0, \text{ for every } \ell \in [p_k],\\
&(T,]\!]^{[j(k,p_k)]}_{\rho,i(k,p_k)} \tilde{u}_{k,p_k}]\!]^{[k]}_\rho, T) && \text{if } p_k > 0.
\end{aligned}$$

The *generator language with respect to* G is $R(G) = L(\mathcal{M}(G))$. The homomorphism $\mathrm{hom}_G \colon \widehat{\Delta} \to \Gamma^*$ is given by

$$\mathrm{hom}_G(\sigma) = \begin{cases} \gamma & \text{if } \sigma = [\![^{[1]}_\gamma \text{ for some } \gamma \in \Gamma \\ \varepsilon & \text{otherwise.} \end{cases}$$ □

From the four types of transitions in $\mathcal{M}(G)$, it is easy to see that $\mathcal{M}(G)$ is deterministic, i.e. for each given state and input, there is at most one successor state. We will denote $L(D_{\Sigma}^{\mathrm{rank}(G)})$ (cf. Definition 3.5) by $mD(G)$ to highlight its connection to the MCFG G.

Example 3.7 (Examples 2.5 and 3.4 continued). Figure 5 shows the FSA $\mathcal{M}(G_{\mathbb{B}})$. An edge labelled with a set L of words denotes a set of transitions each reading a word in L. Note that $R(G_{\mathbb{B}})$ is not finite. □

The following is Theorem 3 of Yoshinaka *et al.* (2010) where "homomorphism" is replaced by "alphabetic homomorphism".

Corollary 3.8. Let L be a language, $k \in \mathbb{N}$, and $r \in \mathbb{N}_+$. Then the following are equivalent:

(i) $L \in (k,r)$-MCFL

(ii) There are an alphabetic homomorphism h_2, a regular language R, and a multiple Dyck language mD of at most dimension k and rank r with $L = h_2(R \cap mD)$.

Proof. The construction of the homomorphism in Yoshinaka *et al.* (2010, Section 3.2) already satisfies the definition of an alphabetic homomorphism. ■

Corollary 3.9. For every MCFG G, there is a bijection between D_G and $R(G) \cap mD(G)$.

Proof. The constructions in Lemmas 1 and 3 in Yoshinaka *et al.* (2010) already hint at the bijection between $R(G) \cap mD(G)$ and D_G, we will merely point out the respective functions toBrackets: $D_G \to R(G) \cap mD(G)$ and fromBrackets: $R(G) \cap mD(G) \to D_G$ here.

Let Δ be the generator set with respect to G and $r = \mathrm{rank}(G)$. We examine the proof of Lemma 1 in Yoshinaka *et al.* (2010). They construct for every rule $A \to f(B_1, \ldots, B_k)$ in G and all tuples $\bar{\tau}_1, \ldots, \bar{\tau}_k$ that are generated by $B_1, \ldots, B_k$ in G, respectively, a tuple $\bar{u} = (u_1, \ldots, u_m)$ that is generated from A_m in G^r_Δ. For each $i \in [m]$, $\mathcal{M}(G)$ recognises u_i on the way from $A^{[i]}$ to T, and $f(\mathrm{hom}_G(\tau_1), \ldots, \mathrm{hom}_G(\tau_k)) = \mathrm{hom}_G(\bar{u})$, where hom_G is applied to tuples component-wise. Now we only look at the initial non-terminal S. Then $\bar{u}$ has only one component and this construction can be conceived as a function toBrackets: $D_G \to R(G) \cap mD(G)$ such that $\mathrm{hom}_G \circ \mathrm{toBrackets} = \mathrm{yield}$.

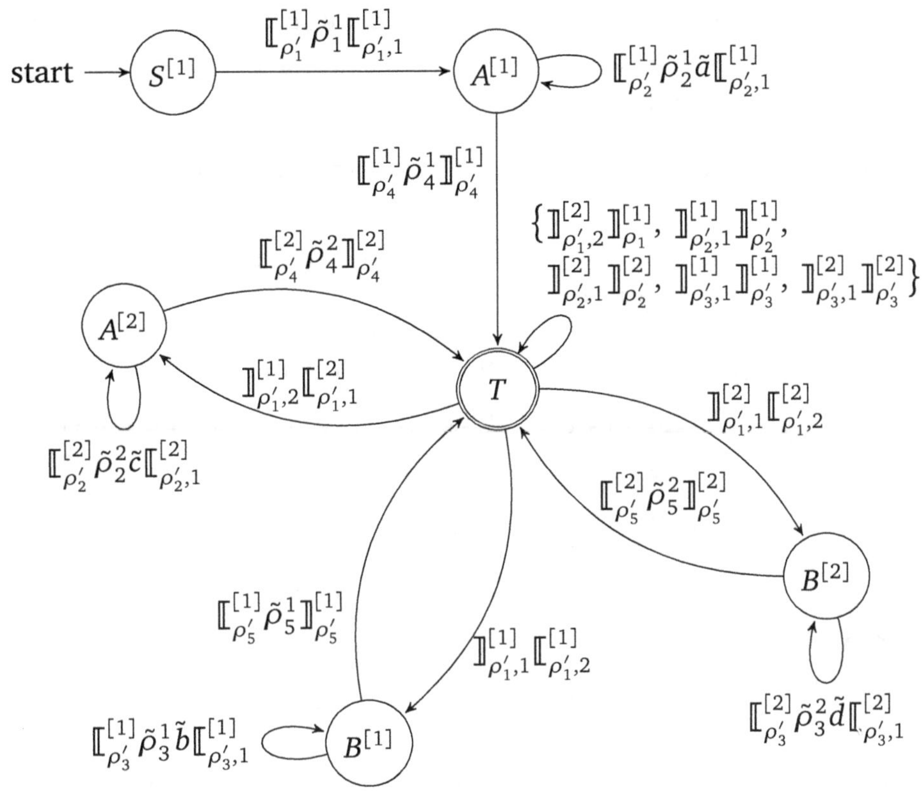

Figure 5: Automaton $\mathcal{M}(G_{\mathbb{B}})$ (cf. Example 3.7)

In Lemma 3, Yoshinaka *et al.* (2010) give a construction for the opposite direction by recursion on the structure of derivations in G_Δ. In a similar way as above, we view this construction as a function fromBrackets: $R(G) \cap mD(G) \to D_G$ such that yield $\circ$ fromBrackets $=$ $\hom_G$. Then we have $\hom_G \circ$ toBrackets $\circ$ fromBrackets $= \hom_G$, and hence toBrackets $\circ$ fromBrackets is the identity on $R(G) \cap mD(G)$. ∎

3.3 *Composing the homomorphisms*

Lemma 3.10. $\alpha\mathrm{HOM}(\mathcal{A}) \circ \alpha\mathrm{HOM} = \alpha\mathrm{HOM}(\mathcal{A})$

Proof. ($\subseteq$) Let $h_1 : \Gamma^* \to (\Delta^* \to \mathcal{A})$ be an alphabetic $\mathcal{A}$-weighted homomorphism and $h_2 : \Sigma^* \to \Gamma^*$ be an alphabetic homomorphism. By the definitions of $\alpha\mathrm{HOM}(\mathcal{A})$ and $\alpha\mathrm{HOM}$, there exist $h_1' : \Gamma \to (\Delta \cup \{\varepsilon\} \to \mathcal{A})$ and $h_2' : \Sigma \to \Gamma \cup \{\varepsilon\}$ such that $\widehat{h_1'} = h_1$ and $\widehat{h_2'} = h_2$. Since $h_1(\mathrm{codom}(h_2')) \subseteq (\Delta \cup \{\varepsilon\} \to \mathcal{A})$ there is some $h \in \alpha\mathrm{HOM}(\mathcal{A})$ such that $h = h_1 \circ h_2$; hence $h_1 \circ h_2 \in \alpha\mathrm{HOM}(\mathcal{A})$.

($\supseteq$) Let $h\colon \Sigma \to (\Gamma^* \to \mathscr{A})$ be an alphabetic $\mathscr{A}$-weighted homomorphism. Clearly $i\colon \Sigma^* \to \Sigma^*$ with $i(w) = w$ for every $w \in \Sigma^*$ is an alphabetic homomorphism. Then we have $h \circ i = h$. ■

Example 3.11 (Examples 3.4 and 3.7 continued). The homomorphism $h\colon (\Sigma \cup \bar{\Sigma})^* \to (\Delta^* \to \mathscr{A})$ obtained from $\text{weights}_G\colon \Gamma^* \to (\Delta^* \to \mathscr{A})$ and $\text{hom}_{G_\mathbb{B}}\colon (\Sigma \cup \bar{\Sigma})^* \to \Gamma^*$ by the construction for $\subseteq$ in Lemma 3.10 is given for every $\sigma \in \Sigma$ and $\omega \in \Delta \cup \{\varepsilon\}$ by

$$h(\sigma)(\omega) = \begin{cases} \mu(\rho_i) & \text{if } \sigma = [\![^{[1]}_{\rho_i} \text{ and } \omega = \varepsilon \text{ for some } i \in [5] \\ 1 & \text{if } \sigma \notin \{[\![^{[1]}_{\rho_i} \mid i \in [5]\} \cup \{[\![^{[1]}_{\delta} \mid \delta \in \Delta\} \text{ and } \omega = \varepsilon \\ 1 & \text{if } \sigma = [\![^{[1]}_{\delta} \text{ and } \omega = \delta \text{ for some } \delta \in \Delta \\ 0 & \text{otherwise.} \end{cases}$$ □

3.4 *The weighted CS characterisation*

Theorem 3.12. Let L be an $\mathscr{A}$-weighted language over Σ, $k \in \mathbb{N}$, and $r \in \mathbb{N}_+$. The following are equivalent:

(i) $L \in (k, r)\text{-MCFL}(\mathscr{A})$

(ii) there are an $\mathscr{A}$-weighted alphabetic homomorphism h, a regular language R, and an multiple Dyck language mD of dimension at most k and rank r with $L = h(R \cap mD)$.

Proof. **(i) ⇒ (ii)** There are some $L' \in (k, r)\text{-MCFL}$, $h, h_1 \in \alpha\text{HOM}(\mathscr{A})$, $h_2 \in \alpha\text{HOM}$, $mD \in k\text{-mDYCK}_c$, and $R \in \text{REC}$ such that

$$\begin{aligned} L &= h_1(L') && \text{(by Lemma 3.3)} \\ &= h_1(h_2(R \cap mD)) && \text{(by Corollary 3.8)} \\ &= h(R \cap mD) && \text{(by Lemma 3.10)} \end{aligned}$$

(ii) ⇒ (i) We use Definition 3.5 and Lemma 3.3, and the closure of (k, r)-MCFG under intersection with regular languages and application of homomorphisms. ■

Corollary 3.13. For every $\mathscr{A}$-weighted MCFG G, there is a bijection between D_G and $R(G_\mathbb{B}) \cap mD(G_\mathbb{B})$.

Proof. There are bijections between D_G and $L(G_\mathbb{B})$ by claims in the proof of Lemma 3.3, between $L(G_\mathbb{B})$ and $D_{G_\mathbb{B}}$ by claims in the proof of Lemma 3.3, and between $D_{G_\mathbb{B}}$ and $R(G_\mathbb{B}) \cap mD(G_\mathbb{B})$ by Corollary 3.9. ■

4 CONGRUENCE MULTIPLE DYCK LANGUAGES

According to Kanazawa (2014, Section 1) there is no definition of multiple Dyck languages using a cancellation law. The congruence multiple Dyck languages (Definition 4.2) close this gap. Even though congruence multiple Dyck languages turn out to be quite different from the multiple Dyck languages by Yoshinaka *et al.* (2010) (see Proposition 4.5 and Observation 4.6), we argue that they are still useful since they allow a CS representation (Theorem 4.11) and they can be utilised more efficiently for CS parsing than multiple Dyck languages (see Section 5.5).

For the rest of this section let Σ be an alphabet. Also let $\overline{\Sigma}$ be a set (disjoint from Σ) and $\overline{(\cdot)}$ be a bijection between Σ and $\overline{\Sigma}$. Intuitively Σ and $\overline{\Sigma}$ are sets of opening and closing parentheses and $\overline{(\cdot)}$ matches an opening to its closing parenthesis.

We define $\equiv_\Sigma$ as the smallest congruence relation on the free monoid $(\Sigma \cup \overline{\Sigma})^*$ where for every $\sigma \in \Sigma$ the cancellation rule $\sigma\overline{\sigma} \equiv_\Sigma \varepsilon$ holds. The *Dyck language with respect to* Σ, denoted by $D(\Sigma)$, is $[\varepsilon]_{\equiv_\Sigma}$. The *set of Dyck languages* is denoted by DYCK.

Example 4.1. Let $\Sigma = \{(, \langle, [, [\![\}$. We abbreviate $\bar{(}$, $\bar{\langle}$, $\bar{[}$, and $\bar{[\![}$ by $)$, $\rangle$, $]$, and $]\!]$, respectively. Then we have for example $[\![()]\!]\langle\rangle() \equiv_\Sigma [\![]\!]\langle\rangle \equiv_\Sigma [\![]\!] \equiv_\Sigma \varepsilon$ and $([\![)]\!]\langle\rangle() \equiv_\Sigma ([\![)]\!]() \equiv_\Sigma ([\![)]\!] \not\equiv_\Sigma \varepsilon$. □

Let $\mathfrak{P}$ be a partition of Σ. We define $\equiv_{\Sigma,\mathfrak{P}}$ as the smallest congruence relation on the free monoid $(\Sigma \cup \overline{\Sigma})^*$ such that if $v_1 \cdots v_\ell \equiv_{\Sigma,\mathfrak{P}} \varepsilon$ with $v_1, \ldots, v_\ell \in D(\Sigma)$, then the *cancellation rule*

$$u_0\sigma_1 v_1 \overline{\sigma_1} u_1 \cdots \sigma_\ell v_\ell \overline{\sigma_\ell} u_\ell \equiv_{\Sigma,\mathfrak{P}} u_0 \cdots u_\ell$$

holds for every $\{\sigma_1, \ldots, \sigma_\ell\} \in \mathfrak{P}$ and $u_0, \ldots, u_\ell \in D(\Sigma)$. Intuitively, every cell of $\mathfrak{P}$ denotes a set of *linked* opening parentheses, i.e. parentheses that must be consumed simultaneously by $\equiv_{\Sigma,\mathfrak{P}}$.

Definition 4.2. The *congruence multiple Dyck language with respect to* Σ *and* $\mathfrak{P}$, denoted by $mD_c(\Sigma, \mathfrak{P})$, is $[\varepsilon]_{\equiv_{\Sigma,\mathfrak{P}}}$. □

Example 4.3. Let $\Sigma = \{(, \langle, [, [\![\}$ and $\mathfrak{P} = \{\mathfrak{p}_1, \mathfrak{p}_2\}$ where $\mathfrak{p}_1 = \{(, \langle\}$ and $\mathfrak{p}_2 = \{[, [\![\}$. We abbreviate $\bar{(}$, $\bar{\langle}$, $\bar{[}$, and $\bar{[\![}$ by $)$, $\rangle$, $]$, and $]\!]$, respectively. Then, using the cancellation rule, we have for example $[\![()]\!][\langle\rangle] \equiv_{\Sigma,\mathfrak{P}} \varepsilon$ since $\mathfrak{p}_2 = \{[, [\![\} \in \mathfrak{P}$, $()\langle\rangle \equiv_{\Sigma,\mathfrak{P}} \varepsilon$, and $u_0 = u_1 = u_2 = \varepsilon$.

But $[\![()]\!]\langle[]\rangle \not\equiv_{\Sigma,\mathfrak{P}} \varepsilon$ since when instantiating the cancellation rule with any of the two cells of $\mathfrak{P}$, we can not reduce $[\![()]\!]\langle[]\rangle$:

(i) If we choose $\{\sigma_1,\sigma_2\} = \{[\![, [\}$ then we would need to set $u_1 = \langle$ and $u_2 = \rangle$, but they are not in $D(\Sigma)$, also $() \not\equiv_{\Sigma,\mathfrak{P}} \varepsilon$;

(ii) If we choose $\{\sigma_1,\sigma_2\} = \{(, \langle\}$ then we would need to set $u_0 = [\![$ and $u_1 =]\!]$, but they are not in $D(\Sigma)$, also $[] \not\equiv_{\Sigma,\mathfrak{P}} \varepsilon$.

Hence $[\![()]\!][\langle\rangle], ()\langle\rangle \in mD_c(\Sigma,\mathfrak{P})$ and $[\![()]\!]\langle[]\rangle \notin mD_c(\Sigma,\mathfrak{P})$. □

Observation 4.4. From the definition of $\equiv_{\Sigma,\mathfrak{P}}$ it is easy to see that for every $u_1,\ldots,u_k \in D(\Sigma)$ and $v_1,\ldots,v_\ell \in D(\Sigma)$ we have that $u_1\cdots u_k$, $v_1\cdots v_\ell \in mD_c(\Sigma,\mathfrak{P})$ implies that every permutation of $u_1,\ldots,u_k$, $v_1,\ldots,v_\ell$ is in $mD_c(\Sigma,\mathfrak{P})$. ■

The *dimension of* $mD_c(\Sigma,\mathfrak{P})$ is $\max_{\mathfrak{p}\in\mathfrak{P}}|\mathfrak{p}|$. The *set of congruence multiple Dyck languages (of at most dimension k)* is denoted by $\mathrm{mDYCK_c}$ (k-$\mathrm{mDYCK_c}$, respectively).

Proposition 4.5. For each $mD \in (k,r)$-mDYCK there is an $mD_c \in k$-$\mathrm{mDYCK_c}$ such that $mD \subseteq mD_c$.

Proof idea. We construct a congruence multiple Dyck language mD_c of dimension at most k such that, if a tuple $(w_1,\ldots,w_m)$ can be generated in G^r_Δ from non-terminal A_m, then $w_1,\ldots,w_m \in D(\Sigma)$ and $w_1\cdots w_m \in mD_e$. We prove this by induction on the structure of derivations in G^r_Δ.

Proof. Let $mD \in (k,r)$-mDYCK. Then there is an $\mathbb{N}$-sorted set Δ such that $mD = mD(\Delta,r)$ and $\max_{\delta\in\Delta}\mathrm{sort}(\delta) \le k$. We define $\mathfrak{p}_\delta = \{\delta^{[i]} \mid i \in [\mathrm{sort}(\delta)]\}$ for every $\delta \in \Delta$, $\Sigma = \bigcup_{\delta\in\Delta}\mathfrak{p}_\delta$, and $\mathfrak{P} = \{\mathfrak{p}_\delta \mid \delta \in \Delta\}$. Clearly $\max_{\mathfrak{p}\in\mathfrak{P}}|\mathfrak{p}| \le k$. Thus $mD_c(\Sigma,\mathfrak{P}) \in k$-$\mathrm{mDYCK_c}$. Let $\mathrm{Tup}(G^r_\Delta,A)$ denote the set of tuples generated in G^r_Δ when starting with non-terminal A where A is not necessarily initial. In the following we show that for every $m \in [\max_{\delta\in\Delta}\mathrm{sort}(\delta)]$ and $w_1,\ldots,w_m \in (\Sigma\cup\bar{\Sigma})^*$:

$$(w_1,\ldots,w_m) \in \mathrm{Tup}(G^r_\Delta,A_m) \Longrightarrow w_1\cdots w_m \in mD_c(\Sigma,\mathfrak{P}) \wedge w_1,\ldots,w_m \in D(\Sigma)\,. \qquad (*)$$

It follows from the definitions of Tup and G^r_Δ that $(w_1,\ldots,w_m) \in \mathrm{Tup}(G^r_\Delta,A_m)$ implies that there are a rule $A_m \to f(A_{m_1},\ldots,A_{m_\ell})$ in G^r_Δ and tuples $\vec{u}_i = (u_i^1,\ldots,u_i^{m_i}) \in \mathrm{Tup}(G^r_\Delta,A_{m_i})$ for every $i \in [\ell]$ such that $f(\vec{u}_1,\dots,\vec{u}_\ell) = (w_1,\dots,w_m)$. By applying the induction hypothesis ℓ times, we also have that $u_1^1,\dots,u_1^{m_1},\dots,u_\ell^1,\dots,u_\ell^{m_\ell} \in D(\Sigma)$ and $u_1^1\cdots u_1^{m_1},\dots,u_\ell^1\cdots u_\ell^{m_\ell} \in mD_c(\Sigma,\mathfrak{P})$. We distinguish three cases (each corresponding to one type of rule in G_Δ^r):

(i) f is linear, non-deleting, and terminal-free. Then we have for every $i \in [m]$ that $w_i \in \{u_1^1,\dots,u_1^{m_1},\dots,u_\ell^1,\dots,u_\ell^{m_\ell}\}^*$ and therefore also $w_i \in D(\Sigma)$. Furthermore, by applying Observation 4.4 $(\ell-1)$ times, we have that $w_1\cdots w_m \in mD_c(\Sigma,\mathfrak{P})$.

(ii) $f = [\delta^{[1]}x_1^1\bar{\delta}^{[1]},\dots,\delta^{[m]}x_1^m\bar{\delta}^{[m]}]$; then $\ell = 1$, $m_1 = m$, and for every $i \in [m]$ we have $w_i = \delta^{[i]}u_1^i\bar{\delta}^{[i]}$ and since $u_1^i \in D(\Sigma)$, also $w_i \in D(\Sigma)$. Furthermore, $w_1\cdots w_m = \delta^{[1]}u_1^1\bar{\delta}^{[1]}\cdots\delta^{[m]}u_1^m\bar{\delta}^{[m]} \in mD_c(\Sigma,\mathfrak{P})$ due to the cancellation rule.

(iii) $f = [u_1,\dots,u_m]$ where $u_i \in \left\{x_i^1,\ x_i^1\delta^{[1]}\bar{\delta}^{[1]},\ \delta^{[1]}\bar{\delta}^{[1]}x_i^1 \mid \delta \in \Delta_1\right\}$ for every $i \in [m]$; then $w_i \in \left\{u_i^1,\ u_i^1\delta^{[1]}\bar{\delta}^{[1]},\ \delta^{[1]}\bar{\delta}^{[1]}u_i^1 \mid \delta \in \Delta_1\right\}$ for every $i \in [m]$, $\ell = 1$, and $m_1 = m$. Since $\equiv_\Sigma$ is a congruence relation (in particular, $\equiv_\Sigma$ respects composition), we have that $w_1,\dots,w_m \in D(\Sigma)$. By applying Observation 4.4 m times, we have that $w_1\cdots w_m \in mD_c(\Sigma,\mathfrak{P})$. ■

From the above proof we can easily see that the rank r of a multiple Dyck language can not be taken into account by a congruence multiple Dyck language. This leads us to the next observation.

Observation 4.6. Let mD be a multiple Dyck language and mD_c be a congruence multiple Dyck language. Then $mD \neq mD_c$. ■

Similar to multiple Dyck languages, the congruence multiple Dyck languages cover the Dyck languages if we set the dimension to 1. Also they form a hierarchy with increasing dimension.

Proposition 4.7. $\text{DYCK} = 1\text{-mDYCK}_c \subsetneq 2\text{-mDYCK}_c \subsetneq \dots$

Proof. We have the equality since the dimension of some partition $\mathfrak{P}$ of Σ is 1 if and only if $\mathfrak{P} = \{\{\sigma\} \mid \sigma \in \Sigma\}$. Then we have $\equiv_\Sigma = \equiv_{\Sigma,\mathfrak{P}}$ and thus $D(\Sigma) = mD_c(\Sigma,\mathfrak{P})$. Hence $\text{DYCK} = 1\text{-mDYCK}_c$. We get "$\subsetneq$" from the definition of $k\text{-mDYCK}_c$. ■

4.1 *Membership in a congruence multiple Dyck language*

We give an algorithm to decide membership in a congruence multiple Dyck language (Algorithm 2). It is closely related to the cancellation

Algorithm 2: Function *isMember* to decide membership in $mD_c(\Sigma, \mathfrak{P})$

Input: Σ, $\mathfrak{P}$, and $w \in (\Sigma \cup \overline{\Sigma})^*$
Output: True if $w \in mD_c(\Sigma, \mathfrak{P})$, False otherwise

1 **function** *isMember*$(\Sigma, \mathfrak{P}, w)$
2   **if** $w \notin D(\Sigma)$ **then** **return** False **end if**
3   let $(\sigma_1 u_1 \overline{\sigma}_1, \ldots, \sigma_\ell u_\ell \overline{\sigma}_\ell) = split(\Sigma, w)$ such that $\sigma_1, \ldots, \sigma_\ell \in \Sigma$
4   let $\mathscr{I} = \varnothing$
5   **for each** $I = \{i_1, \ldots, i_k\} \subseteq [\ell]$ with $\{\sigma_{i_1}, \ldots, \sigma_{i_k}\} \in \mathfrak{P}$ **do**
6   **if** *isMember*$(\Sigma, \mathfrak{P}, u_{i_1} \cdots u_{i_k})$ **then**
7   add I as an element to $\mathscr{I}$
8   **end if**
9   **end for**
10   **for each** $J \subseteq \mathscr{I}$ **do**
11   **if** J is a partition of $[\ell]$ **then** **return** True **end if**
12   **end for**
13   **return** False
14 **end function**

rule and thus provides an algorithmic view on congruence multiple Dyck languages. Although the algorithm is at least exponential in a polynomial of the length of the input word, it becomes quadratic if we only accept input words of a specific form. The parsing algorithm presented in Section 5 will only consider words of that form.

Algorithm 2 works roughly as follows: It is a recursive algorithm. In every call of *isMember*, it checks if the given word can be reduced to ε by applications of the cancellation rule. For substrings $\sigma_1 v_1 \bar{\sigma}_1, \ldots, \sigma_\ell v_\ell \bar{\sigma}_\ell$ to be cancelled, the string $v_1 \cdots v_\ell$ must be an equivalence multiple Dyck word; this is checked with a recursive call to *isMember*. Note that it suffices to only apply the cancellation rule from left to right. To account for all possible applications of the cancellation rule, *isMember* must consider all decompositions of the input string into Dyck words. For this purpose, recall *split* (from Section 4) that splits a given Dyck word into shortest non-empty Dyck words.

Outline of *isMember*

In the following, all line numbers refer to Algorithm 2. We first check if w is in $D(\Sigma)$, e.g. with the context-free grammar in (7.6) in Salomaa (1973). If w is not in $D(\Sigma)$, it is also not in $mD_c(\Sigma, \mathfrak{P})$ and we return False. Otherwise, we split w into shortest non-empty

Dyck words (on line 3), i.e. we compute the tuple $(u_1, \ldots, u_\ell)$ such that $u_1, \ldots, u_\ell \in D(\Sigma) \setminus \{\varepsilon\}$, $u_1 \cdots u_\ell = u$, and for every $i \in [\ell]$ there are no $u_i', v_i' \in D(\Sigma) \setminus \{\varepsilon\}$ with $u_i'v_i' = u_i$. We denote $(u_1, \ldots, u_\ell)$ by *split*(u). Note that *split*(u) can be calculated in time and space linear in $|u|$ with the help of a pushdown transducer (Aho and Ullman 1972, Section 3.1.4): We initially write "(" on the output tape. Whenever we read an element of Σ, we write that element on the output tape and push it on the stack. Whenever we read an element of $\overline{\Sigma}$, we write that element on the output tape and pop it from the stack. Upon reaching the bottom of the stack, we write a "," on the output tape. Finally, we write ")" on the output tape. Then the inscription of the output tape is $(u_1, \ldots, u_\ell)$. Since each of those shortest non-empty Dyck words has the form $\sigma u \overline{\sigma}$ for some $\sigma \in \Sigma$ and $u \in (\Sigma \cup \overline{\Sigma})^*$, we write $(\sigma_1 u_1 \overline{\sigma}_1, \ldots, \sigma_\ell u_\ell \overline{\sigma}_\ell)$ for the left-hand side of the assignment on line 3. On lines 4 to 9 we calculate the set $\mathcal{I}$ of sets of indices $I = \{i_1, \ldots, i_k\}$ such that the outer parenteses of the substrings $\sigma_{i_1} u_{i_1} \overline{\sigma}_{i_1}, \ldots, \sigma_{i_k} u_{i_k} \overline{\sigma}_{i_k}$ of w can be reduced with one step of the cancellation rule. This reduction is possible if there exists an appropriate cell in $\mathfrak{P}$ (checked on line 5) and if $u_{i_1} \cdots u_{i_k}$ is in $mD_{\mathrm{c}}(\Sigma, \mathfrak{P})$ (checked on line 6). Therefore, at the end of line 9, each element of $\mathcal{I}$ represents one possible application of the cancellation rule. In order for $\equiv_{\Sigma,\mathfrak{P}}$ to reduce w to ε, each component of $(\sigma_1 u_1 \overline{\sigma}_1, \ldots, \sigma_\ell u_\ell \overline{\sigma}_\ell)$ needs to be reduced (exactly once) by an application of the cancellation rule. This is equivalent to a subset of $\mathcal{I}$ being a partition of $[\ell]$ (lines 10 to 12). If no such subset exists, then w can not be reduced to ε and we return False on line 13.

Example 4.8 (Example 4.3 continued). Table 1 shows a run of Algorithm 2 on the word $[\![()]\!][\langle\rangle]$ where we report return values and a subset of the variable assignment, when necessary, at the line ending. The recursive calls to *isMember* are indented. Table 2 shows the run of Algorithm 2 on the word $[\![()]\!][][\![]\!][\langle\rangle]$. □

In light of the close link between Algorithm 2 and the relation $\equiv_{\Sigma,\mathfrak{P}}$ we omit the proof of correctness.

Proof of termination for Algorithm 2. If $w = \varepsilon$, then $\ell = 0$, the loop on lines 5 to 9 has no I's to consider, the loop on lines 10 to 13 has only $J = \emptyset$ to consider, which is a partition of $[\ell] = \emptyset$, and hence the algorithm terminates on line 11. If $w \notin D(\Sigma)$, the algorithm terminates

Table 1: Run of Algorithm 2 on the word $[\![()]\!][\langle\rangle]$, cf. Examples 4.3 and 4.8.

isMember$(\Sigma, \mathfrak{P}, [\![()]\!][\langle\rangle])$
line 3: $\ell = 2, \sigma_1 = [\![, \sigma_2 = [, u_1 = (), u_2 = \langle\rangle$
line 5: $\mathscr{I} = \varnothing,\ k = 2, i_1 = 1, i_2 = 2$
line 6: *isMember*$(\Sigma, \mathfrak{P}, ()\langle\rangle)$
  line 3: $\ell = 2, \sigma_1 = (, \sigma_2 = \langle, u_1 = \varepsilon = u_2$
  line 5: $\mathscr{I} = \varnothing,\ k = 2, i_1 = 1, i_2 = 2$
  line 6: *isMember*$(\Sigma, \mathfrak{P}, \varepsilon)$
    line 3: $\ell = 0$
    line 10: $J = \varnothing$
    line 11: **return** True
  line 7: $\mathscr{I} = \{\{1,2\}\}$
  line 10: $J = \varnothing$
  line 10: $J = \{\{1,2\}\}$
  line 11: **return** True
line 7: $\mathscr{I} = \{\{1,2\}\}$
line 10: $J = \varnothing$
line 10: $J = \{\{1,2\}\}$
line 11: **return** True

on line 2. The loop on lines 5 to 9 considers only finitely many values I. Thus there are only finitely many calls to *isMember* on line 6 for each recursion. In the call of *isMember*, the length of the third argument $u_{i_1} \cdots u_{i_k}$ is strictly smaller then the length of w. Therefore, after a finite number of recursions, the fourth argument passed to *isMember* becomes the empty word and the algorithm terminates. ■

Properties of *isMember*

Algorithm 2 is at least exponential in a polynomial of the length of the input word. This is due to the cardinality of $\mathscr{I}$ and the **for**-loop on lines 10 to 12. Let κ be the number of different cells $\mathfrak{p} \in \mathfrak{P}$ that occur in $\sigma_1 \cdots \sigma_\ell$, and let each symbol occurs at most r times. Both κ and r have upper bound ℓ. Let m be the dimension of $\mathfrak{P}$. Then there are at most $\kappa \cdot r^{m-1} \leq \ell^m$ values of I considered in the **for**-loop on lines 5 to 9. Since $\ell < |w|$, we execute this **for**-loop at most $|w|^m$ times. Hence, $\mathscr{I}$ has cardinality at most $|w|^m$. Therefore, the **for**-loop on lines 10 to 12 considers $2^{|\mathscr{I}|} \leq 2^{|w|^m}$ different values of J in the worst case.

Let us now turn to the modification of *isMember* we will use in Section 5. Let $u \in D(\Sigma)$ and $(\sigma_1 u'_1 \overline{\sigma}_1, \ldots, \sigma_\ell u'_\ell \overline{\sigma}_\ell) = split(u)$. For every $\sigma \in \Sigma$, we define $\mathrm{occ}_\sigma u = |\{i \in [\ell] \mid \sigma_i = \sigma\}|$. Furthermore for every $\mathfrak{p} \in \mathfrak{P}$, we define $\mathrm{occ}_\mathfrak{p} u = \max\{\mathrm{occ}_\sigma u \mid \sigma \in \mathfrak{p}\}$ and we define

Table 2: Run of Algorithm 2 on the word $\llbracket()\rrbracket[\,]\llbracket\,\rrbracket[\langle\rangle]$.

isMember$(\Sigma, \mathfrak{P}, \llbracket()\rrbracket[\,]\llbracket\,\rrbracket[\langle\rangle])$

- line 3: $\ell = 4, \sigma_1 = \llbracket = \sigma_3, \sigma_2 = [= \sigma_4, u_1 = (), u_2 = \varepsilon = u_3, u_4 = \langle\rangle$
- line 5: $\mathscr{I} = \varnothing,\ k = 2, i_1 = 1, i_2 = 2$
- line 6: *isMember*$(\Sigma, \mathfrak{P}, ())$
  - line 3: $\ell = 1, \sigma_1 = (, u_1 = \varepsilon$
  - line 9: $\mathscr{I} = \varnothing$
  - line 10: $J = \varnothing$
  - line 13: **return** False
- line 8: $\mathscr{I} = \varnothing$
- line 5: $k = 2, i_1 = 1, i_2 = 4$
- line 6: *isMember*$(\Sigma, \mathfrak{P}, ()\langle\rangle)$
  - line 3: $\ell = 2, \sigma_1 = (, \sigma_2 = \langle, u_1 = \varepsilon = u_2$
  - line 5: $\mathscr{I} = \varnothing,\ k = 2, i_1 = 1, i_2 = 2$
  - line 6: *isMember*$(\Sigma, \mathfrak{P}, \varepsilon)$
    - line 3: $\ell = 0$
    - line 9: $\mathscr{I} = \varnothing$
    - line 10: $J = \varnothing$
    - line 11: **return** True
  - line 7: $\mathscr{I} = \{\{1,2\}\}$
  - line 10: $J = \varnothing$
  - line 10: $J = \{\{1,2\}\}$
  - line 13: **return** True
- line 7: $\mathscr{I} = \{\{1,4\}\}$
- line 5: $k = 2, i_1 = 2, i_2 = 3$
- line 6: *isMember*$(\Sigma, \mathfrak{P}, \varepsilon)$
  - line 3: $\ell = 0$
  - line 10: $\mathscr{I} = \varnothing,\ J = \varnothing$
  - line 11: **return** True
- line 7: $\mathscr{I} = \{\{1,4\},\{2,3\}\}$
- line 5: $k = 2, i_1 = 3, i_2 = 4$
- line 6: *isMember*$(\Sigma, \mathfrak{P}, \langle\rangle)$
  - line 3: $\ell = 1, \sigma_1 = \langle, u_1 = \varepsilon$
  - line 10: $\mathscr{I} = \varnothing,\ J = \varnothing$
  - line 13: **return** False
- line 8: $\mathscr{I} = \{\{1,4\},\{2,3\}\}$
- line 10: $J = \varnothing$
- line 10: $J = \{\{1,4\}\}$
- line 10: $J = \{\{2,3\}\}$
- line 10: $J = \{\{1,4\},\{2,3\}\}$
- line 11: **return** True

$\text{occ}_{\mathfrak{P}}\, u = \sum_{\mathfrak{p}\in\mathfrak{P}} \text{occ}_{\mathfrak{p}}\, u$. We call a word $w \in (\Sigma\cup\bar{\Sigma})^*$ *$\mathfrak{P}$-simple* if $w \notin D(\Sigma)$; or $\text{occ}_{\mathfrak{p}}\, w \leq 1$ for each cell $\mathfrak{p} \in \{\mathfrak{p}' \in \mathfrak{P} \mid |\mathfrak{p}'| \geq 2\}$ and $v_1 \cdots v_\ell$ is $\mathfrak{P}$-simple whenever there are $u_0, \ldots, u_\ell \in D(\Sigma)$, $v_1, \ldots, v_\ell \in D(\Sigma)$, and $\mathfrak{p} = \{\sigma_1, \ldots, \sigma_\ell\} \in \mathfrak{P}$ with $w = u_0\sigma_1 v_1 \bar{\sigma}_1 u_1 \cdots \sigma_\ell v_\ell \bar{\sigma}_\ell u_\ell$. In other words, w is $\mathfrak{P}$-simple if, whenever the cancellation rule can be applied to w to cancel an occurrence of the cell $\mathfrak{p}$ (where $\mathfrak{p}$ has more than one element), then there is only one such occurrence and the string $v_1 \cdots v_\ell$ (from the definition of the cancellation rule) is also $\mathfrak{P}$-simple.

In order for *isMember* to recognise w only if it is $\mathfrak{P}$-simple, we check between lines 1 and 2 in the algorithm whether $\text{occ}_{\mathfrak{p}}\, w \leq 1$ for each cell $\mathfrak{p} \in \{\mathfrak{p}' \in \mathfrak{P} \mid |\mathfrak{p}'| \geq 2\}$. If this is the case, we continue, otherwise we return False. Let us call the function obtained in this manner *isMember'*. Note that the check between lines 1 and 2 can be done in time linear in the input word. Then the I's that Algorithm 2 considers in the **for**-loop on lines 5 to 9 are pairwise disjoint. This means that each u_i (for $i \in [\ell]$) occurs in at most one recursive call on line 6. Then the elements of $\mathscr{I}$ are always pairwise disjoint and we only need to consider $J = \mathscr{I}$ in the **for**-loop on lines 10 to 12. We can decide in time $\mathcal{O}(\ell)$ whether $\mathscr{I}$ is a partition of $[\ell]$. Lines 2 and 3 can be computed in time $\mathcal{O}(|w|)$. Since $\ell < |w|$, we know that for each call of *isMember*, we have to invest time linear in the length of the third argument. The maximum depth of recursion is $|w|/2$ because the third argument in the call on line 6 has at most length $|w|-2$. For every recursion depth, the sum of the lengths of all third arguments is at most $|w|$ because u_i (for $i \in [\ell]$) occurs in at most one recursive call on line 6. Therefore *isMember'*$(\Sigma, \mathfrak{P}, w)$ can be calculated in time $\mathcal{O}(|w|^2)$.

4.2 *A CS representation using congruence multiple Dyck languages*

Definition 4.9. Let $G = (N, \Gamma, S, P)$ be an MCFG. The *congruence multiple Dyck language with respect to* G, denoted by $mD_c(G)$, is $mD_c(\Sigma, \mathfrak{P})$ where $\mathfrak{P}$ is the smallest set such that

- $\mathfrak{p}_\gamma = \{[\![_\gamma^{[1]}\} \in \mathfrak{P}$ for every $\gamma \in \Gamma$,
- $\mathfrak{p}_\rho = \{[\![_\rho^{[j]} \mid j \in [\text{fan-out}(\rho)]\} \in \mathfrak{P}$ for every $\rho \in P$, and
- $\mathfrak{p}_{\rho,i} = \{[\![_{\rho,i}^{[j]} \mid j \in [\text{fan-out}_i(\rho)]\} \in \mathfrak{P}$ for every $\rho \in P$ and $i \in [\text{rank}(\rho)]$,

and $\Sigma = \bigcup_{\mathfrak{p}\in\mathfrak{P}} \mathfrak{p}$. □

Lemma 4.10. $R(G) \cap mD(G) = R(G) \cap mD_c(G)$ for each MCFG G.

Proof. It follows from Definitions 3.5 and 4.9 and Proposition 4.5 that $mD(G) \subseteq mD_c(G)$ and hence $R(G) \cap mD(G) \subseteq R(G) \cap mD_c(G)$. It remains to be shown that $R(G) \cap mD_c(G) \subseteq mD(G)$. Let $G = (N, \Gamma, S, P)$ and Σ and Δ be defined as in Definitions 3.5 and 4.9.

We prove the following statement by induction on the length of $w_1 \cdots w_\ell$: If $B \in N$ and $w_1, \ldots, w_\ell \in D(\Sigma)$ such that $w_1 \cdots w_\ell \in mD_c$ and w_κ is recognised along a path from $B^{[\kappa]}$ to T in $\mathcal{M}(G)$ for every $\kappa \in [\ell]$, then $(w_1, \ldots, w_\ell)$ can be generated by A_ℓ in $G_\Delta^{\mathrm{rank}(G)}$.

By setting $\ell = 1$ and $B = S$, this statement implies our claim. Now let $B \in N$ and $w_1, \ldots, w_k \in D(\Sigma)$ such that $w_1 \cdots w_\ell \in mD_c$ and w_κ is recognised along a path from $B^{[\kappa]}$ to T in $\mathcal{M}(G)$ for every $\kappa \in [\ell]$. By the definitions of $\mathcal{M}(G)$ and $mD_c(G)$, we know that there is some production $\rho = B \to f(B_1, \ldots, B_k) \in P$ with

$$f = [u_{1,0} x_{i(1,1)}^{j(1,1)} u_{1,1} \cdots x_{i(1,p_1)}^{j(1,p_1)} u_{1,p_1}, \ldots, u_{\ell,0} x_{i(\ell,1)}^{j(\ell,1)} u_{\ell,1} \cdots x_{i(\ell,p_\ell)}^{j(\ell,p_\ell)} u_{\ell,p_\ell}]$$

such that for every $\kappa \in [\ell]$ either

(i) $w_\kappa = [\![_\rho^{[\kappa]} \widetilde{u}_{\kappa,0}]\!]_\rho^{[\kappa]}$ or

(ii) $$w_\kappa = [\![_\rho^{[\kappa]} \widetilde{u}_{\kappa,0} \quad [\![_{\rho,i(\kappa,1)}^{[j(\kappa,1)]} \quad v_{i(\kappa,1)}^{j(\kappa,1)} \quad]\!]_{\rho,i(\kappa,1)}^{[j(\kappa,1)]} \quad \widetilde{u}_{\kappa,1} \quad \cdots$$
$$[\![_{\rho,i(\kappa,p_\kappa)}^{[j(\kappa,p_\kappa)]} \quad v_{i(\kappa,p_\kappa)}^{j(\kappa,p_\kappa)} \quad]\!]_{\rho,i(\kappa,p_\kappa)}^{[j(\kappa,p_\kappa)]} \quad \widetilde{u}_{\kappa,p_\kappa} \quad]\!]_\rho^{[\kappa]},$$

and $v_i^j \in D(\Sigma)$ is recognised along a path from $B_i^{[j]}$ to T in $\mathcal{M}(G)$ for every $i \in [k]$ and $j \in [\mathrm{sort}(B_i)]$, and $v_i^1 \cdots v_i^{\mathrm{sort}(B_i)} \in mD_c(G)$ for every $i \in [k]$. Then by induction hypothesis $(v_i^1, \ldots, v_i^{\mathrm{sort}(B_i)})$ can be generated from $A_{\mathrm{sort}(B_i)}$ in $G_\Delta^{\mathrm{rank}(G)}$ for every $i \in [k]$. Using productions of types (ii) and (iii) (cf. Definition 3.5), $A_{\mathrm{sort}(B_1)}, \ldots, A_{\mathrm{sort}(B_k)}$ can generate tuples that together have exactly the components

$$\widetilde{u}_{1,0} [\![_{\rho,i(1,1)}^{[j(1,1)]} v_{i(1,1)}^{j(1,1)}]\!]_{\rho,i(1,1)}^{[j(1,1)]} \widetilde{u}_{1,1}, [\![_{\rho,i(1,2)}^{[j(1,2)]} v_{i(1,2)}^{j(1,2)}]\!]_{\rho,i(1,2)}^{[j(1,2)]} \widetilde{u}_{1,2}, \ldots,$$
$$[\![_{\rho,i(1,p_1)}^{[j(1,p_1)]} v_{i(1,p_1)}^{j(1,p_1)}]\!]_{\rho,i(1,p_1)}^{[j(1,p_1)]} \widetilde{u}_{1,p_1}, \quad \ldots,$$
$$\widetilde{u}_{\ell,0} [\![_{\rho,i(\ell,1)}^{[j(\ell,1)]} v_{i(\ell,1)}^{j(\ell,1)}]\!]_{\rho,i(\ell,1)}^{[j(\ell,1)]} \widetilde{u}_{\ell,1}, [\![_{\rho,i(\ell,2)}^{[j(\ell,2)]} v_{i(\ell,2)}^{j(\ell,2)}]\!]_{\rho,i(\ell,2)}^{[j(\ell,2)]} \widetilde{u}_{\ell,2}, \ldots,$$
$$[\![_{\rho,i(\ell,p_\ell)}^{[j(\ell,p_\ell)]} v_{i(\ell,p_\ell)}^{j(\ell,p_\ell)}]\!]_{\rho,i(\ell,p_\ell)}^{[j(\ell,p_\ell)]} \widetilde{u}_{\ell,p_\ell}.$$

Set $w'_1, \ldots, w'_\ell \in D(\Sigma)$ such that $w_\kappa = [\![_\rho^{[\kappa]} w'_\kappa]\!]_\rho^{[\kappa]}$ for every $k \in [\ell]$. Then we can derive $(w'_1, \ldots, w'_\ell)$ from A_ℓ in $G_\Delta^{\mathrm{rank}(G)}$ by first using a production of type (i) with rank exactly rank(ρ), and for each $\kappa \in [\ell]$ where w_κ has the form $[\![_\rho^{[\kappa]} \widetilde{u}_{\kappa,0}]\!]_\rho^{[\kappa]}$ productions of type (iii). Using a production of type (ii), we finally obtain $(w_1, \ldots, w_\ell)$ from A_ℓ in $G_\Delta^{\mathrm{rank}(G)}$. ■

Theorem 4.11. For every multiple context-free languages L of fan-out at most k, there exist a weighted homomorphism h, a regular language R, and a congruence multiple Dyck language mD_{c} of dimension at most k such that $L = h(R \cap mD_{\mathrm{c}})$.

Proof. This follows immediately from Lemma 4.10 and Theorem 3.12 when taking $h = \mathrm{weights}_G \circ \mathrm{hom}_{G_{\mathbb{B}}}$, $R = R(G_{\mathbb{B}})$, and $mD_{\mathrm{c}} = mD_{\mathrm{c}}(G_{\mathbb{B}})$. ■

5 n-BEST PARSING FOR WEIGHTED MCFGS USING A CHOMSKY-SCHÜTZENBERGER REPRESENTATION

In this section we describe an n-best parsing algorithm (cf. Huang and Chiang 2005; Büchse *et al.* 2010) for a subset of weighted MCFGs, i.e. we want to find the best parses of a given word in a weighted MCFG. In our case, "parse" refers to a derivation in the weighted MCFG. We formalise our intuition of when a derivation is "better" than another derivation by means of a partial order $\trianglelefteq$ on the weights. That is, if we have two derivations d_1 and d_2 with weights μ_1 and μ_2, respectively, we call d_1 "not worse than" d_2 if $\mu_1 \trianglelefteq \mu_2$. Note that we think of weights as *costs* here, i.e. better derivations will get a smaller weight with respect to $\trianglelefteq$. We define the *irreflexive relation with respect to* $\trianglelefteq$ as $\triangleleft = \trianglelefteq \setminus \{(a,a) \mid a \in A\} \subseteq A \times A$. We say that $\mathcal{A}$ *respects* $\trianglelefteq$ if $\cdot$ has the following three properties:

(i) it is *(strictly) increasing*, i.e. $a \triangleleft a \cdot b$ for every $a, b \in \mathcal{A} \setminus \{0,1\}$,

(ii) it has *arbitrarily large powers*, i.e. for every $a, b \in \mathcal{A} \setminus \{0,1\}$ there is a $k \in \mathbb{N}$ with $b \trianglelefteq a^k$ where $a^k = a^{k-1} \cdot a$ for $k \geq 1$ and $a^0 = 1$, and

(iii) it is *monotone*, i.e. $a \trianglelefteq b$ implies $a \cdot c \trianglelefteq b \cdot c$ for every $a, b, c \in \mathcal{A}$.

For the rest of this section let $\mathrm{argmin}^{\trianglelefteq}$ be a function that assigns for every family $f : B \to \mathcal{A}$ a value $\bar{b} \in B$ such that there is no $b' \in B$ with $f(b') \triangleleft \bar{b}$; we write $\mathrm{argmin}^{\trianglelefteq}_{b \in B}(f(b))$ for $\bar{b}$.

Note that we only need multiplication to obtain the weight of a derivation and therefore the sum operation of our complete commutative strong bimonoid becomes irrelevant within this section.

5.1 *n-best parsing*

We will take the n best parses from the possibly infinite sequence of derivations for some word in an MCFG. We therefore need a notion of infinite strings.

Definition 5.1. Let B be a set. The *set of infinite strings over* B, denoted by B^{ω}, is the set of partial functions $u: \mathbb{N} \setminus \{0\} \to B$ where the fact that $u(n)$ is defined implies that $u(n-1)$ is defined as well, for every $n > 1$. □

Every element u of B^* can be construed as an element of B^{ω} where $\mathrm{dom}(u)$ is finite. Let $u \in B^*$ and $v \in B^{\omega}$. The *concatenation of* u *and* v, denoted by $u \cdot^{\omega} v$, is given by

$$(u \cdot^{\omega} v)(n) = \begin{cases} u(n) & \text{if } n \leq |u| \\ v(n - |u|) & \text{otherwise.} \end{cases}$$

To work with infinite strings, we define the following functions:

map applies a function to every element in an infinite list.

$$\begin{aligned} &\mathrm{map}\colon (B \to C) \to (B^{\omega} \to C^{\omega}) \\ &\mathrm{map}(f)(bu) = f(b) \cdot^{\omega} \mathrm{map}(f)(u) && \text{(if } b \in B) \\ &\mathrm{map}(f)(\varepsilon) = \varepsilon \end{aligned}$$

take returns a finite prefix of a given infinite list.

$$\begin{aligned} &\mathrm{take}\colon \mathbb{N} \to (B^{\omega} \to B^*) \\ &\mathrm{take}(n)(bu) = b \cdot^{\omega} \mathrm{take}(n-1)(u') && \text{(if } n > 0 \text{ and } b \in B) \\ &\mathrm{take}(n)(u) = \varepsilon && \text{(if } n = 0 \text{ or } u = \varepsilon) \end{aligned}$$

filter removes elements that are not in a given set from an infinite list.

$$\begin{aligned} &\mathrm{filter}\colon \mathscr{P}(B) \to (B^{\omega} \to B^{\omega}) \\ &\mathrm{filter}(B')(b'u) = b' \cdot^{\omega} \mathrm{filter}(B')(u) && \text{(if } b' \in B') \\ &\mathrm{filter}(B')(bu) = \mathrm{filter}(B')(u) && \text{(if } b \notin B') \\ &\mathrm{filter}(B')(\varepsilon) = \varepsilon \end{aligned}$$

sort returns an infinite list that contains each element of a given set exactly once in an order that respects $\trianglelefteq$.

$$\text{sort}\colon (B \to \mathscr{A}) \times \mathscr{P}(\mathscr{A} \times \mathscr{A}) \to (\mathscr{P}(B) \to B^{\omega})$$

$$\begin{aligned}\text{sort}(f, \trianglelefteq)(B') &= \text{argmin}^{\trianglelefteq}_{b \in B'}(f(b)) \\ &\quad \cdot^{\omega}\ \text{sort}(f, \trianglelefteq)(B' \setminus \text{argmin}^{\trianglelefteq}_{b \in B'}(f(b))) \quad (\text{if } B' \neq \varnothing) \\ \text{sort}(f, \trianglelefteq)(\varnothing) &= \varepsilon\end{aligned}$$

Definition 5.2. Let B be a set, $f : B \to \mathscr{A}$, $n \in \mathbb{N}$, and $\trianglelefteq$ be a partial order on $\mathscr{A}$. We define the *n-best function with respect to f and $\trianglelefteq$* as a function $n\text{-best}(f, \trianglelefteq)\colon \mathscr{P}(B) \to \mathscr{P}(B^*)$ where for every $B' \subseteq B$ we have that $(b_1, \ldots, b_k) \in n\text{-best}(f, \trianglelefteq)(B')$ if the following conditions hold

(i) $k = \min\{n, |B'|\}$,

(ii) $b_1, \ldots, b_k \in B'$ are pairwise different,

(iii) $f(b_1) \trianglelefteq f(b_2) \trianglelefteq \ldots \trianglelefteq f(b_k)$, and

(iv) there is no $b \in B' \setminus \{b_1, \ldots, b_k\}$ with $f(b) \triangleleft f(b_k)$. □

Note that $|n\text{-best}(f, \trianglelefteq)(B')| = 1$ if $n \leq |B'|$.

Definition 5.3. The *parsing problem for $\mathscr{A}$-weighted MCFG* is:

given an $\mathscr{A}$-weighted MCFG $G = (N, \Sigma, S, P, \mu)$, a partial order $\trianglelefteq$ on $\mathscr{A}$, a word $w \in \Sigma^*$, and an integer $n \in \mathbb{N}$,

output an element of $n\text{-best}(\hat{\mu}, \trianglelefteq)(D_G(w))$. □

The following observation is apparent from the definitions of sort, take, and n-best.

Observation 5.4. $\text{take}(n) \circ \text{sort}(f, \trianglelefteq)\big(B'\big) \in n\text{-best}(f, \trianglelefteq)(B')$ for every set B, subset $B' \subseteq B$, function $f\colon B \to \mathscr{B}$, $n \in \mathbb{N}$, and partial order $\trianglelefteq$ on $\mathscr{B}$. ■

5.2 *Specification of the CS parser*

Given an $\mathscr{A}$-weighted MCFG G, we construct the regular language $R(G_{\mathbb{B}})$, the $\mathscr{A}$-weighted homomorphism $h = \text{weights}_G \circ \text{hom}_{G_{\mathbb{B}}}$, and the congruence multiple Dyck language $mD_c(G_{\mathbb{B}})$. Then $L(G) = h\big(R(G_{\mathbb{B}}) \cap mD_c(G_{\mathbb{B}})\big)$. In a more procedural view on this representation of G, we might say that one obtains words (with weights) in $L(G)$ by (i) generating words in $R(G_{\mathbb{B}})$ (called *candidates*), (ii) discarding the candidates that are not in $mD_c(G_{\mathbb{B}})$, and (iii) applying h to the remaining candidates.

Recall that there is a bijection between D_G and $R(G_{\mathbb{B}}) \cap mD_{\mathrm{c}}(G_{\mathbb{B}})$ (Corollary 3.13). Now let w be the word we want to parse. Furthermore, let $R_{h,w}$ be the set of words that h maps to w. Then there is a bijection between $R_{h,w} \cap R(G_{\mathbb{B}}) \cap mD_{\mathrm{c}}(G_{\mathbb{B}})$ and $D_G(w)$. Our strategy to compute the n best derivations is to enumerate the words in $R_{h,w} \cap R(G_{\mathbb{B}})$ in the order given by the weights defined by the homomorphism h and then checking whether each word is in $mD_{\mathrm{c}}(G_{\mathbb{B}})$ until we have found n words. However, this approach will have to be refined to ensure termination of the parsing algorithm.

First we show that the set $R_{h,w}$ of words mapped by h to w is regular.

Definition 5.5. Let $h\colon \Sigma^* \to (\Gamma^* \to \mathcal{A})$ be an $\mathcal{A}$-weighted alphabetic homomorphism and $\gamma_1, \ldots, \gamma_n \in \Gamma$. Furthermore, let $\Sigma_\varepsilon = \{\sigma \in \Sigma \mid h(\sigma) = \mu.\varepsilon$ for some $\mu \in \mathcal{A}\}$, and for every $\gamma \in \Gamma$, define $\sigma_\gamma \in \Sigma$ such that $h(\sigma_\gamma) = \mu.\gamma$ for some $\mu \in \mathcal{A}$. The *domain language of h with respect to* $\gamma_1 \cdots \gamma_n$, is the language

$$R_{h,\gamma_1\cdots\gamma_n} = \{u_0\sigma_{\gamma_1}u_1 \cdots \sigma_{\gamma_n}u_n \mid u_0, \ldots, u_n \in \Sigma_\varepsilon^*\}. \qquad \square$$

Lemma 5.6. $R_{h,w}$ is a regular language for every $\mathcal{A}$-weighted alphabetic homomorphism $h\colon \Sigma^* \to (\Gamma^* \to \mathcal{A})$ and word $w \in \Gamma^*$.

Proof. Since $\{\sigma_{\gamma_1}\}, \ldots, \{\sigma_{\gamma_n}\}$, and Σ_ε are finite sets, $R_{h,w} = \Sigma_\varepsilon^* \cdot \{\sigma_{\gamma_1}\} \cdot \Sigma_\varepsilon^* \cdot \ldots \cdot \{\sigma_{\gamma_n}\} \cdot \Sigma_\varepsilon^*$, and because finite sets are recognisable (Hopcroft and Ullman 1969, Theorem 3.7) and recognisable languages are closed under language concatenation (Hopcroft and Ullman 1969, Theorem 3.8) and Kleene-star (Hopcroft and Ullman 1969, Theorem 3.9), we have that $R_{h,w}$ is regular. ■

Example 5.7 (Examples 3.7 and 3.11 continued). Figure 6 shows a deterministic FSA $\mathcal{M}_{h,ac}$ that recognises $R_{h,ac}$. □

Figure 6: Deterministic FSA $\mathcal{M}_{h,ac}$ that recognises $R_{h,ac}$ (cf. Example 5.7)

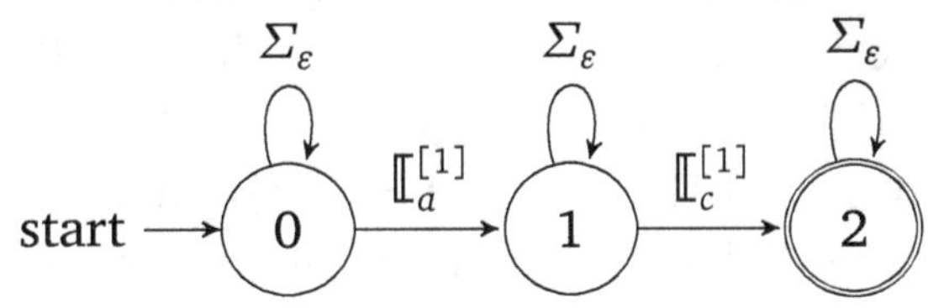

5.3 *Problems and restrictions*

Definition 5.8. Let $\mathcal{M} = (Q, \Delta, q_{\mathrm{i}}, F, T)$ be an FSA and $h: \Delta^* \to (\Gamma^* \to \mathcal{A})$ be an $\mathcal{A}$-weighted homomorphism. The *set of harmful loops in $\mathcal{M}$ with respect to* h is the set of all runs $q_0 u_1 q_1 \cdots u_k q_k$ in $\mathcal{M}$ where $q_1, \ldots, q_k$ are pairwise disjoint elements of Q, $q_0 = q_k$, $u_1, \ldots, u_k \in \Delta^*$, and $h(u_1) = \ldots = h(u_k) = 1.\varepsilon$. □

When examining Example 3.11 and Figure 5, we see that there are seven harmful loops in $\mathcal{M}(G_{\mathbb{B}})$ with respect to h: the five self-loops of T, the loop between T and $A^{[2]}$, and the loop between T and $B^{[2]}$. Harmful loops are problematic for the termination of a parsing algorithm since they cause an infinite set of candidates that are not distinguishable by their image under h. When generating the sequence of candidates for our parsing algorithm, such a situation creates the contingency of never producing a candidate that is accepted by $mD_{\mathrm{c}}(G_{\mathbb{B}})$ even if one exists. To allow our parsing algorithm to solve the above problem, we will

(i) only admit a restricted form of weighted MCFGs and
(ii) require each value in the domain of $\mathcal{A}$ (except 0 and 1) to be viewed as a product of arbitrarily many smaller values from the domain of $\mathcal{A}$.

Restricted weighted MCFG

Definition 5.9. An $\mathcal{A}$-weighted MCFG $G = (N, \Delta, S, P, \mu)$ is called *restricted* if there do not exist a subderivation d in G and a position $\pi = n_1 \cdots n_k \in \mathrm{pos}(d)$ (where $n_1, \ldots, n_k \in \mathbb{N}$) such that $d(\varepsilon) = d(\pi)$, $d(\varepsilon), d(n_1), d(n_1 n_2), \ldots, d(n_1 \cdots n_k)$ are pairwise different, and $\mu(d(\varepsilon)) = \mu(d(n_1)) = \mu(d(n_1 n_2)) = \ldots = \mu(d(n_1 \cdots n_k)) = 1$. □

Restricted weighted MCFG are strictly less powerful than (unrestricted) weighted MCFG, as the next example shows.

Example 5.10. Let us consider an arbitrary $\mathbb{B}$-weighted MCFG G and let m be the number of rules in G. Assume that $L(G)$ is not finite. Then there are subderivations in G of arbitrary height. It is clear that every subderivation d in G with a height greater than $m + 1$ must have a position $\pi \in \mathrm{pos}(d)$ such that $d(\varepsilon) = d(\pi)$. Then, since G has weights from $\mathbb{B}$, we know that 1 is assigned to every production in G and thus G is not restricted. □

Restricted weighted MCFGs are still useful in practice, as the following two observations show.

Definition 5.11. An $\mathscr{A}$-weighted MCFL is called *proper* if $\mathscr{A}$ is the probability semiring, the Viterbi semiring, or one of the algebras Pr_1 or Pr_2 (cf. Example 2.1) and for each non-terminal A the sum (using the usual addition in $\mathbb{R}$) of the weights of all productions with left-hand side A is 1. □

Observation 5.12. Every proper weighted MCFG is restricted.

Proof. Assume that G is proper but not restricted. Then there is a subderivation d in G and a position $\pi \in \mathrm{pos}(d)$ such that the weights of all productions along the path from the root to position π in d are 1 and $d(\varepsilon) = d(\pi) = \rho$. All productions along the path from the root to position π are unique for their respective left-hand side non-terminals since G is probabilistic. This means that every subderivation d' starting from ρ has the position π and $\rho = d'(\varepsilon) = d'(\pi) = d(\varepsilon) = d(\pi)$. But then $\{\varepsilon, \pi, \pi\pi, \pi\pi\pi, \ldots\} \subseteq \mathrm{pos}(d)$ and hence d is not a (finite) term, which contradicts our definition of a subderivation. ■

If we extract a weighted MCFG from a corpus and assign the weights by maximum-likelihood estimation (as for example in Kallmeyer and Maier 2013, p. 107), then we will get a weighted MCFG that is proper and therefore restricted.

The next observation allows us to enrich the weight structure of a $\mathbb{B}$-weighted MCFG to make it suitable for CS-parsing.

Observation 5.13. For every $\mathbb{B}$-weighted MCFG G, there is a restricted weighted MCFG G' such that $\mathrm{supp}(L(G)) = \mathrm{supp}(L(G'))$.

Proof. This can be done by assigning to every $w \in \mathrm{supp}(G)$, the size (i.e. number of productions) of its smallest derivation. To achieve that, we choose the tropical semiring as weight algebra for G', use the productions from G, and give every production the weight 1. Then no production in G' has the semiring-1 (which is 0 for the tropical semiring) as its weight and G' is restricted. ■

Factorisable weight structures

Definition 5.14. Let $\mathscr{A}$ be a complete commutative strong bimonoid and $\trianglelefteq$ be a partial order on $\mathscr{A}$. We say that $\mathscr{A}$ is $\trianglelefteq$-*factorisable* if for every $a \in \mathscr{A} \setminus \{0,1\}$ and natural number $k \geq 2$, there are $a_1, \ldots, a_k \in \mathscr{A} \setminus \{0,1\}$ such that $a_1 \lhd a, \ldots, a_k \lhd a$ and $a_1 \cdot \ldots \cdot a_k = a$. We then call $a_1 \cdot \ldots \cdot a_k$ a *$(\unlhd, k)$-factorisation of a*. □

Some of the complete commutative strong bimonoids mentioned in Example 2.1 are $\unlhd$-factorisable for some suitable partial order $\unlhd$, as Table 3 shows. The examples where multiplication is idempotent, however, have no suitable partial order since $a \cdot a = a$ contradicts $\cdot$ being increasing (in particular $a \lhd a \cdot a$).

Table 3: List of some complete commutative strong bimonoids $\mathscr{A}$ from Example 2.1 together with a partial order $\unlhd$ that $\mathscr{A}$ respects and a $(\unlhd, k)$-factorisation.

example algebra $(\mathscr{A}, +, \cdot, 0, 1)$	partial order $\unlhd$	$(\unlhd, k)$-factorisation of $a \in \mathscr{A} \setminus \{0,1\}$
Viterbi semiring $([0,1], \max, \cdot, 0, 1)$	$\geq$	$\underbrace{\sqrt[k]{a} \cdot \ldots \cdot \sqrt[k]{a}}_{k \text{ times}}$
tropical semiring $(\mathbb{R}_{\geq 0} \cup \{\infty\}, \min, +, \infty, 0)$	$\leq$	$\underbrace{a/k + \ldots + a/k}_{k \text{ times}}$
arctic semiring $(\mathbb{R}_{\geq 0} \cup \{-\infty\}, \max, +, -\infty, 0)$	$\leq$	$\underbrace{a/k + \ldots + a/k}_{k \text{ times}}$
$\mathrm{Pr}_1 = ([0,1], \oplus_1, \cdot, 0, 1)$ and $\mathrm{Pr}_2 = ([0,1], \oplus_2, \cdot, 0, 1)$	$\geq$	$\underbrace{\sqrt[k]{a} \cdot \ldots \cdot \sqrt[k]{a}}_{k \text{ times}}$

For the probability semiring $\mathrm{Pr} = (\mathbb{R}_{\geq 0}, +, \cdot, 0, 1)$ monotonicity and increasingness contradict each other. To show this we first assume that Pr would respect some partial order $\unlhd$. From $1/2 \cdot 1/2 = 1/4$ and $2 \cdot 2 = 4$ follows $1/2 \lhd 1/4$ and $2 \lhd 4$ since $\cdot$ is increasing. By monotonicity then follows $2 \cdot 1/2 \unlhd 4 \cdot 1/2 \unlhd 4 \cdot 1/4$ and hence $1 \unlhd 2 \unlhd 1$. But $\unlhd$ is a partial order and thus antisymmetric.

5.4 *A CS parsing algorithm*

For the remainder of this article let $\mathscr{A}$ be a complete commutative strong bimonoid and $\unlhd$ be a partial order on $\mathscr{A}$ such that $\mathscr{A}$ respects $\unlhd$ and is $\unlhd$-factorisable. Also, we will require our weighted MCFGs to be restricted.

To solve the problem stated in the beginning of Section 5.3, we define a modified generator language and a modified weight function to replace R and h from the CS-theorem (cf. Theorem 3.12).

The modified generator language

Consider an MCFG G with non-terminals N. Then, intuitively, $\mathcal{M}(G)$ has two kinds of states:

(i) For every non-terminal $A \in N$ and every $j \in$ [fan-out(A)] there is a state $A^{[j]}$ that signifies that the automaton *is about to process* the j-th component of a string tuple generated by G with A.

(ii) There is a state T that signifies that the automaton *just finished processing* some component of a string tuple generated by G with some non-terminal.

We split state T from $\mathcal{M}(G)$ up to formalise the following intuition:

(ii') For every non-terminal $A \in N$ and every $j \in$ [fan-out(A)] there is a state $\bar{A}^{[j]}$ that signifies that the automaton *just finished processing* the j-th component of a string tuple generated by G with A.

Definition 5.15. Let $G = (N, \Delta, S, R)$ be an MCFG. The *modified generator automaton with respect to* G, denoted by $\mathcal{M}'(G)$, is the finite state automaton $(Q \cup \bar{Q}, \Sigma, S^{[1]}, \{\bar{S}^{[1]}\}, \tau)$ where Σ is the generator alphabet with respect to G, $Q = \{A^{[j]} \mid A \in N, j \in [\text{fan-out}(A)]\}$, $\bar{Q} = \{\bar{A}^{[j]} \mid A \in N, j \in [\text{fan-out}(A)]\}$, and τ is the smallest set such that for every rule

$$\rho = A \to [u_1^0 y_1^1 u_1^1 \cdots y_1^{n_1} u_1^{n_1}, \ldots, u_s^0 y_s^1 u_s^1 \cdots y_s^{n_s} u_s^{n_s}](B_1, \ldots, B_m)$$

in R we have that

(i) $\big(A^{[j]}, ⟦_\rho^{[j]} \tilde{u}_j^0 ⟧_\rho^{[j]}, \bar{A}^{[j]}\big) \in \tau$ for every $j \in [s]$ with $n_j = 0$,

(ii) $\big(A^{[j]}, ⟦_\rho^{[j]} \tilde{u}_j^0 ⟦_{\rho,i}^{[\ell]}, B_i^{[\ell]}\big) \in \tau$ for every $i \in [m]$, $j \in [s]$, and $\ell \in$ [fan-out(B_i)] with $n_j \neq 0$ and $y_j^1 = x_i^\ell$,

(iii) $\big(\bar{B}_i^{[\ell]}, ⟧_{\rho,i}^{[\ell]} \tilde{u}_j^{\kappa-1} ⟦_{\rho,i'}^{[\ell']}, B_{i'}^{[\ell']}\big) \in \tau$ for every $i, i' \in [m]$, $j \in [s]$, $\kappa \in [n_j]$, $\ell \in$ [fan-out(B_i)], $\ell' \in$ [fan-out($B_{i'}$)] with $n_j \neq 0$, $y_j^{\kappa-1} = x_i^\ell$, $y_j^\kappa = x_{i'}^{\ell'}$, and

(iv) $\big(\bar{B}_i^{[\ell]}, ⟧_{\rho,i}^{[\ell]} \tilde{u}_j^{n_j} ⟧_\rho^{[j]}, \bar{A}^{[j]}\big) \in \tau$ for every $i \in [m]$, $j \in [s]$, and $\ell \in$ [fan-out(B_i)] with $n_j \neq 0$ and $y_j^{n_j} = x_i^\ell$.

The *modified generator language with respect to* G is $R'(G) = L(\mathcal{M}'(G))$. □

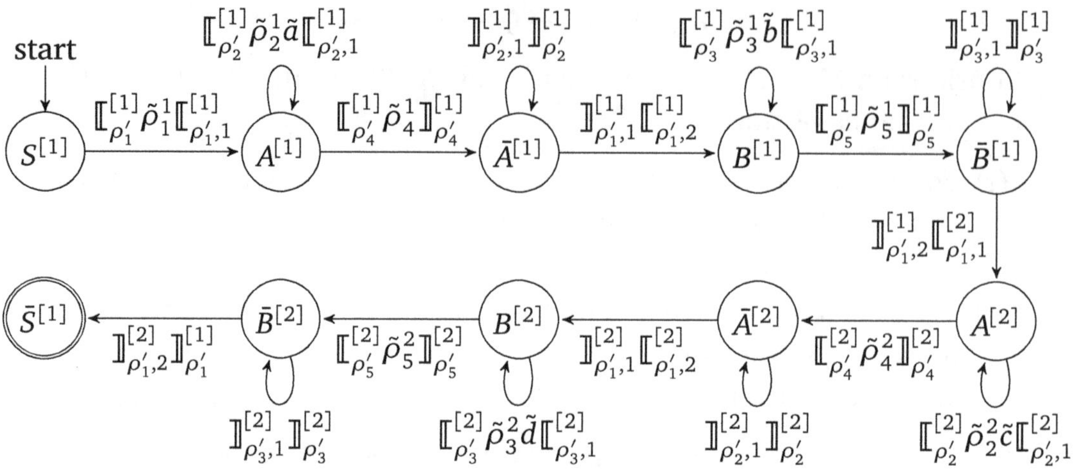

Figure 7: Modified generator automaton $\mathcal{M}'(G')$ with respect to G' from Example 3.4

Lemma 5.16. $R(G) \cap mD_c(G) = R'(G) \cap mD_c(G)$ for every MCFG G.

Proof. Let $G = (N, \Delta, S, P)$ and Σ be the generator alphabet with respect to G.

($\supseteq$) For this we show that $R(G) \supseteq R'(G)$. Let $q_0 u_1 q_1 \cdots u_m q_m$ be a successful run in $\mathcal{M}'(G)$. We define the string $v = t(q_0)u_1 t(q_1) \cdots u_m t(q_m)$ where

$$t(q) = \begin{cases} q & \text{if } q = A^{[j]} \in Q \text{ for some } A \in N \text{ and } j \in \text{fan-out}(A) \\ T & \text{otherwise.} \end{cases}$$

Clearly for every transition (q, u, q') in $\mathcal{M}'(G)$, there is a transition $(t(q), u, t(q'))$ in $\mathcal{M}(G)$. Since $\bar{S}^{[1]}$ is the final state in $\mathcal{M}'(G)$ and $t(\bar{S}^{[1]})$ is a final state in $\mathcal{M}(G)$, we have that v is a successful run in $\mathcal{M}(G)$.

($\subseteq$) Since $R(G) \cap mD_c(G)$ is in bijection with D_G (Corollary 3.9), it suffices to show that $\text{yield}(D_G) \supseteq \text{hom}_G(R'(G))$. We prove the following for every $A \in N$ and $d \in D_G(A)$ by induction on d:

> Let $\text{yield}(d) = (u_1, \ldots, u_m)$. There are $v_1, \ldots, v_m \in \Sigma^*$ such that $\mathcal{M}'(G)$ recognises v_i from $A^{[i]}$ to $\bar{A}^{[i]}$ and $\text{hom}_G(v_i) = u_i$ for every $i \in [m]$.

This statement implies the claim.

Induction base: Let $d = \rho = A \to [u_1, \ldots, u_m]() \in P$. Then for every $i \in [m]$, there is a transition $(A^{[i]}, [\![^{[i]}_{\rho} \tilde{u}_i]\!]^{[i]}_{\rho}, \bar{A}^{[i]})$ in $\mathcal{M}'(G)$. Clearly, $\text{hom}_G([\![^{[i]}_{\rho} \tilde{u}_i]\!]^{[i]}_{\rho}) = u_i$ and $\mathcal{M}'(G)$ recognises $[\![^{[i]}_{\rho} \tilde{u}_i]\!]^{[i]}_{\rho}$ from $A^{[i]}$ to $\bar{A}^{[i]}$.

Step: Let $d = \rho(d_1, \ldots, d_k)$ with $\rho = A \to [u_1, \ldots, u_m](B_1, \ldots, B_k)$ and $m_i = \text{fan-out}(B_i)$ for every $i \in [k]$. By induction hypothesis there are $v^i_1, \ldots, v^i_{m_i}$ for every $i \in [k]$ such that $(\text{hom}_G(v^i_1), \ldots, \text{hom}_G(v^i_{m_i})) = \text{yield}(d_i)$ and $\mathcal{M}'(G)$ recognises v^i_j from $B^{[j]}_i$ to $\bar{B}^{[j]}_i$ for every $j \in [m]$. By the existence of ρ in P and Definition 5.15, we can construct runs in $\mathcal{M}'(G)$ from $A^{[1]}$ to $\bar{A}^{[1]}$, …, $A^{[m]}$ to $\bar{A}^{[m]}$, recognising $v_1, \ldots, v_m$, respectively such that $(\text{hom}_G(v_1), \ldots, \text{hom}_G(v_m)) = \text{yield}(d)$. ■

The modified weight function

Examining $\mathcal{M}'(G_{\mathbb{B}})$ from Figure 7 together with h from Example 3.11 we notice that there are still four harmful loops: the self-loops of $A^{[1]}$, $B^{[1]}$, $A^{[2]}$, and $B^{[2]}$. Therefore, we will define a function $\text{wt}_{G,\trianglelefteq}$ from strings of parentheses to $\mathcal{A}$ that assigns a weight different from 1 to the labels along those loops, but still computes the same weights as h on the subset $mD_c(G_{\mathbb{B}})$. Intuitively, we take the weight attached to a symbol $[\![^{[1]}_\rho$ (for some rule ρ of fan-out s) and distribute it along the $2\cdot s$ symbols $[\![^{[1]}_\rho,]\!]^{[1]}_\rho, \ldots, [\![^{[s]}_\rho,]\!]^{[s]}_\rho$ using the fact that $\mathcal{A}$ is $\trianglelefteq$-factorisable.

Definition 5.17. Let $\mathcal{A}$ be a complete commutative strong bimonoid, $\trianglelefteq$ be a partial order on $\mathcal{A}$, $\mathcal{A}$ be $\trianglelefteq$-factorisable, and $G = (N, \Delta, S, P, \mu)$ be an $\mathcal{A}$-weighted k-MCFG. Furthermore, let Σ be the generator alphabet with respect to G. For every $\rho = A \to [u_1, \ldots, u_s](B_1, \ldots, B_k) \in P$, we set $\rho' = A \to [\rho^1 u_1, \ldots, \rho^s u_s](B_1, \ldots, B_k)$ and fix values $a^\rho_1, \ldots, a^\rho_{2\cdot s} \in \mathcal{A} \setminus \{0\}$ such that

- if $\mu(\rho) \neq 1$ then $a^\rho_1, \ldots, a^\rho_{2\cdot s}$ are not 1, are smaller or equal to $\mu(\rho)$ with respect to $\trianglelefteq$, and $a^\rho_1 \cdot \ldots \cdot a^\rho_{2\cdot s} = \mu(\rho)$; or
- if $\mu(\rho) = 1$ then $a^\rho_1 = \ldots = a^\rho_{2\cdot s} = 1$.

The *weight function with respect to G and* $\trianglelefteq$ is the function $\text{wt}_{G,\trianglelefteq} \colon \Sigma^* \to \mathcal{A}$ defined for every $u_1, \ldots, u_k \in \Sigma$ by

$$\text{wt}_{G,\trianglelefteq}(u_1 \cdots u_k) = \text{wt}'_{G,\trianglelefteq}(u_1) \cdot \ldots \cdot \text{wt}'_{G,\trianglelefteq}(u_k)$$

where $\text{wt}'_{G,\trianglelefteq} \colon \Sigma \to \mathcal{A}$ is given by

$$\text{wt}'_{G,\trianglelefteq}(\sigma) = \begin{cases} a^\rho_{2\cdot i-1} & \text{if } \sigma \text{ is of the form } [\![^{[i]}_\rho \\ a^\rho_{2\cdot i} & \text{if } \sigma \text{ is of the form }]\!]^{[i]}_\rho \\ 1 & \text{otherwise.} \end{cases}$$ □

Example 5.18 (Example 2.5 continued). First, we calculate factorisations of the weights in G as shown in Table 3 for Pr_2:

$$\begin{aligned}
&\text{for } \rho_2 \text{ and } \rho_4: && 1/2 = \sqrt[4]{1/2}\cdot\sqrt[4]{1/2}\cdot\sqrt[4]{1/2}\cdot\sqrt[4]{1/2}\\
&\text{for } \rho_3: && 1/3 = \sqrt[4]{1/3}\cdot\sqrt[4]{1/3}\cdot\sqrt[4]{1/3}\cdot\sqrt[4]{1/3}\\
&\text{for } \rho_5: && 2/3 = \sqrt[4]{2/3}\cdot\sqrt[4]{2/3}\cdot\sqrt[4]{2/3}\cdot\sqrt[4]{2/3}
\end{aligned}$$

Then $\mathrm{wt}_{G,\trianglelefteq}$ is given as follows:

$$\mathrm{wt}_{G,\geq}(\sigma) = \begin{cases} \sqrt[4]{1/2} & \text{if } \sigma \in \{\llbracket^{[j]}_{\rho'}, \rrbracket^{[j]}_{\rho'} \mid \rho' \in \{\rho'_2, \rho'_4\}, j \in [2]\},\\ \sqrt[4]{1/3} & \text{if } \sigma \in \{\llbracket^{[j]}_{\rho'_3}, \rrbracket^{[j]}_{\rho'_3} \mid j \in [2]\},\\ \sqrt[4]{2/3} & \text{if } \sigma \in \{\llbracket^{[j]}_{\rho'_5}, \rrbracket^{[j]}_{\rho'_5} \mid j \in [2]\},\\ 1 & \text{otherwise.} \end{cases}$$ □

Now we examine the FSA $\mathcal{M}'(G_{\mathbb{B}})$ from Figure 7 again, but this time we use the weight function $\mathrm{wt}_{G,\trianglelefteq}$ from Example 5.18 instead of the weights given by the homomorphism h in Example 3.11. For this let $h'\colon(\Sigma \cup \bar{\Sigma})^* \to (\Delta^* \to \mathcal{A})$ be the $\mathcal{A}$-weighted homomorphism defined by $h'(\sigma) = \mathrm{wt}_{G,\trianglelefteq}(\sigma).u_\sigma$ where $h(\sigma) = \mu_\sigma.u_\sigma$ for every $\sigma \in \Sigma \cup \bar{\Sigma}$. Then there are no more harmful loops in $\mathcal{M}'(G_{\mathbb{B}})$ with respect to h'.

Lemma 5.19. Let $G = (N, \Delta, S, P, \mu)$ be a restricted $\mathcal{A}$-weighted MCFG that only has productive non-terminals and $\trianglelefteq$ be a partial order on $\mathcal{A}$ such that $\mathcal{A}$ is $\trianglelefteq$-factorisable. Furthermore, let $h'\colon(\Sigma \cup \bar{\Sigma})^* \to (\Delta^* \to \mathcal{A})$ be the $\mathcal{A}$-weighted homomorphism defined by $h'(\sigma) = \mathrm{wt}_{G,\trianglelefteq}(\sigma).u_\sigma$ where $(\mathrm{weights}_G \circ \mathrm{hom}_{G_{\mathbb{B}}})(\sigma) = \mu_\sigma.u_\sigma$ for every $\sigma \in \Sigma \cup \bar{\Sigma}$. Then $\mathcal{M}'(G_{\mathbb{B}})$ has no harmful loops with respect to h'.

Proof. We show the claim by contradiction. For this assume that $q_0u_1q_1\cdots u_kq_k$ is a harmful loop in $\mathcal{M}'(G_{\mathbb{B}})$ with respect to h' where $q_0,\ldots,q_k$ are states and $u_1,\ldots,u_k \in (\Sigma \cup \bar{\Sigma})^*$. Then $q_0 = q_k$ and $\mathrm{wt}_{G,\trianglelefteq}(u_1) = \ldots = \mathrm{wt}_{G,\trianglelefteq}(u_k) = 1$. We now distinguish two cases:

(Case 1) Let $q_0 = q_k \in Q$ and $I = \{i_0,\ldots,i_m\}$ be the maximal subset of $\{0,\ldots,k\}$ (with $i_0 < \cdots < i_m$) such that

(i) $i_0 = 0$ and $i_m = k$,

(ii) for every $i \in I$ we have that q_i is of the form $B_i^{[j_i]}$ for some $B_i \in N$ and $j_i \in [\text{fan-out}(B_i)]$, and

(iii) for every $\kappa \in [m]$ we have that B_{i_κ} occurs on the right-hand side of $\rho_{i_{\kappa-1}}$ where $[\![^{[j_{i_{\kappa-1}}]}_{\rho_{i_{\kappa-1}}}$ is read in the transition that leaves $q_{i_{\kappa-1}}$.

Since every non-terminal in G is productive there is a derivation d and a position $\pi = n_1 \cdots n_m$ in d such that $n_1, \ldots, n_m \in \mathbb{N}$ and $d(\varepsilon) = \rho_{i_1}$, $d(n_1) = \rho_{i_2}$, ..., $d(n_1 \cdots n_{m-1}) = \rho_{i_m}$, and $d(n_1 \cdots n_m) = \rho_{i_1}$. For every $i \in I$ we know that $\mu(\rho_i) = 1$ since $\mathrm{wt}_{G,\trianglelefteq}([\![^{[j_i]}_{\rho_i}) = 1$ and by Definition 5.17. This contradicts G being restricted.

(Case 2) Let $q_0 = q_k \in \bar{Q}$ and $I = \{i_0, \ldots, i_m\}$ be the maximal subset of $\{0, \ldots, k\}$ (with $i_m < \cdots < i_0$) such that

(i) $i_m = 0$ and $i_0 = k$,

(ii) for every $i \in I$ we have that q_i is of the form $\bar{B}_i^{[j_i]}$ for some $B_i \in N$ and $j_i \in [\text{fan-out}(B_i)]$, and

(iii) for every $\kappa \in [m]$ we have that B_{i_κ} occurs on the right-hand side of $\rho_{i_{\kappa-1}}$ where $]\!]^{[j_{i_{\kappa-1}}]}_{\rho_{i_{\kappa-1}}}$ is read in the transition that reaches $q_{i_{\kappa-1}}$.

Since every non-terminal in G is productive there is a derivation d and a position $\pi = n_1 \cdots n_m$ in d such that $n_1, \ldots, n_m \in \mathbb{N}$ and $d(\varepsilon) = \rho_{i_m}$, $d(n_1) = \rho_{i_{m-1}}$, ..., $d(n_1 \cdots n_{m-1}) = \rho_{i_1}$, and $d(n_1 \cdots n_m) = \rho_{i_m}$. For every $i \in I$ we know that $\mu(\rho_i) = 1$ since $\mathrm{wt}_{G,\trianglelefteq}(]\!]^{[j_i]}_{\rho_i}) = 1$ and by Definition 5.17. This contradicts G being restricted. ∎

Lemma 5.20. Let $G = (N, \Delta, S, P, \mu)$ be an $\mathscr{A}$-weighted MCFG and $\trianglelefteq$ a partial order on $\mathscr{A}$. Then $h = \mathrm{weights}_G \circ \mathrm{hom}_{G_\mathbb{B}}$ assigns the same weight to each word in $mD_\mathrm{c}(G_\mathbb{B}) \cap R'(G_\mathbb{B})$ as $\mathrm{wt}_{G,\trianglelefteq}$.

Proof. Let $\rho \in P$ be an arbitrary production, $m = \text{fan-out}(\rho)$, and $\mathrm{wt}_{G,\trianglelefteq}([\![^{[1]}_{\rho}) = a_{2\cdot i-1}$ and $\mathrm{wt}_{G,\trianglelefteq}(]\!]^{[1]}_{\rho}) = a_{2\cdot i}$ for every $i \in [m]$. By the definition of $R'(G_\mathbb{B})$, we know that symbols of the forms $[\![^{[i]}_{\rho}$, $[\![^{[1]}_{\rho^i}$, and $[\![^{[1]}_{\rho^i}$ occur only as a sequence $[\![^{[i]}_{\rho}[\![^{[1]}_{\rho^i}]\!]^{[1]}_{\rho^i}$ (see the construction in Lemma 3.3 and items (i) and (ii) in Definition 5.15). By the definition of the cancellation rule, we also know that for every symbol $[\![^{[i]}_{\rho}$ there must occur corresponding symbols $[\![^{[1]}_{\rho}, \ldots, [\![^{[i-1]}_{\rho}, [\![^{[i+1]}_{\rho}, \ldots, [\![^{[m]}_{\rho}$ and $]\!]^{[1]}_{\rho}, \ldots,]\!]^{[m]}_{\rho}$ in $mD_\mathrm{c}(G_\mathbb{B})$. Thus in the set $mD_\mathrm{c}(G_\mathbb{B}) \cap R'(G_\mathbb{B})$ we have that $[\![^{[1]}_{\rho}$ occurs iff all the corresponding symbols $[\![^{[2]}_{\rho}, \ldots, [\![^{[m]}_{\rho}$ and $]\!]^{[1]}_{\rho}, \ldots,]\!]^{[m]}_{\rho}$ occur.

Then by the construction of $\mathrm{wt}_{G,\trianglelefteq}$ it follows that

$$\underbrace{\mathrm{wt}_{G,\trianglelefteq}(\llbracket_{\rho}^{[1]})}_{=a_1}\cdot\underbrace{\mathrm{wt}_{G,\trianglelefteq}(\llbracket_{\rho^1}^{[1]}\rrbracket_{\rho^1}^{[1]})}_{=1}\cdot\underbrace{\mathrm{wt}_{G,\trianglelefteq}(\rrbracket_{\rho}^{[1]})}_{=a_2}\cdot\ldots\cdot\underbrace{\mathrm{wt}_{G,\trianglelefteq}(\llbracket_{\rho}^{[m]})}_{=a_{2m-1}}\cdot\underbrace{\mathrm{wt}_{G,\trianglelefteq}(\rrbracket_{\rho}^{[m]})}_{=a_{2m}}$$

is $\mu(\rho)$ and thus exactly the weight assigned to those symbols by h. ∎

The parser

Definition 5.21. Let G be an $\mathcal{A}$-weighted MCFG over Δ, $n \in \mathbb{N}$, and $\trianglelefteq$ be a partial order on $\mathcal{A}$. The *n-best CS parser with respect to G and* $\trianglelefteq$, denoted by CS-parse$(G,n,\trianglelefteq)$, is a function from Δ^* to D_G^* that assigns for every $w \in \Delta^*$ the value

$$\mathrm{take}(n)\circ\mathrm{map}(\mathit{toDeriv}\circ\mathrm{hom}_{G_{\mathbb{B}}})\circ\mathrm{filter}(mD_{\mathrm{c}}(G_{\mathbb{B}}))\\ \circ\,\mathrm{sort}(\mathrm{wt}_{G,\trianglelefteq},\trianglelefteq)\big(R'(G_{\mathbb{B}})\cap R_{h,w}\big)$$

where $h = \mathrm{weights}_G \circ \mathrm{hom}_{G_{\mathbb{B}}}$. □

Theorem 5.22. CS-parse$(G,n,\trianglelefteq)(w) \in n$-best$(\hat{\mu},\trianglelefteq)(D_G(w))$ for every $\mathcal{A}$-weighted MCFG $G=(N,\Delta,S,P,\mu)$, $n\in\mathbb{N}$, partial order $\trianglelefteq$ that respects $\mathcal{A}$, and word $w \in \Delta^*$.

Proof. Let $h = \mathrm{weights}_G \circ \mathrm{hom}_{G_{\mathbb{B}}}$. We prove the claim by verifying the four conditions from Definition 5.2.

(i) This follows from the definition of sort and the bijection between $R(G_{\mathbb{B}})\cap mD_{\mathrm{c}}(G_{\mathbb{B}})$ and D_G (Corollary 3.13).

(ii) $d_1,\ldots,d_k$ are pairwise different since $u_1,\ldots,u_k$ are pairwise different and $R(G_{\mathbb{B}})\cap mD_{\mathrm{c}}(G_{\mathbb{B}})$ and D_G stand in bijection (Corollary 3.13).

(iii) Let $(d_1,\ldots,d_k) =$ CS-parse$(G,n,\trianglelefteq)(w)$ and $(u_1,\ldots,u_k)$ be a prefix of filter$(mD_{\mathrm{c}}(G_{\mathbb{B}}))\circ\mathrm{sort}(\mathrm{wt}_{G,\trianglelefteq},\trianglelefteq)\big(R(G_{\mathbb{B}})\cap R_{h,w}\big)$. Due to the definition of filter, there must be a natural number m such that $(v_1,\ldots,v_m)$ is a prefix of $\mathrm{sort}(\mathrm{wt}_{G,\trianglelefteq},\trianglelefteq)\big(R(G_{\mathbb{B}})\cap R_{h,w}\big)$ for some $v_1,\ldots,v_m \in (\Sigma\cup\bar{\Sigma})^*$ and $u_1,\ldots,u_k$ occur in that order in $v_1,\ldots,v_m$. By the definition of sort, we have that $\mathrm{wt}_{G,\trianglelefteq}(v_1)\trianglelefteq\ldots\trianglelefteq\mathrm{wt}_{G,\trianglelefteq}(v_m)$. Since $u_1,\ldots,u_k$ occur in that order in $v_1,\ldots,v_m$, it follows that $\mathrm{wt}_{G,\trianglelefteq}(u_1)\trianglelefteq\ldots\trianglelefteq\mathrm{wt}_{G,\trianglelefteq}(u_k)$. By Lemma 5.20 we obtain $\hat{\mu}\circ\mathit{toDeriv}\circ\mathrm{hom}_{G_{\mathbb{B}}}(u_1)\trianglelefteq\ldots\trianglelefteq\hat{\mu}\circ\mathit{toDeriv}\circ\mathrm{hom}_{G_{\mathbb{B}}}(u_k)$ and by the definition of map we get $\hat{\mu}(d_1)\trianglelefteq\ldots\trianglelefteq\hat{\mu}(d_k)$.

(iv) There is no $d\in D_G(w)$ with $\hat{\mu}(d)\triangleleft\hat{\mu}(d_k)$ since, by definition of sort, there is no $u\in R(G_{\mathbb{B}})\cap mD_{\mathrm{c}}(G_{\mathbb{B}})$ with $\mathrm{wt}_{G,\trianglelefteq}(u)\triangleleft\mathrm{wt}_{G,\trianglelefteq}(u_k)$. ∎

Algorithm 3: Approximation of CS-parse using a threshold θ

In addition to just implementing CS-parse$(G, n, \trianglelefteq)$, we add a threshold θ for the weight of the found derivations. Then our algorithm will only consider the candidates whose weight is less than or equal to θ. Without such a threshold, the parsing algorithm would not terminate if the intersection of $R'(G_{\mathbb{B}})$ and $R_{h,w}$ had an infinite language and w had less than n derivations in G. On the other hand, if w has a derivation in G with a weight above the threshold, our algorithm will not find it, however large we choose n. Thus the algorithm only approximates CS-parse$(G, n, \trianglelefteq)$.

Input: a restricted $\mathscr{A}$-weighted MCFG $G = (N, \Delta, S, P, \mu)$, a number $n \in \mathbb{N}$, a partial order $\trianglelefteq$ on $\mathscr{A}$ where $\trianglelefteq$ respects $\mathscr{A}$ and $\mathscr{A}$ is $\trianglelefteq$-factorisable, a threshold $\theta \in \mathscr{A}$ with $0 \trianglelefteq \theta$, and a word $w \in \Delta^*$
Output: the subsequence of derivations d in CS-parse$(G, n, \trianglelefteq)(w)$ with $\mu(d) \trianglelefteq \theta$

function *CS-Parse*$(G, n, \trianglelefteq, \theta, w)$
  let $mD_c(\Sigma, \mathfrak{P}) = mD_c(G_{\mathbb{B}})$
  let $h = \text{weights}_G \circ \text{hom}_{G_{\mathbb{B}}}$
  let $parses = \varepsilon$
  while *hasNextCandicate* $\wedge$ $|parses| < n$ **do**
    let $u = nextCandidate$
    if *isMember*$(\Sigma, \mathfrak{P}, u)$ **then**
      append *toDeriv*(u) to the end of *parses*
    end if
  end while
  return *parses*
end function

procedure *hasNextCandicate*
  return whether some $u \in R'(G_{\mathbb{B}}) \cap R_{h,w}$ with $\text{wt}_{G,\trianglelefteq}(u) \trianglelefteq \theta$ was not yet considered
end procedure

procedure *nextCandidate*
  from the elements of $R'(G_{\mathbb{B}}) \cap R_{h,w}$ previously not considered, **return** an element whose image under $\text{wt}_{G,\trianglelefteq}$ is smallest with respect to $\trianglelefteq$
end procedure

To achieve that our algorithm terminates, we require for our input that G is restricted and that $\mathscr{A}$ is $\trianglelefteq$-factorisable. Let us take a closer look at how Algorithm 3 works. Since $\mathrm{sort}(\mathrm{wt}_{G,\trianglelefteq}, \trianglelefteq)$ returns an infinite list, we have a procedure *nextCandidate* that computes only the next element in that list, *hasNextCandicate* returns whether there is such a next element. We utilise those two procedures to only compute the prefix of $\mathrm{sort}(\mathrm{wt}_{G,\trianglelefteq}, \trianglelefteq)(R'(G_{\mathbb{B}}) \cap R_{h,w})$ we need to obtain the first n parses. Since there are deterministic FSA to recognise both $R'(G_{\mathbb{B}})$ and $R_{h,w}$, the computation of $\mathrm{sort}(\mathrm{wt}_{G,\trianglelefteq}, \trianglelefteq)(R'(G_{\mathbb{B}}) \cap R_{h,w})$ amounts to enumerating the paths in a weighted labelled graph ordered by their weights[8] and then replacing each path by the unique word recognised along it, where we take the graph with its labels from a deterministic FSA recognising $R'(G_{\mathbb{B}}) \cap R_{h,w}$ and the weights from $\mathrm{wt}_{G,\trianglelefteq}$.

Proof of termination for Algorithm 3. Let $h = \mathrm{weights}_G \circ \mathrm{hom}_{G_{\mathbb{B}}}$ and M be the set of all weights assigned by $\mathrm{wt}_{G,\trianglelefteq}$ to each of the words read in the transitions along one pass of every loop in the product of $\mathscr{M}'(G_{\mathbb{B}})$ and $\mathscr{M}_{h,w}$. Then M contains neither 0 nor 1 because $\mathscr{M}'(G_{\mathbb{B}})$ has no harmful loops. Since $\cdot$ has arbitrarily large powers, we know that for every element $a \in M$, there is a natural number k such that $\theta \trianglelefteq a^k$. Let $\hat{k}$ be the maximum of all such k's. There are only finitely many runs in the product of $\mathscr{M}'(G_{\mathbb{B}})$ and $\mathscr{M}_{h,w}$ that contain every loop less than $\hat{k}$ times. Hence *hasNextCandicate* is false after a finite number of iterations of the **while**-loop (lines 6 to 11), and Algorithm 3 terminates. ■

Example 5.23 (Examples 2.5, 3.7, and 5.7 continued)**.** Consider the word $w = ac$. The product of $\mathscr{M}'(G_{\mathbb{B}})$ and $\mathscr{M}_{h,w}$ together with $\mathrm{wt}_{G,\trianglelefteq}$ is shown in Figure 8 (for the product construction see Hopcroft and Ullman 1979, after Theorem 3.3). It suffices to consider at most 8 candidates to find the (only) derivation of w in G, as is shown in Table 4. The candidates themselves are not shown, instead we see their weight, their corresponding path in the graphical representation of the product of $\mathscr{M}'(G_{\mathbb{B}})$ and $\mathscr{M}_{h,w}$, and whether they are in $mD_{\mathrm{c}}(G_{\mathbb{B}})$. Candidate 7 is exactly $\mathrm{toBrackets}(\rho_1'(\rho_2'(\rho_4'), \rho_5'))$. □

[8] This is described for example in Hoffman and Pavley 1959 for graphs with edge weights from the real numbers. However, their algorithm works also for complete commutative strong bimonoids $\mathscr{A}$ with a partial order on $\mathscr{A}$ that respects $\mathscr{A}$.

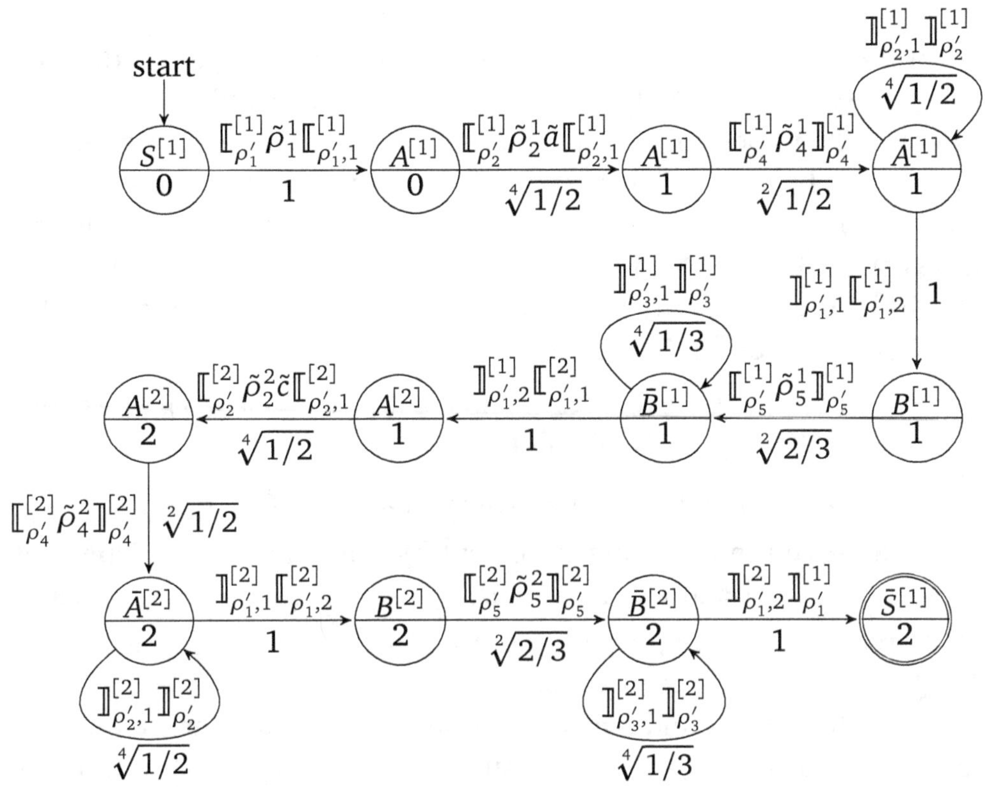

Figure 8: Product of $\mathcal{M}'(G_{\mathbb{B}})$ and $\mathcal{M}_{h,w}$ with the weight assigned by $\mathrm{wt}_{G,\trianglelefteq}$ to words read in each transition

Table 4: First eight paths (sorted by their image under $\mathrm{wt}_{G,\trianglelefteq}$) in the product of $\mathcal{M}'(G_{\mathbb{B}})$ and $\mathcal{M}_{h,w}$ and whether the corresponding candidate u_i is in $mD_c(G_{\mathbb{B}})$

i	$\mathrm{wt}_{G,\trianglelefteq}(u_i)$	path corresponding to u_i	$u_i \in mD_c(G_{\mathbb{B}})$?
1	$\frac{1}{3\sqrt{2}}$	without using any loops	no
2	$\frac{1}{3\sqrt[4]{8}}$	use the loop of $(\bar{A}^{[1]}, 1)$	no
3		use the loop of $(\bar{A}^{[2]}, 2)$	no
4	$\frac{1}{3\sqrt[4]{12}}$	use the loop of $(\bar{B}^{[1]}, 1)$	no
5		use the loop of $(\bar{B}^{[2]}, 2)$	no
6	$\frac{1}{6}$	use the loop of $(\bar{A}^{[1]}, 1)$ twice	no
7		use the loops of $(\bar{A}^{[1]}, 1)$ and $(\bar{A}^{[2]}, 2)$	yes
8		use the loop of $(\bar{A}^{[2]}, 2)$ twice	no

5.5 *Analysis of CS-Parse*

From the proof of termination of Algorithm 3 we can gather that the complexity of the algorithm depends on how many candidates are considered. The upper bound for the number of considered candidates is determined by n, θ, and the number $\widehat{k}$. In particular, it does not depend on the input word w. Therefore we cannot expect to get a meaningful time complexity for Algorithm 3.

Instead we will only determine the time complexity of the evaluation of *isMember* on line 7.

Lemma 5.24. Let G be an MCFG and $mD_c(\Sigma, \mathfrak{P}) = mD_c(G)$. The every element of $R'(G) \cap mD_c$ is $\mathfrak{P}$-simple.

Proof. Let $G = (N, \Gamma, S, P)$ and Σ and $\mathfrak{P}$ be defined as in Definition 4.9.

We prove the following statement by induction on the length of $w_1 \cdots w_\ell$: If $B \in N$ and $w_1, \ldots, w_\ell \in D(\Sigma)$ such that $w_1 \cdots w_\ell \in mD_c$ and w_κ is recognised along a path from $B^{[\kappa]}$ to $\overline{B}^{[\kappa]}$ in $\mathcal{M}'(G)$ for every $\kappa \in [\ell]$, then $w_1 \cdots w_\ell$ is $\mathfrak{P}$-simple.

By setting $\ell = 1$ and $B = S$, this statement implies our claim. Now let $B \in N$ and $w_1, \ldots, w_k \in D(\Sigma)$ such that $w_1 \cdots w_\ell \in mD_c$ and w_κ is recognised along a path from $B^{[\kappa]}$ to $\overline{B}^{[\kappa]}$ in $\mathcal{M}'(G)$ for every $\kappa \in [\ell]$. By the definitions of $\mathcal{M}'(G)$ and $mD_c(G)$, we know that there is some production $\rho = B \to f(B_1, \ldots, B_k) \in P$ with

$$f = [u_{1,0} x_{i(1,1)}^{j(1,1)} u_{1,1} \cdots x_{i(1,p_1)}^{j(1,p_1)} u_{1,p_1}, \ldots, u_{\ell,0} x_{i(\ell,1)}^{j(\ell,1)} u_{\ell,1} \cdots x_{i(\ell,p_\ell)}^{j(\ell,p_\ell)} u_{\ell,p_\ell}]$$

such that for every $\kappa \in [\ell]$ either

(i) $w_\kappa = \llbracket_\rho^{[\kappa]} \widetilde{u}_{\kappa,0} \rrbracket_\rho^{[\kappa]}$ or

(ii) $$w_\kappa = \llbracket_\rho^{[\kappa]} \widetilde{u}_{\kappa,0} \quad \llbracket_{\rho,i(\kappa,1)}^{[j(\kappa,1)]} \quad v_{i(\kappa,1)}^{j(\kappa,1)} \quad \rrbracket_{\rho,i(\kappa,1)}^{[j(\kappa,1)]} \quad \widetilde{u}_{\kappa,1} \quad \cdots \quad \llbracket_{\rho,i(\kappa,p_\kappa)}^{[j(\kappa,p_\kappa)]} \quad v_{i(\kappa,p_\kappa)}^{j(\kappa,p_\kappa)} \quad \rrbracket_{\rho,i(\kappa,p_\kappa)}^{[j(\kappa,p_\kappa)]} \quad \widetilde{u}_{\kappa,p_\kappa} \quad \rrbracket_\rho^{[\kappa]},$$

and $v_i^j \in D(\Sigma)$ is recognised along a path from $B_i^{[j]}$ to $\overline{B}_i^{[j]}$ in $\mathcal{M}'(G)$ for every $i \in [k]$ and $j \in [\text{sort}(B_i)]$, and $v_i^1 \cdots v_i^{\text{sort}(B_i)} \in mD_c(G)$ for every $i \in [k]$. Set $w'_1, \ldots, w'_\ell \in D(\Sigma)$ such that $w_\kappa = \llbracket_\rho^{[\kappa]} w'_\kappa \rrbracket_\rho^{[\kappa]}$ for each $\kappa \in [\ell]$. Then by induction hypothesis the string $v_i^1 \cdots v_i^{\text{sort}(B_i)}$ is $\mathfrak{P}$-simple for every $i \in [k]$. By analysing the form of w_κ for each $\kappa \in [\ell]$, we observe that $\text{occ}_\mathfrak{p}\, w'_1 \cdots w'_\ell \leq 1$ and $\text{occ}_\mathfrak{p}\, w_1 \cdots w_\ell \leq 1$ for each cell $\mathfrak{p} \in \{\mathfrak{p}' \in \mathfrak{P} \mid |\mathfrak{p}'| \geq 2\}$. Hence, $w_1 \cdots w_\ell$ is $\mathfrak{P}$-simple. ■

Let G be an MCFG and $mD_c(\Sigma, \mathfrak{P} = mD_c(G)$. Since every element of $R'(G) \cap mD_c(G)$ is $\mathfrak{P}$-simple, we can use *isMember'* on line 7 instead of *isMember*. Then line 7 can be done in time quadratic in the length of the candidate u.

6 RELATED PARSING APPROACHES

An established approach to speed up the parsing of MCFGs for practical applications is to use a formalism with lower parsing complexity than MCFGs to guide the exploration of the search space. In the following, we will focus on four such approaches.

The parsers in Barthélemy *et al.* (2001); Burden and Ljunglöf (2005); van Cranenburgh (2012) work as follows: Suppose that we want to parse a given word w with a grammar G of a formalism A. We first construct a grammar (or automaton) G' in a formalism B that has a lower parsing complexity than A. This can be done offline. Then, we parse w with G'. Lastly, we parse w with G, but while doing so, we consult the parses of w in G' to *guide* the exploration of the search space (of possible parses). The three papers differ in their choice of formalisms for G and G', and in their use of the parses of w in G' while parsing w in G:

(i) Barthélemy *et al.* (2001) have a positive range concatenation grammar (short: PRCG) (Boullier 1998) of arbitrary arity for G and use a PRCG of arity 1 for G'. They extract from the parse forest F of w in G' a so-called *guiding structure* and query this structure while parsing w in G. The guiding structure can range from a set of instantiated clauses that occur in F to F itself. In their experiments they used as a guiding structure the function that assigns for each instantiated clause the number of its occurrences in F.

(ii) Burden and Ljunglöf (2005, Section 4) have a linear context-free rewriting system (short: LCFRS) (Vijay-Shanker *et al.* 1987) for G and a context-free grammar for G'. They use deductive parsing. The *parse chart* C' of w in G' is created. While creating the parse chart of w in G, only items are created that are consistent with the items in C'. The algorithm is therefore an instance of *coarse-to-fine parsing* (Charniak *et al.* 2006).

(iii) Van Cranenburgh (2012) has a probabilistic LCFRS (of arbitrary fan-out) for G and a probabilistic LCFRS of fan-out 1 for G'. As

Burden and Ljunglöf (2005), he uses deductive parsing: First, a parse chart C' of w in G' is created. Then the probabilities of G' are used to restrict C' to the n best parses, obtaining a new parse chart $\widehat{C}$, this step is called *pruning*. A value of $n = 50$ was used in the experiments. Then, while creating the parse chart of w in G, only items are created that are consistent with the items in $\widehat{C}$. The algorithm is an instance of coarse-to-fine parsing.

Kallmeyer and Maier (2015) present a different approach:

(iv) They construct an FSA G' as the predict/resume-closure of *thread automaton thread stores* (Villemonte de la Clergerie 2002) where the corresponding thread automaton is constructed from the given LCFRS G. The addresses in the thread stores are represented by regular expressions to keep the set of states of G' finite. Then, a *parse table* is read off of G'. As opposed to Items (i) to (iii), w is *not* parsed with G'. Instead, while parsing w with G using a shift-reduce parser, the parse table is consulted directly at each shift or reduce operation to determine the successor state. Their algorithm is an instance of LR-parsing.

With the Chomsky-Schützenberger parsing presented in this article, we construct from the given weighted LCFRS G *three* devices (instead of just one): the deterministic FSA $\mathcal{M}'(G_{\mathbb{B}})$ together with the weight assignment $\mathrm{wt}_{G,\trianglelefteq}$, the congruence multiple Dyck language $mD_{\mathrm{c}}(G_{\mathbb{B}})$, and the alphabetic homomorphism $\mathrm{hom}_{G_{\mathbb{B}}}$. For the given word w we construct a deterministic FSA, let us call it $\mathcal{M}$, that recognises $\mathrm{hom}_{G_{\mathbb{B}}}^{-1}(w) \cap L(\mathcal{M}'_{G_{\mathbb{B}}})$. Constructing $\mathcal{M}$ is an additional preprocessing step in comparison to Items (i) to (iv). In contrast to Item (iii), we do not use the weight assignment $\mathrm{wt}_{G,\trianglelefteq}$ for pruning. We instead use it to enumerate the elements of $L(\mathcal{M})$ in increasing order of their costs. Finally, we filter the list of those elements with $mD_{\mathrm{c}}(G_{\mathbb{B}})$. Note that w is never actually parsed with G as in Items (i) to (iv).

7 CONCLUSION AND OUTLOOK

We obtained a weighted version of the Chomsky-Schützenberger characterisation of MCFLs for complete commutative strong bimonoids (Theorem 3.12) by separating the weights from the weighted MCFG and using Yoshinaka *et al.* (2010, Theorem 3) for the unweighted part.

We defined a variant of multiple Dyck languages that uses congruence relations (Definition 4.2), gave an algorithm to decide whether a word is in a given congruence multiple Dyck language in Algorithm 2, and derived a CS representation using congruence multiple Dyck languages.

Following the idea of Hulden (2011), we used this CS representation for weighted MCFL to describe a parsing algorithm (Algorithm 3) that approximates n-best parsing for restricted weighted MCFGs with a weight structure that is partially ordered and factorisable.

The utility of Algorithm 3 can *not* be judged based on theoretical considerations alone. The author therefore plans to implement it and evaluate it empirically.

ACKNOWLEDGEMENTS

The author is very grateful to the anonymous reviewers, as well as Mark-Jan Nederhof and Toni Dietze for their insightful comments, which helped improve this article.

REFERENCES

Alfred Vaino AHO and Jeffrey D. ULLMAN (1972), *The Theory of Parsing, Translation, and Compiling*, Prentice-Hall, Inc., Upper Saddle River, NJ, USA, ISBN 0-13-914556-7, http://dl.acm.org/citation.cfm?id=SERIES11430.578789.

Krasimir ANGELOV (2009), Incremental parsing with parallel multiple context-free grammars, in *Proceedings of the 12th Conference of the European Chapter of the Association for Computational Linguistics*, pp. 69–76, Association for Computational Linguistics, http://dl.acm.org/citation.cfm?id=1609074.

François BARTHÉLEMY, Pierre BOULLIER, Philippe DESCHAMP, and Éric DE LA CLERGERIE (2001), Guided parsing of range concatenation languages, in *Proceedings of the 39th Annual Meeting on Association for Computational Linguistics - ACL '01*, Association for Computational Linguistics (ACL), doi:10.3115/1073012.1073019.

Pierre BOULLIER (1998), A generalization of mildly context-sensitive formalisms, in *Proceedings of the Fourth International Workshop on Tree Adjoining Grammars and Related Formalisms (TAG+ 4)*, pp. 17–20, Citeseer.

Sabine BRANTS, Stefanie DIPPER, Peter EISENBERG, Silvia HANSEN-SCHIRRA, Esther KÖNIG, Wolfgang LEZIUS, Christian ROHRER, George SMITH, and Hans

USZKOREIT (2004), TIGER: Linguistic Interpretation of a German Corpus, *Research on Language and Computation*, 2(4):597–620, doi:10.1007/s11168-004-7431-3.

Håkan BURDEN and Peter LJUNGLÖF (2005), Parsing Linear Context-free Rewriting Systems, in Harry BUNT, Robert MALOUF, and Alon LAVIE, editors, *Proceedings of the Ninth International Workshop on Parsing Technology*, Parsing '05, pp. 11–17, Association for Computational Linguistics, Stroudsburg, PA, USA, `http://dl.acm.org/citation.cfm?id=1654494.1654496`.

Matthias BÜCHSE, Daniel GEISLER, Torsten STÜBER, and Heiko VOGLER (2010), n-Best Parsing Revisited, in Frank DREWES and Marco KUHLMANN, editors, *Proceedings of the 2010 Workshop on Applications of Tree Automata in Natural Language Processing*, pp. 46–54, Association for Computational Linguistics, `http://www.aclweb.org/anthology/W10-2506`.

Eugene CHARNIAK, Michael POZAR, Theresa VU, Mark JOHNSON, Micha ELSNER, Joseph AUSTERWEIL, David ELLIS, Isaac HAXTON, Catherine HILL, R. SHRIVATHS, and Jeremy MOORE (2006), Multilevel coarse-to-fine PCFG parsing, in *Proceedings of the main conference on Human Language Technology Conference of the North American Chapter of the Association of Computational Linguistics* -, Association for Computational Linguistics (ACL), doi:10.3115/1220835.1220857.

Noam CHOMSKY and Marcel Paul SCHÜTZENBERGER (1963), The algebraic theory of context-free languages, pp. 118–161, doi:10.1016/S0049-237X(09)70104-1.

Tobias DENKINGER (2015), A Chomsky-Schützenberger representation for weighted multiple context-free languages, in *Proceedings of the 12th International Conference on Finite-State Methods and Natural Language Processing (FSMNLP 2015)*, `http://aclweb.org/anthology/W15-4803`.

Manfred DROSTE, Torsten STÜBER, and Heiko VOGLER (2010), Weighted finite automata over strong bimonoids, *Information Sciences*, 180(1):156–166, doi:10.1016/j.ins.2009.09.003.

Manfred DROSTE and Heiko VOGLER (2013), The Chomsky-Schützenberger Theorem for Quantitative Context-Free Languages, in Marie-Pierre BÉAL and Olivier CARTON, editors, *Developments in Language Theory*, volume 7907 of *Lecture Notes in Computer Science*, pp. 203–214, Springer Berlin Heidelberg, ISBN 978-3-642-38770-8, doi:10.1007/978-3-642-38771-5_19.

Jürgen DUSKE, Rainer PARCHMANN, and Johann SPECHT (1979), A Homomorphic Characterization of Indexed Languages, 15(4):187–195.

Séverine FRATANI and El Makki VOUNDY (2015), Context-free characterization of Indexed Languages, abs/1409.6112, `http://arxiv.org/abs/1409.6112`.

Séverine FRATANI and El Makki VOUNDY (2016), Homomorphic Characterizations of Indexed Languages, in Adrian-Horia DEDIU, Jan

JANOUŠEK, Carlos MARTÍN-VIDE, and Bianca TRUTHE, editors, *Proceedings of the 10th International Conference on Language and Automata Theory and Applications (LATA 2015)*, pp. 359–370, Springer Science + Business Media, doi:10.1007/978-3-319-30000-9_28.

Luisa HERRMANN and Heiko VOGLER (2015), A Chomsky-Schützenberger Theorem for Weighted Automata with Storage, in Andreas MALETTI, editor, *Proceedings of the 6th International Conference on Algebraic Informatics (CAI 2015)*, volume 9270, pp. 90–102, Springer International Publishing, ISBN 978-3-319-23021-4, doi:10.1007/978-3-319-23021-4_11.

Walter HOFFMAN and Richard PAVLEY (1959), A Method for the Solution of the Nth Best Path Problem, 6(4):506–514, doi:10.1145/320998.321004.

John Edward HOPCROFT and Jeffrey David ULLMAN (1969), *Formal languages and their relation to automata*, Addison-Wesley Longman Publishing Co., Inc.

John Edward HOPCROFT and Jeffrey David ULLMAN (1979), *Introduction to Automata Theory, Languages and Computation*, Addison-Wesley, 1st edition.

Liang HUANG and David CHIANG (2005), Better k-best Parsing, in *Proceedings of the Ninth International Workshop on Parsing Technology*, Parsing '05, pp. 53–64, Association for Computational Linguistics, Stroudsburg, PA, USA, http://dl.acm.org/citation.cfm?id=1654494.1654500.

Mans HULDEN (2011), Parsing CFGs and PCFGs with a Chomsky-Schützenberger Representation, in Zygmunt VETULANI, editor, *Human Language Technology. Challenges for Computer Science and Linguistics*, volume 6562 of *Lecture Notes in Computer Science*, pp. 151–160, Springer Berlin Heidelberg, ISBN 978-3-642-20094-6, doi:10.1007/978-3-642-20095-3_14.

Laura KALLMEYER and Wolfgang MAIER (2013), Data-driven parsing using probabilistic linear context-free rewriting systems, *Computational Linguistics*, 39(1):87–119, doi:10.1162/COLI_a_00136.

Laura KALLMEYER and Wolfgang MAIER (2015), LR Parsing for LCFRS, in *Proceedings of the 2015 Conference of the North American Chapter of the Association for Computational Linguistics: Human Language Technologies*, Association for Computational Linguistics (ACL), doi:10.3115/v1/n15-1134.

Makoto KANAZAWA (2014), Multidimensional trees and a Chomsky-Schützenberger-Weir representation theorem for simple context-free tree grammars, ISSN 1465-363X, doi:10.1093/logcom/exu043.

Marco KUHLMANN and Giorgio SATTA (2009), Treebank Grammar Techniques for Non-projective Dependency Parsing, in *Proceedings of the 12th Conference of the European Chapter of the Association for Computational Linguistics*, EACL '09, pp. 478–486, Association for Computational Linguistics, Stroudsburg, PA, USA, http://dl.acm.org/citation.cfm?id=1609067.1609120.

Wolfgang MAIER and Anders SØGAARD (2008), Treebanks and mild context-sensitivity, in *Proceedings of Formal Grammar*, p. 61, http://web.stanford.edu/group/cslipublications/cslipublications/FG/2008/maier.pdf.

Jens MICHAELIS (2001a), Derivational Minimalism Is Mildly Context-Sensitive, in Michael MOORTGAT, editor, *Logical Aspects of Computational Linguistics*, volume 2014 of *Lecture Notes in Computer Science*, pp. 179–198, Springer Berlin Heidelberg, ISBN 978-3-540-42251-8, doi:10.1007/3-540-45738-0_11.

Jens MICHAELIS (2001b), Transforming Linear Context-Free Rewriting Systems into Minimalist Grammars, in Philippe GROOTE, Glyn MORRILL, and Christian RETORÉ, editors, *Logical Aspects of Computational Linguistics*, volume 2099 of *Lecture Notes in Computer Science*, pp. 228–244, Springer Berlin Heidelberg, ISBN 978-3-540-42273-0, doi:10.1007/3-540-48199-0_14.

Mehryar MOHRI (2000), Minimization algorithms for sequential transducers, 234(1–2):177–201, ISSN 0304-3975, doi:10.1016/s0304-3975(98)00115-7.

Arto SALOMAA (1973), *Formal languages*, Academic Press, ISBN 978-0126157505.

Arto SALOMAA and Matti SOITTOLA (1978), *Automata-Theoretic Aspects of Formal Power Series*, Springer New York, ISBN 978-1-4612-6266-4, doi:10.1007/978-1-4612-6264-0.

Hiroyuki SEKI, Takashi MATSUMURA, Mamoru FUJII, and Tadao KASAMI (1991), On multiple context-free grammars, 88(2):191–229, ISSN 0304-3975, doi:10.1016/0304-3975(91)90374-B.

Hiroyuki SEKI, Ryuichi NAKANISHI, Yuichi KAJI, Sachiko ANDO, and Tadao KASAMI (1993), Parallel Multiple Context-free Grammars, Finite-state Translation Systems, and Polynomial-time Recognizable Subclasses of Lexical-functional Grammars, in *Proceedings of the 31st Annual Meeting on Association for Computational Linguistics*, ACL '93, pp. 130–139, Association for Computational Linguistics, Stroudsburg, PA, USA, doi:10.3115/981574.981592.

Andreas VAN CRANENBURGH (2012), Efficient Parsing with Linear Context-free Rewriting Systems, in Walter DAELEMANS, editor, *Proceedings of the 13th Conference of the European Chapter of the Association for Computational Linguistics*, EACL '12, pp. 460–470, Association for Computational Linguistics, Stroudsburg, PA, USA, ISBN 978-1-937284-19-0, http://dl.acm.org/citation.cfm?id=2380816.2380873.

Krishnamurti VIJAY-SHANKER (1988), *A study of tree adjoining grammars*, Ph.D. thesis, http://citeseerx.ist.psu.edu/viewdoc/download?doi=10.1.1.401.1695&rep=rep1&type=pdf.

Krishnamurti VIJAY-SHANKER, David Jeremy WEIR, and Aravind K. JOSHI (1986), Tree adjoining and head wrapping, in *Proceedings of the 11th Conference on Computational Linguistics*, pp. 202–207, Association for Computational Linguistics, doi:10.3115/991365.991425.

Krishnamurti VIJAY-SHANKER, David Jeremy WEIR, and Aravind K. JOSHI (1987), Characterizing Structural Descriptions Produced by Various Grammatical Formalisms, in *Proceedings of the 25th Annual Meeting on Association for Computational Linguistics*, ACL '87, pp. 104–111, Association for Computational Linguistics, Stroudsburg, PA, USA, doi:10.3115/981175.981190.

Éric VILLEMONTE DE LA CLERGERIE (2002), Parsing Mildly Context-Sensitive Languages with Thread Automata, in *Proceedings of the 19th International Conference on Computational Linguistics (COLING '02)*, volume 1, pp. 1–7, Association for Computational Linguistics, Stroudsburg, PA, USA, doi:10.3115/1072228.1072256.

David Jeremy WEIR (1988), *Characterizing mildly context-sensitive grammar formalisms*, Ph.D. thesis, `http://repository.upenn.edu/dissertations/AAI8908403`.

David Jeremy WEIR and Aravind K. JOSHI (1988), Combinatory categorial grammars: Generative power and relationship to linear context-free rewriting systems, in *Proceedings of the 26th annual meeting on Association for Computational Linguistics*, pp. 278–285, Association for Computational Linguistics, doi:10.3115/982023.982057.

Ryo YOSHINAKA, Yuichi KAJI, and Hiroyuki SEKI (2010), Chomsky-Schützenberger-type characterization of multiple context-free languages, in Adrian-Horia DEDIU, Henning FERNAU, and Carlos MARTÍN-VIDE, editors, *Language and Automata Theory and Applications*, pp. 596–607, Springer, ISBN 978-3-642-13088-5, doi:10.1007/978-3-642-13089-2_50.

4

Implementing semantic frames as typed feature structures with XMG

Timm Lichte[1] *and Simon Petitjean*[2]
[1] University of Düsseldorf, Germany
[2] Université d'Orléans, LIFO, France

Keywords: metagrammar, typed feature structures, models of type constraints, type hierarchy, unification

ABSTRACT

This work[1] presents results on the integration of frame-based representations into the framework of eXtensible MetaGrammar (XMG). Originally XMG allowed for the description of tree-based syntactic structures and underspecified representations of predicate-logical formulae, but the representation of frames as a sort of typed feature structure, particularly type unification, was not supported. Therefore, we introduce an extension that is capable of handling frame representations directly by means of a novel `<frame>`-dimension. The aim is not only to make possible a straightforward specification of frame descriptions, but also to offer various ways to specify constraints on types, be it as a connected type hierarchy or a loose set of feature structure con-

[1] This article is a substantially revised and extended version of Lichte *et al.* (2013). It has greatly benefited from discussions with Laura Kallmeyer, Rainer Osswald, Christof Rumpf and Yulia Zinova. We also thank both the reviewers of the ESSLLI 2013 workshop on High-level Methodologies in Grammar Engineering (HMGE) and the the reviewers of the JLM for detailed and helpful comments. The work presented in this paper was financed by the Deutsche Forschungsgemeinschaft (DFG) within the CRC 991. It was also financially supported by the scientific network PARSEME (COST Action IC1207) with a travel grant for Simon Petitjean. When finishing this article we learned with great sadness of the passing of our friend and colleague Christof Rumpf. We dedicate this article to his memory.

straints. The presented extensions to XMG are fully operational in a new prototype.

1 INTRODUCTION

Recent work (Kallmeyer and Osswald 2012a,b, 2013; Zinova and Kallmeyer 2012) has shown increasing interest in coupling a frame-based semantics with a tree-based syntax such as Tree Adjoining Grammar (TAG, Joshi and Schabes 1997). While having led to promising results on the theoretic side, it is still unclear how to implement these ideas with existing grammar engineering tools, let alone how to bring them alive in natural language parsing. In this article, we present results on the integration of frame-based representations into the framework of eXtensible MetaGrammar (XMG, Crabbé *et al.* 2013).[2] XMG originally allowed for the description of tree-based syntactic structures and underspecified representations of predicate-logical formulae, but the representation of frames as a sort of typed feature structure, particularly type unification, was not supported. Therefore we extend XMG by a novel `<frame>`-dimension, among other tools, that makes it capable of handling frame representations as formalized in Petersen (2007) and Kallmeyer and Osswald (2013), i.e. as extended typed feature structures, directly.[3] This capability also paves the way for implementing recent work on morphological decomposition, such as in Zinova and Kallmeyer (2012), where morphemes are linked to a frame-semantic representation.

These efforts might seem redundant, given that there exists a multitude of works on dealing with typed feature structures in grammar implementation and parsing, notably in the framework of HPSG (e.g. Carpenter 1992; Götz *et al.* 1997; Malouf *et al.* 2000; Flickinger 2000; Copestake 2002; Carpenter *et al.* 2003). As far as we can see, however, our approach differs from previous work in several respects: first and

[2] `https://sourcesup.renater.fr/xmg/`

[3] The reviewers suggested to focus more on typed feature structures and less on semantic frames. While this is a reasonable advice, we consider the application to be the driving force of this whole endeavour, which also crucially motivates our choice of a typed feature structure logic that is, from our perspective, uncommon in linguistic applications.

foremost, it allows for a choice between minimal and maximal models of type constraints. As a consequence of this, our approach also allows for anonymous types, hence types that result from the conjunction of defined types, but that are not defined themselves in the type signature. We will precisely explicate this distinction in Section 4. Finally, our work aims at providing the grammar writer with multiple means of expression, for example, in permitting him/her to make use of loose type constraints or connected type hierarchies, or both. This degree of flexibility is often not found in other grammar implementation frameworks that support typed feature structures. We hypothesize that other frameworks are mainly concerned with the syntactic component of the grammar, while we focus on the conceptual semantics whose structure (and how it comes about) seems to be much less predetermined.

The paper proceeds as follows. The next section briefly illustrates the grammatical objects that we are concerned with, and Section 3 then shows the proposed factorization, which crucially guides the implementation with XMG and also justifies the employment of frame unification. After this, we explain the formalization of frames as a sort of typed feature structure in Section 4, and the basic concepts of XMG in Section 5. This will be essential to understand the usage and compilation details of the new `<frame>`-dimension, the presentation of which follows in Section 6. Finally, Section 7 concludes the article. Moreover, a complete code example based on analyses from Section 2 and Section 3 is presented in the Appendix.

2 A FRAME-BASED SEMANTICS FOR LTAG

We will use the state-of-the-art work of Kallmeyer and Osswald (2013) on integrating frame semantics into Lexicalized Tree-Adjoining Grammars (LTAG) as a starting point. One important motivation for developing a frame-based semantics for LTAG is found in the straightforward account for the well-established distinction between lexical and constructional contributions to the overall meaning. An example of this sort of contrast is displayed in (1):

(1) a. The ball rolled into the goal.
b. John rolled the ball into the goal.

Both sentences involve the same verb of directed motion, *rolled*, but the two instances nevertheless differ with respect to the linking of the subject with the conveyed event semantics. While in (1a) the subject *the ball* is the moved object, in (1b) the subject *John* is causing the motion rather than undergoing it. The trigger for this semantic shift seems to be the lack or existence of the direct object (both under the presence of a directional PP), hence the construction type, as this constitutes the crucial syntactic difference between (1a) and (1b).

In the framework of Kallmeyer and Osswald (2013), the syntax of these constructions lies in the scope of the LTAG component. An LTAG consists of a finite set of phrase structure trees, the *elementary trees*, that can be combined (by means of two basic operations, substitution and adjunction) to generate larger trees.[4] Since we are dealing with a lexicalized TAG, each elementary tree must include at least one non-terminal leaf, the *lexical anchor*. Furthermore elementary trees are constrained through the valency properties of their anchors. Usually each non-terminal leaf corresponds to exactly one syntactic argument, and vice versa.

The proposed LTAG analyses of (1a) and (1b), shown in Figure 1, differ with respect to the elementary trees that are associated with the two instances of *rolled*, say the intransitive $\textit{rolled}_{\text{int}}$ and the transitive $\textit{rolled}_{\text{tr}}$:[5] since syntactic arguments are represented as non-terminal leaves, the elementary tree for $\textit{rolled}_{\text{int}}$ lacks the object NP slot that the elementary tree for $\textit{rolled}_{\text{tr}}$ has. The difference in meaning is therefore attributed to the different elementary trees that a given verb may anchor.

Since elementary trees, but not the anchoring verbs, are held responsible for different linking patterns, it is straightforward to abstract away from the concrete anchor by just considering the yet unanchored elementary tree, which is commonly called the *tree template*. An example of such a tree template is shown on the left in Figure 2, wherein the site of lexical insertion, here of *rolled*, is marked by the ◇-symbol. The

[4] Since in the present paper we mainly focus on single elementary trees, we skip most details of the formalism here. See Joshi and Schabes (1997) or Abeillé and Rambow (2000a) for comprehensive presentations.

[5] Note that dashed arrows indicate combinatorial operations, which in this case only involve substitution, i.e. the rewriting of a leaf node in the target tree.

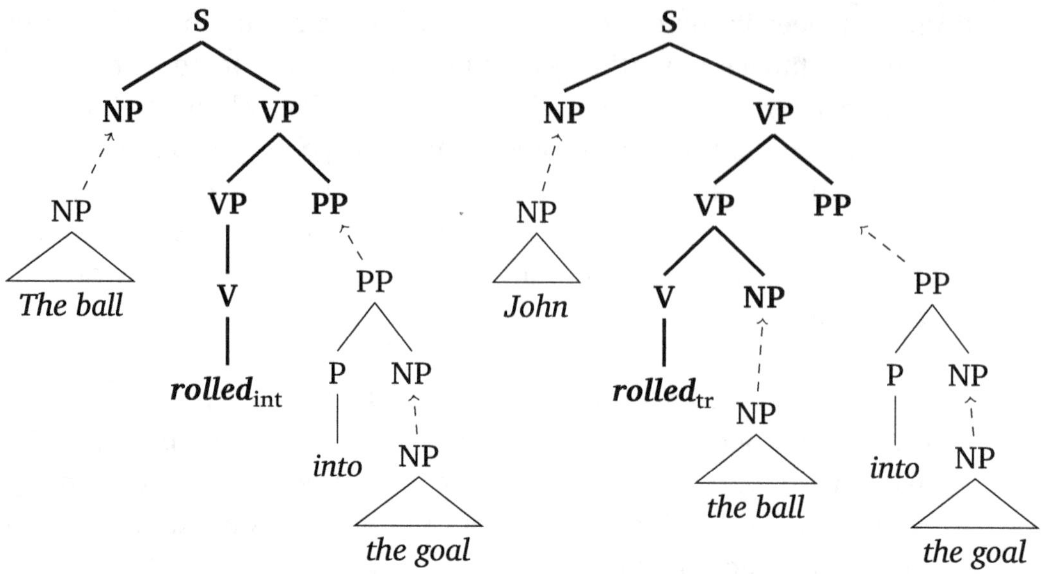

Figure 1: LTAG derivation for (1a) and (1b) with intransitive versus transitive *rolled*

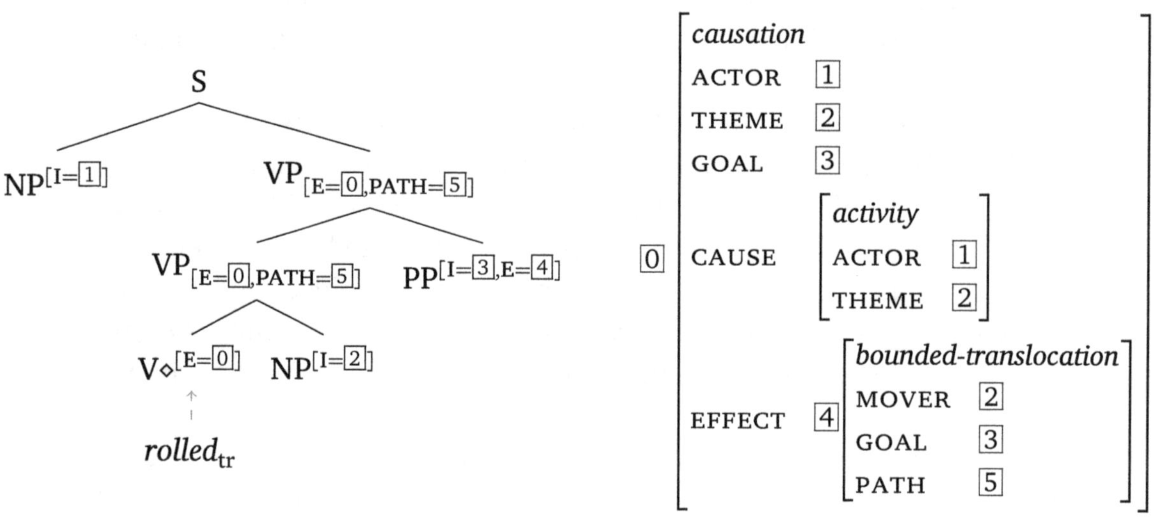

Figure 2: Tree template and frame-semantic representation of the transitive motion construction from Figure 1, taken from Kallmeyer and Osswald (2013, Fig. 26)

complex node labels will be explained presently. The right side of Figure 2 shows the event semantic contribution of the tree template in the format of a typed feature structure, here represented as an attribute value matrix (AVM). Typed feature structures are a common representation format of *frames* (see Petersen 2007), which, according to

Fillmore (1982), Barsalou (1992) and others, are considered a proper representation of mental concepts.[6] As can be seen from the example, features describe semantic participants and components (AGENT, THEME, ...), while feature structures correspond to conceptual objects, restricted by the type (*causation, activity,* ...) that they are associated with. The boxed numbers, finally, are *base labels* which serve to mark inequalities and correspondences in the syntax-frame interface. Furthermore, they guide the unification of (subparts of) frames, as can be seen in the next section.

Because tree templates, just as elementary trees, span an extended domain of locality,[7] the linking of positions within the tree template to positions within the frame-semantic representation can be achieved rather directly. In Figure 2 it is indicated by co-occurring boxed numbers. For example, the subject NP-leaf is linked with the ACTOR role(s) of the frame, eventually causing the unification of the ACTOR role and the frame of the substituting NP-tree. Note that the nodes of tree templates carry (non-recursive, non-typed) feature structures, which include, among others, interface features such as I(NDIVIDUAL) and E(VENT).[8] Following the terminology in Kallmeyer and Osswald (2013), we call couples of tree template and frame-semantic representation an *elementary construction.*

The composition of frame representations is moreover guided by a globally defined type hierarchy, which determines (i) the unifiability of types and the resulting type, and (ii) the set of appropriate features

[6] Note that FrameNet (Fillmore 2007), despite being declared as an implementation of Fillmore's frame semantics, deals with flat lexical frame representations that are generally less expressive (Osswald and Van Valin 2014).

[7] The extended domain of locality (EDL) is one of the central properties of the TAG formalism (cf. Joshi *et al.* 1990). It amounts to the capability of arguments to immediately attach to the elementary tree of their governor; see again Figure 1. In connection with TAG, EDL presupposes the availability of the adjunction operation (i.e. the rewriting of inner nodes), in order to account for discontinuity effects such as long distance dependencies.

[8] The approach to let the syntax-semantics interface rely on the unification of interface features can already be found in, e.g., Stone and Doran (1997), Frank and van Genabith (2001), Gardent and Kallmeyer (2003). The proposal for linking nodes of an elementary tree with positions in some semantic representation, and thus to derive syntax and semantics in parallel, dates back at least to Shieber and Schabes (1990).

(and their value types) of a type, the *appropriateness conditions*. Regarding event types, Kallmeyer and Osswald (2013) work with the partial type hierarchy in Figure 3. It has to be read top-down, with

Figure 3: Partial type hierarchy for event types proposed in Kallmeyer and Osswald (2013, Fig. 16).

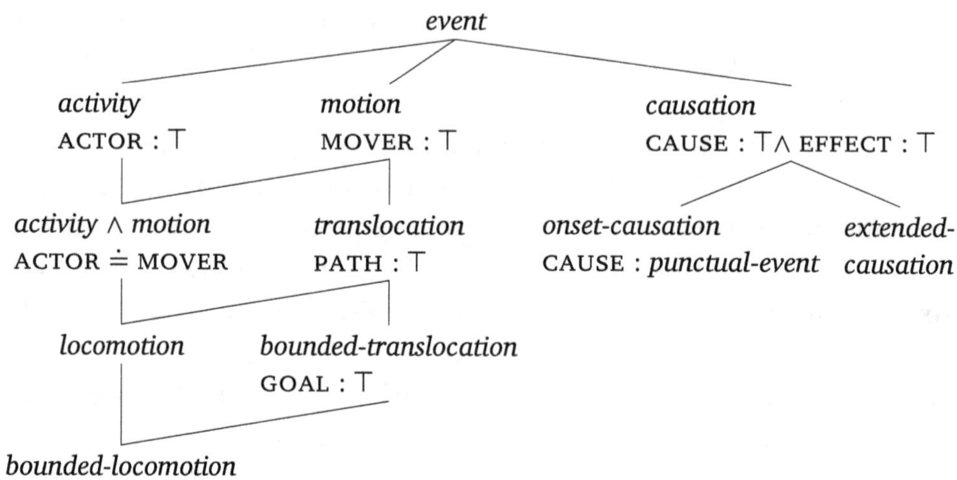

the more general types dominating the more specific types. Note that the type hierarchy may also contain anonymous types, e.g. *activity* ∧ *motion*, which are usually not available in other frameworks. Roughly speaking, anonymous types make it possible to assign appropriateness conditions to a conjunction of types rather than just to a single type. The details will be explained in Section 4.

In this work we are neither concerned with the unification of frame representations following syntactic composition, nor with the preceding process of lexical insertion that triggers the unification of lexical and constructional frame components (see Kallmeyer and Osswald 2013, Fig. 13), but rather with the metagrammatical framework of XMG. Metagrammars are a tool to describe static elementary constructions such as in Figure 2, consisting of a tree template and a fixed typed feature structure. It might therefore seem unnecessary to employ all aspects of typed feature structures in metagrammars, particularly unification. However, this assumption is not warranted. Unification of types and feature structures is also found in the metagrammatical domain once the factorization of elementary constructions of the kind in Figure 2 is taken into account. This will be shown in the next section.

3 FACTORIZATION OF TREE TEMPLATES AND FRAMES

Richly structured grammatical objects like those in Figure 2 make necessary some kind of metagrammatical factorization, once a large coverage grammar gets compiled and maintained (Xia *et al.* 2010). Metagrammatical factorization is a process to define recurring subcomponents of grammatical objects, which can then be combined in at least two ways: in a transformation-based fashion, known as the metarule approach (Becker 1994, 2000; Prolo 2002), or in a purely constraint-based, monotonic fashion as is the case in XMG (following Candito 1996). In addition to the benefit in terms of grammar engineering, however, Kallmeyer and Osswald (2012a,b, 2013) claim that metagrammar factorization can be also used to reflect constructional analyses in the spirit of Construction Grammar (Kay 2002; Goldberg 2006). By this perspective, both the lexical material and the "constructions" used contribute meaning.

Taking these two aspects into account, Kallmeyer and Osswald (2013) propose to factorize the tree template and the frame in Figure 2 along the lines of Figure 4.[9] Boxes stand for the resulting factors or classes (i.e. classes in the sense of XMG), consisting of descriptions of a tree and a frame fragment. The inclusion relation between boxes is to be understood as a representation of inheritance or instantiation, so that the class of the comprising box inherits from, or instantiates, the class of the included box. Double edges (indicating identity constraints over nodes or base labels), dashed edges (non-strict dominance), $\prec^*$ (non-strict precedence), and $\vee$ (disjunction) are elements of the description language. Figure 4 then illustrates that the tree-frame couple in Figure 2 is a model of the class n0Vn1pp(dir), which combines the classes n0Vn1 and DirPrepObj. Combining two classes essentially means that all associated information is unified, from which a minimal model is resolved (see Section 5). Note that Figure 4 shows only a part of the proposed factorization. For example, the class n0Vn1, also taken from Kallmeyer and Osswald (2013, Fig. 4), results from combining three other classes (Subj, VSpine, DirObj), as shown in Figure 5.[10] Furthermore note that the class n0Vn1pp(dir) bears a con-

[9] The boxes-and-pipes notation in Figures 4 and 5 is of our invention.

[10] Kallmeyer and Osswald (2013) conjecture that class n0V has exactly one

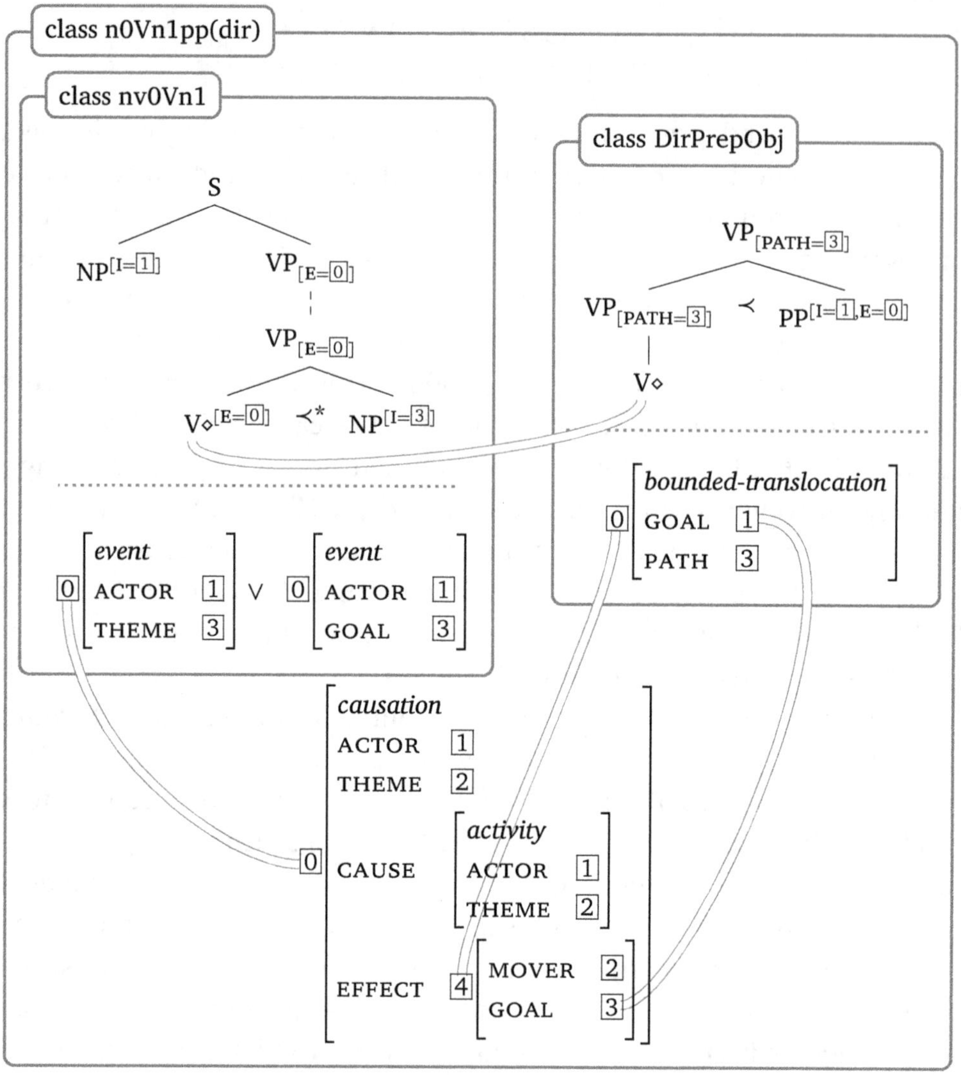

Figure 4: Metagrammatical factorization of the elementary construction from Figure 2. Boxes stand for the resulting factors or classes. Double edges indicate identity constraints, dashed edges indicate non-strict dominance, $\prec^*$ is non-strict precedence, and $\vee$ is disjunction.

minimal model, which only holds, however, if minimal models are said to consist of the smallest set of nodes that satisfy the description. In XMG, by contrast, minimal models just consist of a set of nodes mentioned in the description, and nothing more. Hence, from point of view of XMG, n0V has two minimal models, one with one VP node, and one with two VP nodes. In order to resolve only the former one, one could additionally apply polarization, or "colours" (Crabbé and Duchier 2005), onto the nodes. Fortunately, the question how many minimal models there are is irrelevant for the point made here and throughout the article.

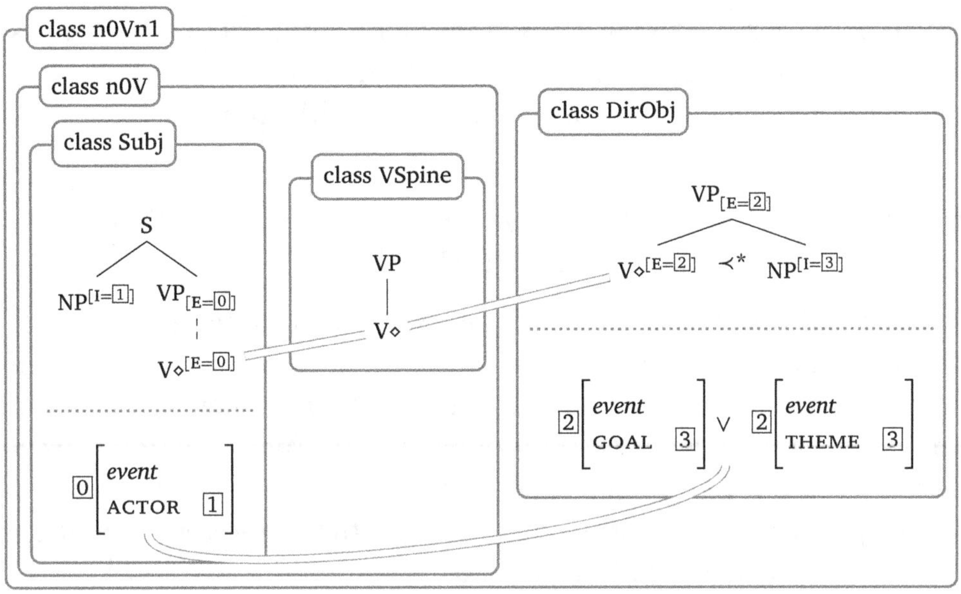

Figure 5: Metagrammatical factorization for the transitive elementary construction.

structional facet: it only contributes to the frame representation, but no tree descriptions.

Now the question is whether the combination of frame representations, following the combination of two classes, should be considered a unification of typed feature structures. It is not hard to see that this is justified. A particularly good example is found in the combination of the frame representations of n0Vn1 and n0Vn1pp(dir) in Figure 4. Even though they have different types, namely *event* and *causation*, the resulting type is supposed to be *causation*. According to the type hierarchy in Figure 3, *causation* is a subtype of *event*. Hence this is in line with regular type unification, but exceeds a plain union of feature structures. Therefore the unification of typed feature structures should be already supported at the metagrammatical level. The same holds for the verification of appropriateness conditions, of course. Note that, as can be seen from Figure 4, the flexibility of frame unification is fostered by base labels when unifying the frame of DirPrepObj with a subpart of the frame of n0Vn1pp(dir).

The graphic representation of the metagrammatical factorization in Figure 4 and Figure 5 remains at a rather informal level and the question arises: how could this be translated into XMG code? Since the original XMG did not give a satisfying answer due to reasons of usability and completeness (which we will cover in Section 5) we will develop and justify a new `<frame>`-dimension in Section 6. But first we will review the underlying notions: frames as typed feature structure with base labels, type hierarchies and unification.

4 BASE-LABELLED TYPED FEATURE STRUCTURES: FORMAL DEFINITIONS

In what follows we largely, but not exclusively, adhere to the definitions in Kallmeyer and Osswald (2013), while streamlining them according to our terminology and taste. What is not needed from Kallmeyer and Osswald (2013), however, are (non-functional) relations, because they do not appear in the frame representations of elementary constructions, other than, e.g., in the frame representations of the anchor lexicon (Kallmeyer and Osswald 2013, Fig. 13).[11] So we will ignore the notion of (non-functional) relations, and instead dwell on type inference and the minimal and maximal models of feature structure constraints. It is this choice between minimal and maximal models, as well as the general availability of anonymous types, which makes the presented extension to XMG particularly flexible at describing a type system. And it is this flexibility, among other things, which sets our extension to XMG apart from current frameworks for HPSG.

Let us start with the building blocks of typed feature structures, which are settled in the *signature*:

Definition 1 (Signature) *A signature is a tuple $\langle A, T, B \rangle$ with a finite set of attributes (or features) A, a finite set of elementary types T, and an infinitely countable set of base labels B.*

The set of elementary types is accompanied by special types $\top$ and $\bot$ that are useful in feature structure descriptions and feature structure constraints (see below). $\top$ is the most general type, unifiable with every other type, whereas $\bot$ is unifiable with none of them. Within Boolean expressions, $\top$ corresponds to 'true' and $\bot$ to 'false'. *Base labels* are commonly boxed natural numbers, thus $B = \{\boxed{0}, \boxed{1}, \boxed{2}, \ldots\}$.

Based on a given signature, typed feature structures are defined as follows:

---

[11] Kallmeyer and Osswald (2013) make use of the part-of relation when dealing with directional prepositions such as *to, into,* and *along.*

Definition 2 (Base-labelled typed feature structure) *Given a signature* $\langle A, T, B\rangle$, *a base-labelled typed feature structure is a tuple* $\langle V, \delta, \tau, \beta\rangle$ *with*

- V, *a finite set of nodes,*
- $\delta : (V \times A) \to V$, *a partial transition function,*
- $\tau : V \to 2^T$, *a total typing function, and*
- $\beta : B \to V$, *a partial base-labelling function.*

We call types in 2^T, i.e. elements of the powerset of T, *conjunctive types* in order to distinguish them from elementary types.

We follow Kallmeyer and Osswald (2013) in that we do not specify a type hierarchy immediately, but treat it as a model of feature structure constraints, i.e. generalized feature structure descriptions.[12] Therefore the following notations can be directly borrowed from Kallmeyer and Osswald (2013, (3)), omitting only those parts of their definition that deal with relations. Note that we extend δ by feature paths in the usual way.[13]

Definition 3 (Unlabelled feature structure description) *Let* $\langle V, \delta, \tau, \beta\rangle$ *be a feature structure over the signature* $\langle A, T, B\rangle$ *with* $v, w \in V$, $t \in 2^T$ *and* $p, q \in A^+$, *then the satisfaction relation* $\models$ *between nodes and feature structure descriptions is defined as follows:*

- $v \models t$ *iff* $t \in \tau(v)$
- $v \models p : t$ *iff* $\delta(v, p) \models t$
- $v \models p \doteq q$ *iff* $\delta(v, p) = \delta(v, q)$
- $\langle v, w\rangle \models p \triangleq q$ *iff* $\delta(v, p) = \delta(w, q)$

As such, unlabelled feature structure descriptions apply to nodes of a feature structure. For example, the root node of the causation frame in Figure 4 satisfies the following conjunction of descriptions:

(2) $\mathit{causation} \wedge \text{ACTOR} \doteq \text{CAUSE ACTOR} \wedge \text{THEME} \doteq \text{CAUSE THEME} \wedge \text{THEME} \doteq \text{EFFECT MOVER} \wedge \text{CAUSE} : \mathit{activity} \wedge \text{EFFECT GOAL} : \top$

By adding base labels, we can explicitly assign descriptions to nodes within a feature structure. Therefore, in contrast to unlabelled ones,

[12] However, XMG also allows one to specify a type signature explicitly; see Section 6.

[13] $\delta(v, p\ a)$ with $p \in A^+$ and $a \in A$ is a shorthand for $\delta(\delta(v, p), a)$.

the labelled feature structure descriptions are satisfied by feature structures as a whole:[14]

Definition 4 (Labelled feature structure description) *Let* $F = \langle V, \delta, \tau, \beta \rangle$ *be a feature structure over the signature* $\langle A, T, B \rangle$ *with* $p, q \in A^+$ *and* $l, k \in B$*, and let* ϕ *be an unlabelled feature structure description. The satisfaction relation* $\models$ *between feature structures and labelled feature structure descriptions is defined in the following way:*

- $F \models l\ \phi$ *iff* $\beta(l) \models \phi$
- $F \models l\ p \triangleq k\ q$ *iff* $\langle \beta(l), \beta(k) \rangle \models p \triangleq q$

The unlabelled descriptions in (2) can be straightforwardly labelled in order to be satisfied by the causation frame as a whole:

(3) $\boxed{0}$ *causation* $\wedge$ $\boxed{0}$ ACTOR $\doteq$ CAUSE ACTOR $\wedge$ $\boxed{0}$ THEME $\doteq$ CAUSE THEME $\wedge$ $\boxed{0}$ THEME $\doteq$ EFFECT MOVER $\wedge$ $\boxed{0}$ CAUSE : *activity* $\wedge$ $\boxed{0}$ EFFECT GOAL : $\top$

Note that $\boxed{0}$ ACTOR $\doteq$ CAUSE ACTOR is equivalent with $\boxed{0}$ ACTOR $\triangleq$ $\boxed{0}$ CAUSE ACTOR (see Kallmeyer and Osswald 2013, fn. 14). We adopt the convention to write l instead of $l\ \epsilon$ for some label l. This allows us to write $\boxed{1} \triangleq \boxed{2}$ for expressing the value identity of labels $\boxed{1}$ and $\boxed{2}$.

Concerning the subsumption relation on feature structures, we can transfer the fairly standard definition from Kallmeyer and Osswald (2013), which they extend by base labels.

Definition 5 (Subsumption, $\sqsubseteq$) *Given feature structures* $F_1 = \langle V_1, \delta_1, \tau_1, \beta_1 \rangle$ *and* $F_2 = \langle V_2, \delta_2, \tau_2, \beta_2 \rangle$ *over the signature* $\langle A, T, B \rangle$*,* F_1 *subsumes* F_2*, if there is a function* $h : V_1 \to V_2$ *so that*

- *if* $\delta_1(v, a)$ *is defined for* $v \in V_1$ *and* $a \in A$*, then* $\delta_2(h(v), a) = h(\delta_1(v, a))$*;*
- *for every* $v \in V_1$*,* $\tau_1(v) \subseteq \tau_2(h(v))$*;*
- *if* $\beta_1(l)$ *is defined for* $l \in B$*, then* $\beta_2(l) = h(\beta_1(l))$*.*

As usual, the definition of unification builds on subsumption:

[14] From the general shape of labelled feature structure descriptions it follows that they can only describe feature structures where every node is reachable from some labelled node via a (potentially empty) attribute path. In fact, this is why these labels are called base labels.

Definition 6 (Unification, $\sqcup$) *Let F_1, F_2, F_3 be feature structures. F_3 is the result of the unification of F_1 and F_2, iff F_3 is the least specific feature structure such that $F_1 \sqsubseteq F_3$ and $F_2 \sqsubseteq F_3$.*

The specificity of feature structures is determined by the number of nodes, the specificity of the assigned types and the size of the base labelling function. Note that, in cases of unification such as in Figure 4, feature structures (and corresponding interface variables) are relabelled beforehand, so that they come with disjoint sets of labels. The identity of certain labels can then be imposed through additional identity statements.

Feature structure constraints consist of universally quantified, unlabelled features structure descriptions, i.e. descriptions that hold for every node in the feature structure. Kallmeyer and Osswald (2013) restrict them to Horn clauses for reasons of tractability.[15]

Definition 7 (Feature structure constraint) *Given unlabelled feature structure descriptions $\phi_1, \ldots, \phi_n, \psi$, a feature structure constraint is $\phi_1 \wedge \ldots \wedge \phi_n \preceq \psi$, which is equivalent to the universally quantified implication $\forall(\phi_1 \wedge \ldots \wedge \phi_n \rightarrow \psi)$ where quantification is over the nodes of the described feature structure.*

The following list shows different kinds of feature structure constraints (mostly taken from Kallmeyer and Osswald 2013, (12)):[16]

(4) a. *activity* $\preceq$ *event*
b. *causation* $\preceq \neg$*activity* $\Leftrightarrow$ *causation* $\wedge$ *activity* $\preceq \bot$
c. *locomotion* $\preceq$ *activity* $\wedge$ *translocation*
$\Leftrightarrow$ (*locomotion* $\preceq$ *activity*) $\wedge$ (*locomotion* $\preceq$ *translocation*)
d. *activity* $\preceq$ ACTOR: $\top$
e. AGENT: $\top \preceq$ AGENT $\doteq$ ACTOR

The first three feature structure constraints in (4a)–(4c) consist of descriptions over types, which is why we call them *type constraints*. The simplest type constraint in (4a) relates two elementary types and cor-

[15] Horn clauses are disjunctive clauses with at most one non-negative literal, all others being negative. Hence they are of the form $\neg\phi_1 \vee \ldots \vee \neg\phi_n \vee \psi$, which has the implicational equivalent $\phi_1 \wedge \ldots \wedge \phi_n \rightarrow \psi$.

[16] Note that $\Leftrightarrow$ in (4) is not part of the description language but indicates the equivalence of descriptions.

responds to an ISA-relation, namely *activity* being also an *event*. An ISNOTA-relation can be expressed by type constraints of the kind in (4b). Note that the use of negation in the consequent is equivalent to a clause with a conjunctive antecedent and a 'false' ($\bot$) consequent. Not only can the antecedent be complex, but also the consequent, even though this is reducible to a conjunction of simpler implications, as shown in (4c). The last two examples in (4d) and (4e) contain attribute-value terms. Constraint (4d) represents an *appropriateness condition*, namely a condition on the type *activity* concerning the value type of its attribute ACTOR. Finally, (4e) adds a constraint about the token identity of the values of the attributes AGENT and ACTOR (if AGENT has a value). Constraints of this sort, where every conjunct consists of a feature-value description or a path equation, can be characterized as *feature-value constraints*.[17]

A crucial decision concerns the model of feature structure constraints, as it can be seen as maximal or minimal. The difference is made visible in Figure 6 with type hierarchies based on $\preceq$.

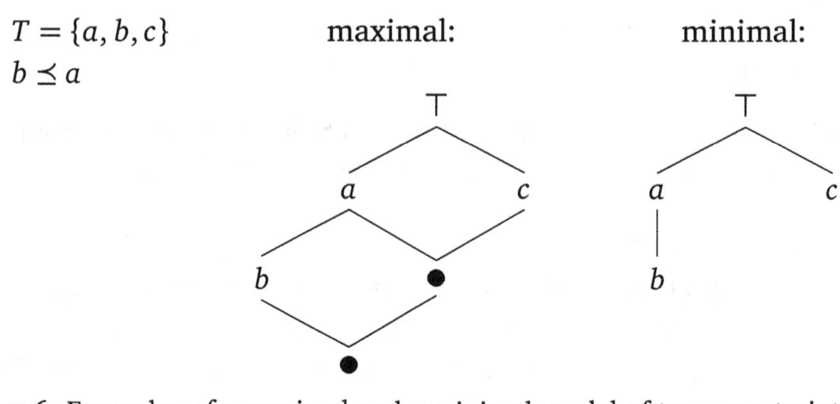

Figure 6: Examples of a maximal and a minimal model of type constraint

Roughly speaking, a maximal model of type constraints allows for *anonymous types* (indicated with dots in Figure 6) as long as they are not explicitly excluded. With minimal models it is the other way

[17] Other sorts of feature structure constraints, for example those in (i), are not discussed in Kallmeyer and Osswald (2013):

(i) a. $p : t_1 \preceq t_2$
b. $p : t_1 \wedge t_2 \preceq t_3$

We therefore concentrate on feature structure constraints in the shape of type constraints, appropriateness conditions and feature-value constraints.

around: anonymous types are forbidden as long as they are not explicitly allowed. In both cases they could be introduced (or excluded) by constraints such as in (5a), where the antecedent consists of a conjunction of elementary types. In Figure 6, $a \wedge c$ and $a \wedge b \wedge c$ are anonymous types. It is shown in (5b) that these anonymous types can bear feature-value constraints as well.[18]

(5) a. $a \wedge c \preceq \top$

b. *action* $\wedge$ *motion* $\preceq$ ACTOR $\doteq$ MOVER
(Kallmeyer and Osswald 2013, (12e))

The preceding remarks were concerned with elementary types. However, as we learned in Definition 2, the typing function τ assigns sets of elementary types, the conjunctive types. They are included for good reason, since they help to treat elementary types and anonymous types in a uniform way, and eventually to facilitate the definition and implementation of unification.[19] In the following, we treat conjunctive types as a model of type constraints, and, on this basis, explicate what it means to be minimal or maximal.

Definition 8 (Model of type constraints) *Given type constraints TC over a signature $\langle A, T, B\rangle$, a set $\hat{T}$ of conjunctive types over T is a model of TC, if $\hat{T}$ satisfies the type constraints from TC in the following way:*

- $\hat{T} \models t_1 \wedge \ldots \wedge t_n \preceq \bot$ *iff* $\{t_1, \ldots, t_n\} \not\subseteq \hat{t}$ *for all* $\hat{t} \in \hat{T}$;
- $\hat{T} \models t_1 \wedge \ldots \wedge t_n \preceq t_m$ *iff if* $\{t_1, \ldots, t_n\} \subseteq \hat{t}$, *then* $\{t_m\} \subseteq \hat{t}$.

The model $\hat{T}$ of given type constraints is said to be *maximal,* if $\hat{T}$ is the largest set of conjunctive types that satisfies them. On the other

[18] Note that anonymous types are generally ruled out in major implementation tools for HPSG such as LKB (Copestake and Flickinger 2000; Copestake 2002) and TRALE (Götz *et al.* 1997; Carpenter *et al.* 2003), from which it follows that models from type constraints are always minimal.

[19] Note however that Carpenter (1992, 23–25) defines conjunctive types differently as he adds the condition that p, but not q, is included whenever the relation $p \preceq q$ is considered. Hence, following his conception, there is no co-occurrence of elementary types and their elementary subtypes within a conjunctive type. On the other hand, our definition of conjunctive type rather coincides with the notion of "conjunctive concepts" in Carpenter and Pollard (1991), or with the notions of "entity types" and "generic entities" in Osswald (2003, 24f).

hand, $\hat{T}$ is said to be the *minimal* model, if $\hat{T}$ includes just those conjunctive types of the maximal model that correspond (i) to elementary types, and (ii) to conjunctive types that make up the left side (i.e. the condition) of a type constraint.

The type hierarchies from Figure 6 for elementary types are repeated in Figure 7 for conjunctive types. They are now based on $\subseteq$ rather than $\preceq$. We say that conjunctive type $\hat{t}_1$ is the subtype of $\hat{t}_2$, if $\hat{t}_1 \supset \hat{t}_2$. The definition of the most general common subtype is equally simple.

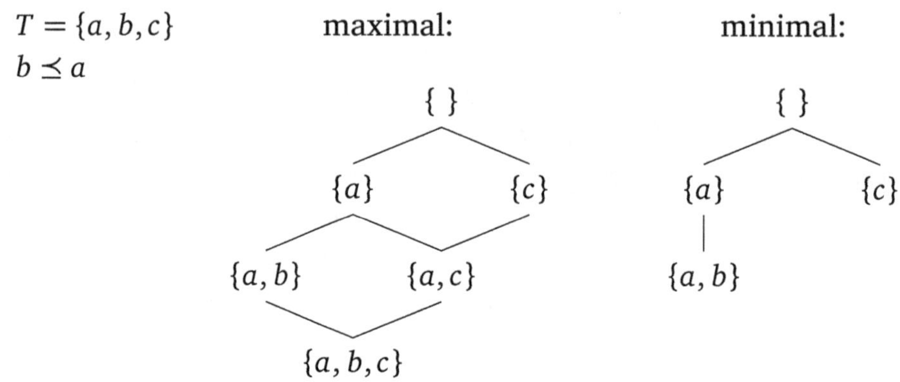

Figure 7: Example of maximal and minimal models of type constraints over conjunctive types

Definition 9 (Most general common subtype) *The most general common subtype of two conjunctive types $\hat{t}_1, \hat{t}_2 \in \hat{T}$ is the smallest set $\hat{t}_3 \in \hat{T}$ such that $\hat{t}_1 \cup \hat{t}_2 \subseteq \hat{t}_3$.*

It is easy to see that, whenever type constraints have the shape of Horn clauses, the maximal model over conjunctive types $\hat{T}$ forms a meet semi-lattice (a bounded complete partially ordered set) $\langle \hat{T}, \subseteq \rangle$. Hence, there is a most general common subtype for any two unifiable types. This does not necessarily hold for minimal models that are confined to elementary and certain anonymous types.[20] In order to obtain uniqueness of the most general common subtype for any two unifiable types, it can be necessary to add further anonymous types to $\hat{T}$ (the Dedekind-McNeille completions). Theses completions are computed by the compiler that will be described in Section 6.3.2.

[20] For example, say $T = \{a, b, c, d\}$, $TC = \{c \preceq a \wedge b,\ d \preceq a \wedge b\}$, then $\hat{T} = \{\{\}, \{a\}, \{b\}, \{a, b, c\}, \{a, b, d\}\}$ satisfies TC and only contains the conjunctive types that correspond to elementary types in T. However, $\{a\}$ and $\{b\}$ have more than one most general common subtype in $\hat{T}$, namely $\{a, b, c\}$ and $\{a, b, d\}$.

A conjunctive type $\hat{t}$ corresponds to an elementary type t, if $\hat{t}$ is the smallest set that contains t according to the model. Otherwise, if there is no t to which $\hat{t}$ corresponds, $\hat{t}$ is an anonymous type. Similarly, $\hat{t}$ corresponds to some conjunctive type $\hat{t}'$, if $\hat{t}$ is the smallest set of a model that contains $\hat{t}'$. Moreover, it can be useful to also express subtype relations among elementary types $t_1, t_2 \in T$. We say that t_1 is the subtype of t_2, if for $\hat{t}_1, \hat{t}_2 \in \hat{T}$ that correspond to t_1 and t_2 it holds that $\hat{t}_1$ is a subtype of $\hat{t}_2$.

Before proceeding to the next section, two further aspects of the feature logic used here and in Kallmeyer and Osswald (2013) should be mentioned. Firstly, it cannot account for reverse type constraints, which refer to dominating nodes (Rainer Osswald, personal communication, July 23, 2014). A case in point is the set of relational concepts such as the *mother* example from Petersen and Osswald (2014, Fig. 11.5), where *mother* is said to constrain the existence of a dominating node, connected with a MOTHER edge. Hence, if *mother* was treated as a type (a subtype of, e.g., *person*), this constraint could not be expressed, at least not as a part of its appropriateness conditions. Secondly, what seems to be missing so far from the definition in Petersen (2007) is the notion of the central node of a frame, i.e. the node that tells us what the frame "represents" or "refers to". We think, however, that the notion of central nodes is reflected, and generalized, in the present formalization by the notion of base labels. By reappearing in the interface features on the syntactic side, they serve to connect frame nodes with linguistic entities, and nothing else seems to be expressed by central nodes.

5 A BRIEF INTRODUCTION TO XMG

XMG (eXtensible MetaGrammar, Crabbé *et al.* 2013) stands both for metagrammatical descriptions and the compiler for these descriptions. Such descriptions are organized into classes that can be reused (i.e. "imported" or instantiated) by other classes. Borrowing from object oriented programming, classes are encapsulated, which means that each class can handle the scopes of their variables explicitly, by declaring variables and choosing which ones to make accessible for (i.e. to "export to") other instantiating classes. The namespace of a class is

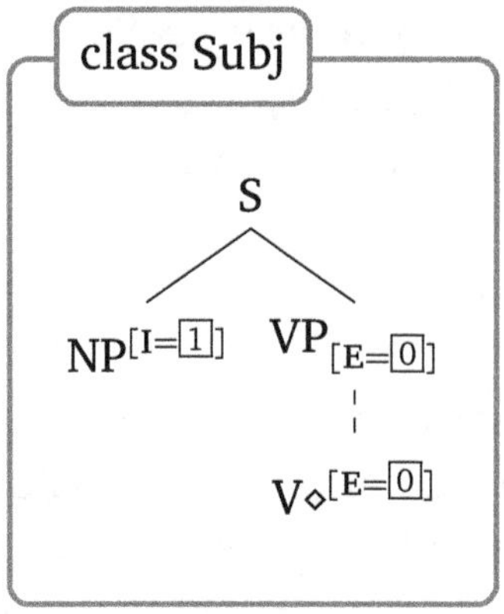


```
class Subj
...
<syn>{
  node ?S [cat=s];
  node ?SUBJ [cat=np,
              top=[i=?1]];
  node ?VP [cat=vp,bot=[e=?0]];
  node ?V (mark=anchor)
          [cat=v,top=[e=?0]];
  ?S->?SUBJ; ?S->?VP; ?VP->*?V;
  ?SUBJ>>?VP
}
...
```

Figure 8: The <syn>-dimension of class Subj

then composed of the declared variables and all the variables exported by the imported classes.

Dimensions are the crucial elements of a class. They can be equipped with specific description languages and are compiled independently, thereby enabling the grammar writer to treat the levels of linguistic information separately. The standard dimensions are <syn> for the syntax, and <sem> for the semantics.[21]

The <syn>-dimension allows one to describe TAG tree templates (or fragments thereof). An example is shown in Figure 8 for the <syn>-dimension of class Subj from Figure 4. It includes two sorts of statements, namely those like 'node ?S [cat=s]' that instantiate nodes of the trees, and those like '?S->?SUBJ' which determine the relative position of two nodes in the trees by referring to dominance and linear precedence.[22] Note that variable names are prefixed with a question mark ('?'). The <sem>-dimension, on the other hand, includes descriptions of a different language, for which a different compiler is used. Since this could be a candidate for hosting frame descriptions, we will have a look at <sem> more closely below. Different as they may be, one crucial commonality of all the dimensions pertains to the joint access

[21] Crabbé *et al.* (2013, 601) also mention the fairly technical dimension <dyn>, more commonly called *interface*, which helps to express the coreference of variables from different dimensions. Recently Duchier *et al.* (2012) have introduced a dimension for morphology; see also Lichte *et al.* (2013).

[22] There is also available a notational alternative with bracket structure.

to local variables declared in the same class. These shared variables constitute a direct interface between otherwise separated dimensions.

The combination of classes takes place outside the <syn>- and <sem>-dimensions. Figure 9 shows an example where the two classes Subj and VSpine are reused by the class n0V. First Subj and VSpine are instantiated and assigned a variable, then the encapsulated, yet exported, variables from Subj and VSpine can be accessed via the dot operator (e.g. to impose identity).

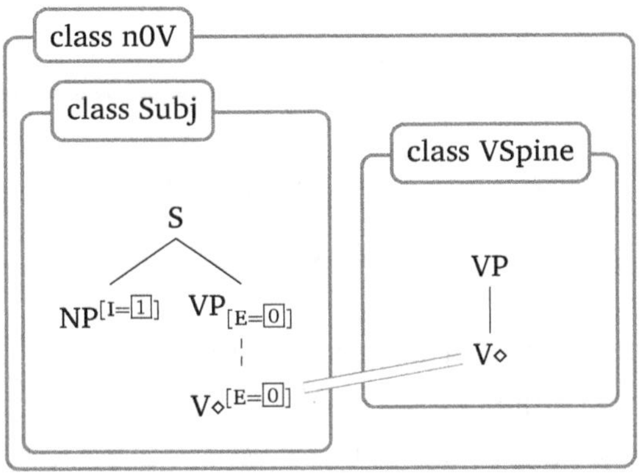


```
class n0V
...
?Subj = Subj[];
?VSpine = VSpine[];
?Subj.?V = ?VSpine.?V;
...
value n0v
```

Figure 9: Example of the combination of classes

When the metagrammar is compiled, first a set of descriptions for each class under evaluation (triggered by `value` statements such as in Figure 9) is accumulated, and then the accumulated descriptions are resolved to yield minimal models. In the case of <syn>, the solver computes tree templates as minimal models, which is to say that only those nodes that are mentioned in the description are included. The final result can be explored with a viewer, or exported as an XML file in order to use it for parsing (e.g. with the TuLiPA parser, Kallmeyer *et al.* 2008).

Frame descriptions in the <sem>*-dimension?*

As mentioned before, the <sem>-dimension is designed to contain underspecified, flat formulae of predicate logic (borrowing from Bos 1996). In fact, it is rather straightforward to reformulate frame descriptions in first-order predicate logic (Kallmeyer and Osswald 2013, Sec. 3.3.3). Concerning the signature, attributes can be represented with two-place predicates, while types can be seen as one-place predicates. The functionality of attributes is imposed by the following axiom for all $a \in A$, given some signature $\langle A, T \rangle$:

(6) $\forall x \forall y \forall z (a(x,y) \wedge a(x,z) \rightarrow y = z)$
(Kallmeyer and Osswald 2013, (6a))

The reformulation of feature structure descriptions and feature structure constraints is equally unproblematic:

(7)
a. $p : t$ $\quad \lambda x \exists y (p(x,y) \wedge t(y))$
b. $p \doteq q$ $\quad \lambda x \exists y (p(x,y) \wedge q(x,y))$
c. $a\ p$ $\quad \lambda x \lambda z \exists y (a(x,y) \wedge q(y,z))$
(Kallmeyer and Osswald 2013, (7))

(8)
a. $t_1 \preceq t_2$ $\quad \forall x (t_1(x) \rightarrow t_2(x))$
b. $t_1 \preceq p : t_2$ $\quad \forall x \exists y (t_1(x) \rightarrow p(x,y) \wedge t_2(y))$
c. $t \preceq p \doteq q$ $\quad \forall x \exists y (t(x) \rightarrow p(x,y) \wedge q(x,y))$

Following this approach, a frame representation such as $\boxed{0}$[ACTOR $\boxed{1}$] would be translated into the two-place predicate *actor*(?0, ?1), using regular XMG variables. A more detailed example based on the class n0Vn1pp(dir) is shown in Figure 10.

While the reformulation of frame descriptions via two-place predicates is straightforward, it is far less obvious how to account for feature structure constraints and the axiom of functionality. As far as type constraints and the type hierarchy are concerned, there seems to be a chance to simulate them with sets of type predicates. This approach is pursued in Figure 10. The construction of those *type simulating sets* (TSSs), as we call them, could proceed as follows: given a signature $\langle A, T \rangle$ and a type hierarchy $\mathcal{T}$ such as the one in Figure 10, we say that $t \in T$ is simulated by the minimal set of predicates $P_t(?X)$ for some variable $?X$, if $P_t(?X)$ is assembled in the following way: for every $t' \in T$, if t' reflexively and transitively dominates t in $\mathcal{T}$, then $t'(?X) \in P_t(?X)$; else if t and t' have no common subtype, then $\sim t'(?X) \in P_t(?X)$, where '$\sim$' stands for negation. To give an example, $P_{locomotion}(?X)$ for the type *locomotion* in the type hierarchy of Figure 10 would be the set $\{activity(?X), motion(?X), \sim causation(?X), locomotion(?X)\}$. It is easily seen that the size of some $P_t(?X)$ crucially depends on the position of t in $\mathcal{T}$, and on the size of T. Note that TSSs do not fully match conjunctive types, due to the insertion of negated type predicates.

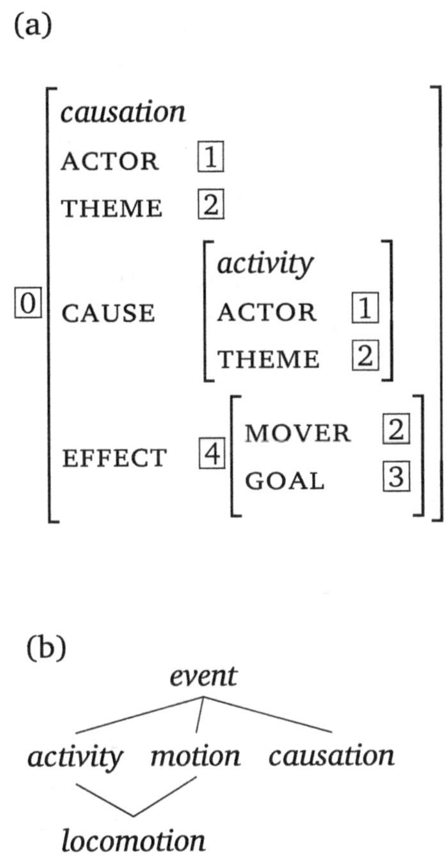

(c)

```
class n0Vn1pp(dir)
...
<sem>{
  actor(?0,?1);
  theme(?0,?2);
  cause(?0,?5);
  actor(?5,?1);
  theme(?5,?2);
  effect(?0,?4);
  goal(?4,?3);

  %% causation type
    event(?0);
   ~activity(?0);
   ~motion(?0);
   ~locomotion(?0);
    causation(?0);
  %% activity type
    event(?5);
    activity(?5);
   ~causation(?5)
}
...
```

Figure 10: The feature structure of n0Vn1pp(dir) (repeated from Figure 4), the global type hierarchy (partially repeated from Figure 2), and its reformulation inside the <sem>-dimension

One basic problem of this approach is that so far XMG does not interpret the predicates of the <sem>-dimension, but merely accumulates them for later use. Hence XMG allows for, e.g., the coexistence of predicates $theme(x_1, x_2)$ and $theme(x_1, x_3)$ with $x_2 \neq x_3$, which conflicts with the required functionality of feature predicates. But even if XMG was enhanced to verify the functionality of predicates, at least three disadvantages would remain: (i) TSSs have to be provided by the grammar writer, (ii) they have to be included in the XMG descriptions as a whole, and (iii) unifying sister types with a common subtype will yield a TSS that does not immediately reveal the elementary type of the common subtype. The latter disadvantage might be more of an aesthetic kind, but the first and the second one clearly have an impact on usability. Modifying the type hierarchy in the context of a large grammar would make necessary a meta-metagrammar, that would automatically recompute the TSSs and adapt the parts of the XMG descriptions, where TSSs were used. Rather than considerably modifying and extending the solver of the `<sem>`-dimension, let alone the available description language, we present a novel `<frame>`-dimension in the next section, which is closely adjusted to the peculiarities of frame representations and frame composition.

6 THE IMPLEMENTATION OF TYPED FEATURE STRUCTURE DESCRIPTIONS AND CONSTRAINTS

Implementation entails two operations: specification and compilation. We will deal with the first one in Section 6.2, when introducing specification languages for feature structure descriptions and constraints. The compilation of frame models based on these specifications is then covered in Section 6.3. First, however, the technical prerequisites for extending the XMG compiler are to be outlined.

6.1 *Architecture and extensibility of XMG*

The XMG project started in 2003 with the goal of providing a means to write large scale tree-based grammars, i.e. Tree Adjoining Grammars and Interaction Grammars (Perrier 2000). Originally, the compiler was written in Oz/Mozart, a language which is not maintained anymore. For this reason, and in order to build a compiler more in line with the project's ambitions (regarding modularity and extensibility), it was necessary to restart the implementation from scratch. The new implementation started in 2010 and is sometimes called XMG-NG or XMG2.[23] The compiler is now written in YAP (Yet Another Prolog) with bindings to Gecode for solving constraints. The extensibility is provided by automatic code generation using Python.

With this new version, an XMG compiler can be built from a combination of elementary compiler units. These elementary units are

[23] See `https://sourcesup.renater.fr/xmg/`.

called bricks, and correspond to the set of compiling steps of a metagrammatical language. A brick can correspond to a description language (e.g. the TAG description language of the <syn>-dimension), to a subpart thereof (e.g. the feature structure language used by the <syn>-dimension), or to a solver (e.g. the tree solver used by the same dimension). Every part of the compiler is a brick, even the control language allowing one to express conjunction and disjunction, and a compiler is built by picking bricks and plugging them together. In this process, the parser for a new metagrammatical language, and all the other compiling steps, can be automatically assembled according to the way the bricks are plugged together, to generate a whole compiler for this language. The idea is that every brick holds a fragment of compiler, dedicated to a fragment of language (described by a set of context-free rules). Whilst combining these language fragments to build a full language, the compiler fragments are also contributed to a full compiler.

Hence, when extending XMG by components that are able to handle typed feature structures, we can take advantage of the compiler's modularity to add another module, dedicated to this new task. Such a module, for example a new dimension, can be equipped with a dedicated specification language and compiler.

6.2 *Specification languages*

The design of the specification languages that we present in the following subsections is guided by certain goals, ideas and examples. Firstly, we try to adhere to the notation in the definitions in Section 4 as closely as possible. Secondly, we try to remain consistent with the coding style that already exists in XMG, though being largely unrestricted in principle from a technical point of view. Thirdly, and most importantly, we aim at specification languages that are inherently consistent, lightweight, transparent, and at the same time flexible. In doing so, we share certain elements from specification languages proposed in other work, but, as far as we know, our combination of these elements has not been presented elsewhere.

A complete code example based on the type hierarchy from Section 2 and the factorization from Section 3 is presented in the Appendix.

6.2.1 Specification of the signature

For the specification of the signature, that is to say attributes, types and base labels, the global fields `frame_types` and `frame_attributes` are available:

```
frame_types = {event,activity,motion,causation,...}
frame_attributes = {actor,theme,goal,...}
```

Base labels correspond to XMG variables and do not need to be declared globally.

6.2.2 Specification language for feature structure descriptions

Feature structure descriptions are specified within the `<frame>`-dimension of a class, which comes with a dedicated specification language and compiler. The mode of operation of the compiler is detailed below in Section 6.3.1. We make use of the following description language, which is basically a simple bracket notation:[24]

```
<frame>{Descriptions;Descriptions;...}
Descriptions ::= var? '[' Description (',' Description)* ']'
Description  ::= type | PathEquation | AVPair
PathEquation ::= attr+ '=' var? attr+ (':' Value)?
AVPair ::= attr+ ':' Value
Value  ::= var | type | Descriptions
```

Unsurprisingly, `type` and `attr` stand for a type and an attribute from the signature, while `var` is an XMG variable. Borrowing the notation from Definition 7, `attr:type` is an attribute-value pair. Figure 11 then shows the description language in action, while mimicking the AVM representation of the frame. Note that the order of descriptions within a pair of brackets is generally unrestricted, as well as the number of type expressions (in order to fully support conjunctive types). The specification language furthermore follows the definitions in Section 4 in that it allows for the abbreviated specification of paths, namely as a sequence of attributes separated by whitespaces. Hence, `[cause:[actor:?1]]` and `[cause actor:?1]` have the same meaning. Path equations are similarly constructed using the equality sym-

[24] In the following we use a simplified Backus-Naur form to define the syntax of specification languages. Disjunction (|), optionality (?) and the Kleene operators (*,+) are encoded as usual.

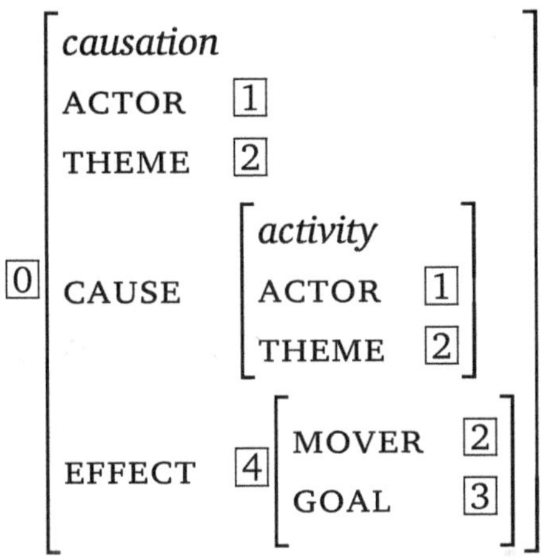

```
<frame>{
?0[causation,
    actor:?1,
    theme:?2,
    cause:[activity,
           actor:?1,
           theme:?2],
    effect:?4[mover:?2,
              goal:?3]
]}
```

Figure 11: Specification of the frame component of n0Vn1pp(dir)

bol =. For example, the meaning of `[actor:?1,cause actor:?1]` could also be expressed with `[actor=cause actor:?1]`.[25]

The use of XMG variables not only enables one to avoid path equations, and eventually to mimic AVM representations, as we just demonstrated, but they may also serve to link semantic components with positions in the syntactic tree, as can be seen from Figure 12, where the ACTOR role and the NP-slot of the subject are linked in this way. It shows that XMG variables may play the role of base labels in labelled feature structure descriptions (see Section 4).

Finally, it might be instructive to compare the specification language for feature structure descriptions proposed here with alternatives that are used elsewhere, particularly in grammar development tools for HPSG. The ALE/TRALE system (Götz *et al.* 1997; Carpenter *et al.* 2003), for example, is rather similar in this respect. The only major difference is found in the path specification, where attributes are separated with the colon, which happens to be also the attribute-value separator. This overloading might be disadvantageous – and in fact path equations then entail a different way of specifying paths.[26]

[25] Note that, in the <syn>-dimension, the symbol = has a different meaning for historical reasons; there it acts as a attribute-value separator.

[26] Another case of overloading can be observed in PATR-II (Shieber 1984), where the operator for path equations and attribute-value pairs coincides. As a consequence, paths are enclosed by angled brackets to distinguish them from regular (atomic) values. Nevertheless, the notation of feature structures in Shieber (1984) bears similarity to our specification language. Indeed, one could say that we basically merge, and extend, the path and feature structure representations from PATR-II. See also the PC-PATR manual (McConnel 1995).

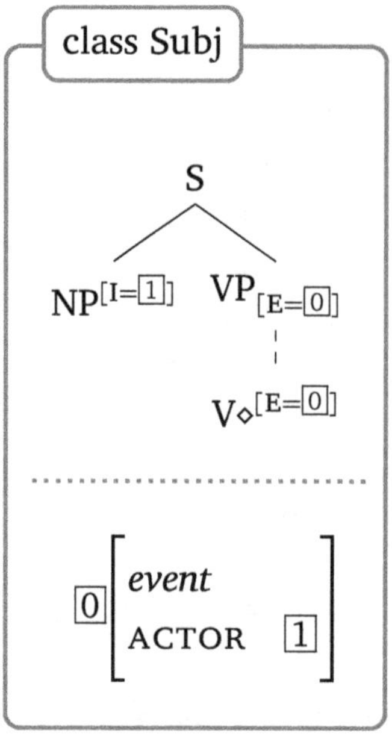


```
class Subj
...
<syn>{
  node ?S [cat=s];
  node ?SUBJ [cat=np,
              top=[i=?1]];
  node ?VP [cat=vp,bot=[e=?0]];
  node ?V (mark=anchor)
          [cat=v,top=[e=?0]];
  ?S->?SUBJ; ?S->?VP; ?VP->*?V;
  ?SUBJ>>?VP
}
<frame>{
?0[event,
    actor:?1]
}
...
```

Figure 12: Implementation of class Subj

In LKB (Copestake 2002), on the other hand, paths are encoded with dots instead of colons, while the whitespace acts as the separator in attribute-value pairs. This being merely an alphabetical variant of our proposal, there are other differences, notably the types being placed outside the feature structure brackets. Still, these differences seem rather marginal.

6.2.3 Specification language for feature structure constraints

We have seen in Section 4 that feature structure constraints can be – and in practice are – specified in different ways, namely either on the basis of a set of single constraint statements, or on the basis of a connected type hierarchy. Therefore one important aspect of the specification language for feature structure constraints is its versatility. Instead of dictating what direction to follow, the grammar writer should have several options at hand from which a suitable one may be chosen on a case-by-case basis.

Concerning the specification of feature structure constraints, two options are provided: a loose set of constraint statements, or a type hierarchy. The former are collected in the global field `frame_constraints`:

```
frame_constraints = {Constraint,Constraint,...}
Constraint ::=
  %% type constraint
  type+ '->' type+ |
  %% appropriateness condition
  type+ '->' Descriptions+  |
  %% feature-value constraint
  ('[' (AVPair|PathEquation) (',' AVPair|',' PathEquation)* ']')+
    '->' Descriptions+
Descriptions ::= '[' Description (',' Description)* ']'
Description  ::= type | PathEquation | AVPair
PathEquation ::= attr+ '=' attr+ (':' Value)?
AVPair ::= attr+ ':' Value
Value  ::= type | Descriptions
```

The specification language for constraints largely integrates the specification language for (unlabelled) descriptions, while it adds -> as a symbol for generalized implication ($\preceq$ in Definition 7). Similarly, a distinction is made between type constraints, appropriateness conditions and feature-value constraints, to which we confine ourselves in the following. An example is provided in Figure 13. Note that the antecedent and the consequent of -> may consist of more than one description separated by whitespaces, in which case the descriptions form a Cartesian product in the following way: t_1 t_2 -> t_3 t_4 iff t_1 -> t_3, t_1 -> t_4, t_2 -> t_3, t_2 -> t_4. Furthermore it is possible to reverse ->, hence to use t_2 <- t_1 instead of t_1 -> t_2.

The other option is to specify feature structure constraints in the shape of a connected type hierarchy. For this the field `frame_type_hierarchy` is available and should be used in the following way:

```
frame_type_hierarchy = {Hierarchy,Hierarchy,...}
Hierarchy ::= '[' type (',' (Description|Hierarchy))* ']'
Descriptions ::= '[' Description (',' Description)* ']'
Description  ::= type | PathEquation | AVPair
PathEquation ::= attr+ '=' attr+ (':' Value)?
AVPair ::= attr+ ':' Value
Value  ::= type | Descriptions
```

An example of this way of specifying a type hierarchy was already included in Figure 13. Similarly to `frame_constraints`, only unlabelled feature structure descriptions are admitted, but unlike `frame_constraints`, the implication symbol -> is missing. Instead squared

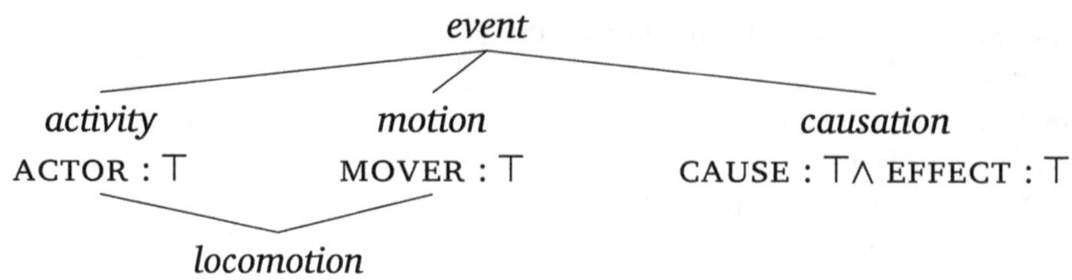


```
frame_constraints = {
    activity -> event, activity -> [actor:+],
    motion -> event, motion -> [mover:+],
    causation -> event, causation -> [cause:+,effect:+],
    locomotion -> activity motion}

frame_type_hierarchy = {
    [event, [activity, actor:+, [locomotion]],
            [motion, mover:+, [locomotion]],
            [causation, cause:+, effect:+]]}
```

Figure 13: Examples of the specification of feature structure constraints. The type hierarchy is a fraction of the type hierarchy shown above in Figure 3 from Kallmeyer and Osswald (2013)

brackets receive a second interpretation where they correspond to types. In other words, the set of feature structure constraints enclosed by a pair of brackets constitute the type constraints and appropriateness conditions for exactly one type. If there are several type expressions, then they form a conjoined type. And if another pair of type-denoting brackets is embedded, then this is a subtype of the embedding type. This squared bracket notation is introduced in the `Hierarchy` part of the syntax definition of `frame_type_hierarchy`, and it is also the only one that is used in the example in Figure 13.

Note here that `frame_type_hierarchy` can only express a proper subset of feature structure constraints, since constraints with feature structures in their antecedents are excluded from this representational format in general. Fortunately, constraints like these may be specified in parallel in the `frame_constraints` field.

Finally, there is the possibility to set a flag to trigger either the maximal or the minimal model of feature structure constraints:

```
use hierarchy (maximal|minimal) with dims (frame)
```

At the time of writing, minimal models are compiled by default.

6.3 *Compilation*

Within XMG2, the compilation of feature structure descriptions and constraints leads to representations which are used in the Prolog component of the system. Therefore we will be mainly concerned with Prolog data structures in the following. Note that, other than with tree descriptions in the <syn>-dimension, no underspecification is involved, and therefore the compiler for feature structure descriptions and constraints employs no constraint solving in the proper sense.

6.3.1 Compilation of feature structure descriptions

Typed feature structures are decomposed into two parts during compilation: types are compiled separately from feature structures. For the latter, we can reuse the XMG module (or brick) for untyped feature structures, which is already applied to feature structures in the <syn>-dimension. The module falls back on *attributed variables* and *association lists*, which are predefined data structures in Prolog. Attributed variables behave like common variables, the only difference being that they come with encapsulated attributes that can be accessed with dedicated commands only, and for which the standard unification algorithm can be customized. They are basically used here in order to replace the standard list (or term) unification by type unification and set union. Association lists, on the other hand, consist of key-value pairs with unique keys, thereby supporting the functionality of features within feature structures.

When a typed feature structure is declared, an attributed variable with two attributes is created: one attribute for the type and one for the feature-value pairs. Types are represented by bit vectors, basically Prolog lists over $\{0, 1\}$, that get unified by means of element-wise Boolean operations (see the next section). A set of feature-value pairs, on the other hand, is represented by an association list, whose values can be attributed variables again and thus induce recursion, i.e. feature structures of arbitrary depth. When two declared feature structures are unified, the compiler unifies their attributed variables in two different ways, namely with type unification on their type attribute and with set union on their association lists.

The check on the well-formedness of the generated structures is performed dynamically during their creation. This includes checking the appropriateness conditions (i.e. for invalid features or specific types of feature values) and computing type unifications. Contrary to the `<syn>`-dimension, the `<frame>`-dimension does not come with a description solver.

When the descriptions in the frame dimension are compiled, a number of instantiations and unifications of attributed variables is executed. It is important to note that the unification has to be explicitly specified by means of variable equations. Hence the compilation result may consist of several unconnected feature structures, as the compiler does not search for a minimal connected model that satisfies the processed feature structure descriptions. Furthermore note that, as unification is deterministic, there is at most one model for each accumulation.

6.3.2 Compilation of feature structure constraints

We are dealing with conjunctive types in the sense of Definition 8. Following a widespread approach (Aït-Kaci *et al.* 1989; Penn 1999; Kilbury *et al.* 2006; Skala *et al.* 2010), conjunctive types are internally represented by bit vectors (or "bit strings"), more precisely by Prolog lists over $\{0, 1\}$. The length of these lists is at least the number of elementary types in the signature. Every position in a bit vector stands for the membership of an elementary type in the conjunctive type, which means that a bit vector composed only of zeros is the most generic type (the empty set) and a bit vector composed only of ones is the conjunction of all elementary types.

We will present two methods to determine the set of valid bit vectors for a set of type constraints. The first one is a brute-force method that basically applies top-down filtering. The second one is based on subsumption matrices (Aït-Kaci *et al.* 1989; Penn 1999) and turns out to be more efficient. In the following let $T = \{a, b, c, d\}$ be the set of elementary types and # a bijective positioning function for bit vectors with $\# = \{(a, 1), (b, 2), (c, 3), (d, 4)\}$.

The top-down filtering on bit vector representations proceeds in the following way:

1. Generate the set of *virtual* (conjunctive) types, namely the bit vectors that represent the powerset of the set of elementary types:

$\{[1,0,0,0],[1,1,0,0],\ldots\}$.

2. Translate type constraints into bit vector patterns of *nonvalid* types:

$$a \preceq b \quad \rightsquigarrow \quad [1,0,\_,\_]$$
$$a \wedge c \preceq \bot \quad \rightsquigarrow \quad [1,\_,1,\_]$$
$$a \wedge b \preceq d \quad \rightsquigarrow \quad [1,1,\_,0]$$

3. Maximal model: Filter the set of bit vectors (representing the virtual types) based on the bit vector patterns in order to identify the valid types. Consequently, if no constraint is expressed, the set of valid types is the powerset of elementary types.

To compute the minimal model it needs an extra step:

3′. Minimal model: Translate elementary types and conjunctive types (on the left side of type constraints) into bit vector patterns of *declared* types:

$$a \quad \rightsquigarrow \quad [1,\_,\_,\_]$$
$$a \wedge b \preceq d \quad \rightsquigarrow \quad [1,1,\_,\_]$$

Then, for each declared type, determine the set of compatible bit vectors from the maximal model and select the bit vector with the fewest 1s. If there is more than one such bit vector, compute the bitwise AND over all these bit vectors and add the resulting bit vector to the set of declared types.

4. Assign bit vector patterns to elementary types: $a \rightarrow [1,\_,\_,\_]$, $b \rightarrow [\_,1,\_,\_]$, …
5. Based on the set of valid bit vectors, unification of two types proceeds as list unification, after which the set of valid types is filtered with the resulting bit vector pattern. Finally the matching bit vector with the fewest 1s gets selected.

It is not hard to see that this method gets intractable for larger sets of elementary types, since the set of virtual types grows exponentially, namely with 2^n where n is the number of elementary types.

Fortunately, methods based on subsumption matrices tend to be much more space-efficient, although they still come with at least quadratic growth in terms of the number of elementary types. In the following, we adapt the procedure of Aït-Kaci *et al.* (1989) (see also Penn 1999), and only add to it anonymous types and maximal models:

1. Generate a boolean matrix where rows and columns correspond to elementary types and anonymous types that are subject to type

constraints. An element a_{ij} in the ith row and the jth column has value 1 iff $t_i \preceq t_j$ is a valid type constraint.[27] Otherwise it has value 0. For example, given type constraints $d \preceq c$ and $a \wedge b \preceq d$, the following preliminary matrix is generated:

$$\begin{array}{c} \\ a \\ b \\ c \\ d \\ a \wedge b \end{array} \begin{array}{c} \begin{array}{ccccc} a & b & c & d & a \wedge b \end{array} \\ \begin{pmatrix} 1 & 0 & 0 & 0 & 1 \\ 0 & 1 & 0 & 0 & 1 \\ 0 & 0 & 1 & 1 & 0 \\ 0 & 0 & 0 & 1 & 1 \\ 0 & 0 & 0 & 0 & 1 \end{pmatrix} \end{array}$$

2. Multiply the matrix by itself until a fixpoint is reached.[28] This ensures that transitive subsumption relations are taken into account. When applied to the preliminary matrix above, we receive the following matrix, where c furthermore subsumes $a \wedge b$:

$$\begin{array}{c} \\ a \\ b \\ c \\ d \\ a \wedge b \end{array} \begin{array}{c} \begin{array}{ccccc} a & b & c & d & a \wedge b \end{array} \\ \begin{pmatrix} 1 & 0 & 0 & 0 & 1 \\ 0 & 1 & 0 & 0 & 1 \\ 0 & 0 & 1 & 1 & 1 \\ 0 & 0 & 0 & 1 & 1 \\ 0 & 0 & 0 & 0 & 1 \end{pmatrix} \end{array}$$

3. Each type is assigned two vectors: a subsumption vector taken from the row, and an ISA vector taken from the column (which was also used in the previous filtering approach). Hence the bit vector representation for type a consists of the subsumption vector $[1,0,0,0,1]$ and the ISA vector $[1,0,0,0,0]$. The difference of the minimal and maximal model emerges in the use of these vector pairs.

4. Minimal model: During unification the subsumption vectors are combined with bitwise AND in order to determine the most general common subtype (Aït-Kaci *et al.* 1989). To give an example, the unification of the subsumption vectors assigned to a and d results in the subsumption vector of $a \wedge b$:

---

[27] We tacitly assume that tautologies (e.g. $t_i \preceq t_i$ and $t_i \wedge t_j \preceq t_i$) are taken into account.

[28] According to Aït-Kaci *et al.* (1989), this takes at most $log_2 n$ iterations.

$$\begin{array}{ll} a & [1,0,0,0,1] \\ d & [0,0,0,1,1] \\ \hline a \wedge b & [0,0,0,0,1] \end{array}$$

Otherwise, if the resulting bit vector was not found among the bit vectors of the matrix, the unification does not necessarily fail. It only fails if the resulting bit vector only consists of 0s.

4′. Maximal model: During unification, the ISA vectors are combined with bitwise OR, while the subsumption vectors are ignored. Hence the unification of a and d yields an ISA vector not found in the matrix:

$$\begin{array}{ll} a & [1,0,0,0,0] \\ d & [0,0,1,1,0] \\ \hline (a \wedge d) & [1,0,1,1,0] \end{array}$$

In order to account for constraints on anonymous types, further unification steps can be necessary. For example, upon unifying the ISA vectors of a and b, the ISA vector of $a \wedge b$ has to be added as well:

$$\begin{array}{ll} a & [1,0,0,0,0] \\ b & [0,1,0,0,0] \\ \hline & [1,1,0,0,0] \\ a \wedge b & [1,1,1,1,1] \\ \hline & [1,1,1,1,1] \end{array}$$

Types that are explicitly ruled out in the type constraints are accounted for by means of extra filtering. For example, a type constraint such as $a \wedge d \preceq \perp$ would give rise to a filter based on the pattern $[1,\_,\_,1,\_]$, which would be applied to the resulting ISA vector after unification.

For each one of the computed valid types, i.e. the assigned ISA vectors, XMG also computes the set of appropriateness conditions. Once again, this step uses the technique of vector pattern matching: when a valid type matches a pattern corresponding to a appropriateness condition, the appropriateness condition is added to the list of appropriateness conditions for this type. These lists can be used in other precompilation steps to check for cyclicity in the feature structure constraints, and for their incompatibility.

At the end of the compilation process, the bit vectors can be easily mapped back to conjunctive types and the corresponding elementary type, if it exists.

7 DISCUSSION AND CONCLUSION

In this article, we presented recent efforts to extend the grammar engineering framework XMG in order to deal with frame representations in the format of typed feature structures. Because metagrammatical factorization involves the composition of feature structures and types along given feature structure constraints, the full power of unification on typed feature structures is needed in XMG. We showed that the simulation of typed feature structures within the `<sem>`-dimension comes with severe disadvantages concerning the implementation of types and type unification. Therefore a new toolkit was developed, including a novel `<frame>`-dimension, which is adjusted to the peculiarities of typed feature structures and type unification, and which should eventually reduce the burden for the grammar writer. The article explained the main components of this toolkit: the specification language, for which a comprehensive code example is included in the appendix, and the compilation procedure, which uses bit vector encodings of types.

While the focus was on the theoretic foundation of the proposed extension and its proof of concept, aspects of computational complexity and the possibilities for optimization (e.g. regarding the size of bit vectors) were largely set aside. Undoubtedly, there is room for future improvements of the compiler. It has to be stressed, however, that compilation with XMG is not as time-critical as parsing, because XMG compilation is part of the preprocessing (Kallmeyer and Osswald 2013, 56). Nevertheless it would be interesting to see how compilation time scales as a function of the size and structure of the type hierarchy, and whether this is relevant given theoretically justified conceptual type systems. As no complex examples of the latter kind are known to us, this remains to be seen.[29] We are aware, of course, that the issue of complexity will become more critical once these resources are used for parsing. Note that, while the presented extensions to XMG are fully

[29] Just for comparison, Skala and Penn (2011) count some 3412 elementary types in the English Resource Grammar (ERG, Copestake and Flickinger 2000).

operational in a recent prototype, a compatible lexical component as well as a parser have yet to be implemented.

Regardless of complexity issues, it could be useful to separate the sources and compilation procedures for global feature structure constraints on the one hand, and local feature structure descriptions within the `<frame>`-dimension on the other hand. The reason is that at some point the feature structure constraints should stabilize, given that they represent cognitive concepts, and therefore constant recompilation triggered by changes in other parts of the metagrammar would be superfluous. At the current stage of research, however, as the development of frame representations is still ongoing, we think that metagrammars are the right place to implement and to experiment with feature structure constraints.

Finally it remains to be stressed that the combination of the `<frame>`-dimension with the `<syn>`-dimension is by no means privileged. The `<frame>`-dimension can also be used to implement standalone frames, or to implement recent frame-based accounts to morphological decomposition (e.g. Zinova and Kallmeyer 2012), thereby considerably widening the scope of XMG.

APPENDIX: COMPLETE CODE EXAMPLE

The following code example covers the implementation of the type hierarchy in Figure 3 and the factorization of the prepositional object construction in Figures 4 and 5.

```
%%%%%%%%%%%%%%%%%%%%%%%%%%%%%%%%%%%%%%%%%%%%%%%%%%%%%
% HEADER:
%%%%%%%%%%%%%%%%%%%%%%%%%%%%%%%%%%%%%%%%%%%%%%%%%%%%%
type MARK = {subst, nadj, foot, anchor, coanchor, flex, lex}
type CAT = {np,v,vp,s,pp}
type VAR !
property mark : MARK
feature cat : CAT
feature top : VAR
feature bot : VAR
feature i : VAR
```

```
feature e : VAR
feature path : VAR

frame_types = {event,activity,motion,causation,translocation,
    onset-causation,extended-causation,locomotion,bounded-
    translocation,bounded-locomotion}
frame_attributes = {actor,theme,goal,mover,path,cause,effect}
frame_constraints = { activity -> event,
  activity -> actor:+,
  motion -> event,
  motion -> mover:+,
  causation -> event,
  causation -> cause:+,
  causation -> effect:+,
  [activity,motion] -> actor=mover,
  translocation -> motion,
  translocation -> path:+,
  bounded-translocation -> translocation,
  bounded-translocation -> goal:+,
  locomotion -> activity translocation,
  bounded-locomotion -> locomotion bounded-translocation
}
%%%%%%%%%%%%%%%%%%%%%%%%%%%%%%%%%%%%%%%%%%%%%%%%%%
% TREE FRAGMENTS:
%%%%%%%%%%%%%%%%%%%%%%%%%%%%%%%%%%%%%%%%%%%%%%%%%%
class VSpine
export ?V
declare  ?VP ?V ?X0
{<syn>{
  node ?VP [cat=vp] {
      node ?V (mark=anchor)[cat=v]
} } }
%%%%%%%%%%%%%%%%%%%%%%%%%%%%%%%%%%%%%%%%%%%%%%%%%%
class Subj
export ?V ?X0
declare ?S ?NP ?VP ?V ?X0 ?X1
{ <syn>{
    node ?S [cat = s];
    node ?NP (mark=subst)[cat=np,top=[i=?X1]];
    node ?VP [cat=vp,bot=[e=?X0]];
    node ?V (mark=anchor)[cat=v,top=[e=?X0]];
    ?S -> ?NP; ?S -> ?VP; ?VP ->* ?V; ?NP >> ?VP
  };
```

```
    <frame> {
    ?X0[event,
      actor:?X1]
  } }
  %%%%%%%%%%%%%%%%%%%%%%%%%%%%%%%%%%%%%%%%%%%%%%%%%%%%%
  class DirObj
  export ?V ?X0
  declare ?VP ?NP ?V ?X0 ?X2
  { <syn>{
    node ?VP [cat = vp,bot=[e=?X0]]{
      node ?V [cat=v,top=[e=?X0] ]
      ,,,node ?NP (mark=subst)[cat=np,top=[i=?X2] ]
    } };
    <frame>{
    ?X0[event,goal:?X2]
    |
    ?X0[event,theme:?X2]
  } }
  %%%%%%%%%%%%%%%%%%%%%%%%%%%%%%%%%%%%%%%%%%%%%%%%%%%%%
  class DirPrepObj
  export ?V ?X0
  declare ?VP1 ?VP2 ?PP ?V ?X0 ?X1 ?X2 ?X3
  { <syn>{
    node ?VP1 [cat = vp,bot=[path=?X3] ]{
      node ?VP2 [cat = vp,bot=[path=?X3] ]{
        node ?V (mark=anchor)[cat=v]}
      node ?PP (mark=subst)[cat=pp,top=[i=?X1,e=?X0] ]
    } };
    <frame>{
    ?X0[bounded-translocation,
      goal:?X1,
      path:?X3]
  } }
  %%%%%%%%%%%%%%%%%%%%%%%%%%%%%%%%%%%%%%%%%%%%%%%%%%%%%
  % TREE TEMPLATES:
  %%%%%%%%%%%%%%%%%%%%%%%%%%%%%%%%%%%%%%%%%%%%%%%%%%%%%
  class n0V
  export ?V ?X0
  declare ?V ?SSubj ?Spine ?X0
  {
    ?SSubj = Subj[];
    ?Spine = VSpine[];
    ?SSubj.?V = ?V;
```

```
  ?Spine.?V = ?V;
  ?SSubj.?X0 =?X0
}
%%%%%%%%%%%%%%%%%%%%%%%%%%%%%%%%%%%%%%%%%%%%%%%%%%%%%%
class n0Vn1
import n0V[]
declare ?Obj
{
  ?Obj = DirObj[];
  ?Obj.?V = ?V
}
%%%%%%%%%%%%%%%%%%%%%%%%%%%%%%%%%%%%%%%%%%%%%%%%%%%%%%
class n0Vn1pp-dir
import n0Vn1[]
declare ?PPObj ?X1 ?X2 ?X3 ?X4
{
  ?PPObj = DirPrepObj[];
  ?PPObj.?V = ?V;
  ?PPObj.?X0 = ?X4;
  <frame>{
  ?X0[causation,
    actor:?X1,
    theme:?X2,
    cause:[activity,
        actor:?X1,
        theme:?X2],
    effect:?X4[
      mover:?X2,
      goal:?X3]
  ]
} }
%%%%%%%%%%%%%%%%%%%%%%%%%%%%%%%%%%%%%%%%%%%%%%%%%%%%%%
% EVALUATION:
%%%%%%%%%%%%%%%%%%%%%%%%%%%%%%%%%%%%%%%%%%%%%%%%%%%%%%
value n0V
value n0Vn1
value n0Vn1pp-dir
```

REFERENCES

Anne ABEILLÉ and Owen RAMBOW (2000a), Tree Adjoining Grammar: An overview, in Abeillé and Rambow (2000b), pp. 1–68.

Anne ABEILLÉ and Owen RAMBOW, editors (2000b), *Tree Adjoining Grammars: Formalisms, linguistic analyses and processing*, number 107 in CSLI Lecture Notes, CSLI Publications, Stanford, CA.

Hassan AÏT-KACI, Robert BOYER, Patrick LINCOLN, and Roger NASR (1989), Efficient implementation of lattice operations, *ACM Transactions on Programming Languages and Systems (TOPLAS)*, 11(1):115–146.

Lawrence BARSALOU (1992), Frames, concepts, and conceptual fields, in Adrienne LEHRER and Eva Feder KITTEY, editors, *Frames, fields, and contrasts: New essays in semantic and lexical organization*, pp. 21–74, Lawrence Erlbaum Associates, Hillsdale, NJ.

Tilman BECKER (1994), *HyTAG: A new type of Tree Adjoining Grammars for hybrid syntactic representations of free word order languages*, Ph.D. thesis, Universität des Saarlandes, `http://www.dfki.de/~becker/becker.diss.ps.gz`.

Tilman BECKER (2000), Patterns in metarules for TAG, in Abeillé and Rambow (2000b), pp. 331–342.

Johan BOS (1996), Predicate logic unplugged, in Paul DEKKER and Martin STOKHOF, editors, *Proceedings of the tenth Amsterdam Colloquium*, pp. 133–143, Amsterdam, Netherlands.

Marie-Hélène CANDITO (1996), A principle-based hierarchical representation of LTAGs, in *Proceedings of the 16th International Conference on Computational Linguistics (COLING 96)*, Copenhagen, Denmark, `http://aclweb.org/anthology-new/C/C96/C96-1034.pdf`.

Bob CARPENTER (1992), *The logic of typed feature structures with applications to unification grammars, logic programs and constraint resolution*, number 32 in Cambridge Tracts in Theoretical Computer Science, Cambridge University Press, Cambridge, UK.

Bob CARPENTER, Gerald PENN, and Mohammad HAJI-ABDOLHOSSEINI (2003), *The Attribute Logic Engine user's guide with TRALE extensions*, version 4.0 beta edition.

Bob CARPENTER and Carl POLLARD (1991), Inclusion, disjointness and choice: The logic of linguistic classification, in *Proceedings of the 29th annual meeting of the Association for Computational Linguistics*, pp. 9–16, Berkeley, CA, `http://acl.ldc.upenn.edu/P/P91/P91-1002.pdf`.

Ann COPESTAKE (2002), *Implementing typed feature structure grammars*, CSLI Publications, Stanford, CA.

Ann A. COPESTAKE and Dan FLICKINGER (2000), An open source grammar development environment and broad-coverage English grammar using HPSG, in *Proceedings of the second Conference on Language Resources and Evaluation (LREC 2000)*, Athens, Greece.

Benoit CRABBÉ and Denys DUCHIER (2005), Metagrammar redux, in Henning CHRISTIANSEN, Peter Rossen SKADHAUGE, and Jørgen VILLADSEN, editors, *Constraint solving and language processing*, number 3438 in Lecture Notes in Computer Science, pp. 32–47, Springer, Berlin, Germany.

Benoit CRABBÉ, Denys DUCHIER, Claire GARDENT, Joseph LE ROUX, and Yannick PARMENTIER (2013), XMG: eXtensible MetaGrammar, *Computational Linguistics*, 39(3):1–66, `http://hal.archives-ouvertes.fr/hal-00768224/en/`.

Denys DUCHIER, Brunelle Magnana EKOUKOU, Yannick PARMENTIER, Simon PETITJEAN, and Emmanuel SCHANG (2012), Describing morphologically rich languages using metagrammars: A look at verbs in Ikota, in *Workshop on Language Technology for Normalisation of Less-Resourced Languages (SALTMIL 8 - AfLaT 2012)*, pp. 55–59, Istanbul, Turkey, `http://www.tshwanedje.com/publications/SaLTMiL8-AfLaT2012.pdf#page=67`.

Charles J. FILLMORE (1982), Frame Semantics, in The Linguistic Society of Korea, editor, *Linguistics in the morning calm*, pp. 111–137, Hanshin Publishing, Seoul, South Korea.

Charles J. FILLMORE (2007), Valency issues in FrameNet, in Thomas HERBST and Katrin GÖTZ-VOTTELER, editors, *Valency: Theoretical, descriptive and cognitive issues*, pp. 129–162, Mouton de Gruyter, Berlin, Germany.

Dan FLICKINGER (2000), On building a more effcient grammar by exploiting types, *Natural Language Engineering*, 6(1):15–28.

Anette FRANK and Josef VAN GENABITH (2001), GlueTag. Linear Logic based Semantics for LTAG – and what it teaches us about LFG and LTAG, in Miriam BUTT and Tracy Holloway KING, editors, *Proceedings of the LFG01 conference*, CSLI Publications, Hong Kong.

Claire GARDENT and Laura KALLMEYER (2003), Semantic construction in Feature-Based TAG, in *Proceedings of the 10th meeting of the European Chapter of the Association for Computational Linguistics*, pp. 123–130.

Adele GOLDBERG (2006), *Constructions at work. The nature of generalizations in language*, Oxford University Press, Oxford, UK.

Thilo GÖTZ, Detmar MEURERS, and Dale GERDEMANN (1997), *The ConTroll manual*, Seminar für Sprachwissenschaft, Universität Tübingen, Tübingen, Germany, `http://www.sfs.uni-tuebingen.de/controll/controll-manual.ps.gz`, draft of 17. September 1997 for ConTroll v.1.0b and XTroll v.5.0b.

Aravind K. JOSHI and Yves SCHABES (1997), Tree-Adjoining Grammars, in Grzegorz ROZENBERG and Arto SALOMAA, editors, *Handbook of Formal Languages*, volume 3, pp. 69–124, Springer, Berlin, Germany.

Aravind K. JOSHI, K.Vijay SHANKER, and David WEIR (1990), The convergence of mildly context-sensitive grammar formalisms, Technical Report MS-CIS-90-01, Department of Computer and Information Science, University of Pennsylvania, http://repository.upenn.edu/cis_reports/539/.

Laura KALLMEYER, Timm LICHTE, Wolfgang MAIER, Yannick PARMENTIER, Johannes DELLERT, and Kilian EVANG (2008), TuLiPA: Towards a multi-formalism parsing environment for grammar engineering, in *Proceedings of the workshop on Grammar Engineering Across Frameworks (GEAF '08)*, pp. 1–8, Manchester, UK.

Laura KALLMEYER and Rainer OSSWALD (2012a), An analysis of directed motion expressions with Lexicalized Tree Adjoining Grammars and frame semantics, in Luke ONG and Ruy DE QUEIROZ, editors, *Proceedings of WoLLIC*, number 7456 in Lecture Notes in Computer Science (LNCS), pp. 34–55, Springer, Berlin, Germany.

Laura KALLMEYER and Rainer OSSWALD (2012b), A frame-based semantics of the dative alternation in Lexicalized Tree Adjoining Grammars, in Christopher PIÑÓN, editor, *Empirical Issues in Syntax and Semantics 9*, pp. 167–184, Paris, France.

Laura KALLMEYER and Rainer OSSWALD (2013), Syntax-driven semantic frame composition in Lexicalized Tree Adjoining Grammar, *Journal of Language Modelling*, 1:267–330.

Paul KAY (2002), An informal sketch of a formal architecture for Construction Grammar, *Grammars*, 5:1–19.

James KILBURY, Wiebke PETERSEN, and Christof RUMPF (2006), Inheritance-based models of the lexicon, in Dieter WUNDERLICH, editor, *Advances in the theory of the lexicon*, number 13 in Interface Explorations, pp. 429–478, De Gruyter, Berlin, Germany.

Timm LICHTE, Alexander DIEZ, and Simon PETITJEAN (2013), Coupling trees, words and frames through XMG, in *Proceedings of the ESSLLI 2013 workshop on high-level methodologies for grammar engineering*, Düsseldorf, Germany.

Robert MALOUF, John CARROLL, and Ann COPESTAKE. (2000), Efficient feature structure operations without compilation, *Natural Language Engineering*, 6(1):29–46.

Stephen MCCONNEL (1995), *PC-PATR reference manual*, http://www.sil.org/pcpatr/manual/pcpatr.html, version 0.97a9.

Rainer OSSWALD (2003), *A logic of classification with applications to linguistic theory*, Dissertation, FernUniversität Hagen.

Rainer OSSWALD and Robert D. VAN VALIN, Jr. (2014), FrameNet, frame structure, and the syntax-semantics interface, in Thomas GAMERSCHLAG, Doris GERLAND, Rainer OSSWALD, and Wiebke PETERSEN, editors, *Frames and concept types*, number 94 in Studies in Linguistics and Philosophy, pp. 125–156, Springer, Cham, Switzerland.

Gerald PENN (1999), An optimized Prolog encoding of typed feature structures, Arbeitspapiere des SFB 340 138, University of Tübingen.

Guy PERRIER (2000), Interaction Grammars, in *Proceedings of the 18th International Conference on Computational Linguistics (COLING 2000)*, pp. 600–606, Saarbrücken, Germany.

Wiebke PETERSEN (2007), Representation of concepts as frames, *The Baltic International Yearbook of Cognition, Logic and Communication*, 2:151–170.

Wiebke PETERSEN and Tanja OSSWALD (2014), Concept composition in frames: Focusing on genitive constructions, in Thomas GAMERSCHLAG, Doris GERLAND, Rainer OSSWALD, and Wiebke PETERSEN, editors, *Frames and concept types*, number 94 in Studies in Linguistics and Philosophy, pp. 243–266, Springer, Cham, Switzerland.

Carlos A. PROLO (2002), Generating the XTAG English grammar using metarules, in *Proceedings of the 19th International Conference on Computational Linguistics (COLING 2002)*, pp. 814–820, Taipei. Taiwan.

Stuart M. SHIEBER (1984), The design of a computer language for linguistic information, in *Proceedings of the 10th International Conference on Computational Linguistics and 22nd annual meeting of the Association for Computational Linguistics*, pp. 362–366, Stanford, CA, http://www.aclweb.org/anthology/P84-1075.

Stuart M. SHIEBER and Yves SCHABES (1990), Synchronous Tree-Adjoining Grammars, in *Proceedings of the 13th International Conference on Computational Linguistics (COLING 1990)*, pp. 253–258, Helsinki, Finland.

Matthew SKALA, Victoria KRAKOVNA, János KRAMÁR, and Gerald PENN (2010), A generalized-zero-preserving method for compact encoding of concept lattices, in *Proceedings of the 48th annual meeting of the Association for Computational Linguistics*, pp. 1512–1521, Uppsala, Sweden.

Matthew SKALA and Gerald PENN (2011), Approximate bit vectors for fast unification, in Makoto KANAZAWA, András KORNAI, Marcus KRACHT, and Hiroyuki SEKI, editors, *The mathematics of language*, number 6878 in Lecture Notes in Computer Science, pp. 158–173, Springer, Berlin, Germany.

Matthew STONE and Christine DORAN (1997), Sentence planning as description using Tree Adjoining Grammar, in *Proceedings of the eighth conference of the European Chapter of the Association for Computational Linguistics (EACL'97)*, pp. 198–205.

Fei XIA, Martha PALMER, and K. VIJAY-SHANKER (2010), Developing Tree-Adjoining Grammars with lexical descriptions, in Srinivas BANGALORE and Aravind K. JOSHI, editors, *Using complex lexical descriptions in natural language processing*, pp. 73–110, MIT Press, Cambridge, UK.

Yulia ZINOVA and Laura KALLMEYER (2012), A frame-based semantics of locative alternation in LTAG, in *Proceedings of the 11th international workshop on Tree Adjoining Grammars and Related Formalisms (TAG+11)*, pp. 28–36, Paris, France, `http://www.aclweb.org/anthology-new/W/W12/W12-4604`.

5

The Bulgarian National Corpus: Theory and Practice in Corpus Design

Svetla Koeva, Ivelina Stoyanova, Svetlozara Leseva, Tsvetana Dimitrova, Rositsa Dekova, and Ekaterina Tarpomanova
Department of Computational Linguistics, Institute for Bulgarian Language, Bulgarian Academy of Sciences, Sofia, Bulgaria

Keywords: corpus design, Bulgarian National Corpus, computational linguistics

ABSTRACT

The paper discusses several key concepts related to the development of corpora and reconsiders them in light of recent developments in NLP. On the basis of an overview of present-day corpora, we conclude that the dominant practices of corpus design do not utilise the technologies adequately and, as a result, fail to meet the demands of corpus linguistics, computational lexicology and computational linguistics alike.

We proceed to lay out a data-driven approach to corpus design, which integrates the best practices of traditional corpus linguistics with the potential of the latest technologies allowing fast collection, automatic metadata description and annotation of large amounts of data. Thus, the gist of the approach we propose is that corpus design should be centred on amassing large amounts of mono- and multilingual texts and on providing them with a detailed metadata description and high-quality multi-level annotation.

We go on to illustrate this concept with a description of the compilation, structuring, documentation, and annotation of the Bulgarian National Corpus (BulNC). At present it consists of a Bulgarian part of 979.6 million words, constituting the corpus kernel, and 33 Bulgarian-X language corpora, totalling 972.3 million words, 1.95 billion words (1.95×10^9) altogether. The BulNC is supplied with a comprehensive metadata description, which allows us to organise the texts according to different principles. The Bulgarian part of the BulNC is automatically processed (tokenised and sentence split) and annotated at several levels: morphosyntactic tagging, lemmatisation, word-sense annotation, annotation of noun phrases and named entities. Some levels of annotation are also applied to the Bulgarian-English parallel corpus with the prospect of expanding multilingual annotation both in terms of linguistic levels and the number of languages for which it is available. We conclude with a brief evaluation of the quality of the corpus and an outline of its applications in NLP and linguistic research.

1 INTRODUCTION

Since the first structured electronic corpus, the Brown Corpus (Francis and Kučera, 1964), corpora have been increasingly used as a source of authentic linguistic data for theoretical and applied research. Corpus-based studies have been employed in various areas of linguistics, such as lexicology, lexicography, grammar, stylistics, sociolinguistics, as well as in diachronic and contrastive studies (Meyer, 2002).

Traditional definitions of a corpus emphasise different aspects. A corpus is typically viewed as a collection of authentic linguistic data that may be used in linguistic research (Garside *et al.*, 1997). Sinclair (2005) adds to this definition the storage format and the selection criteria: "*A corpus is a collection of pieces of language text in electronic form, selected according to external criteria to represent, as far as possible, a language or language variety as a source of data for linguistic research.*" Finally, annotation at different linguistic levels (phonological, lexical, morphological, morphosyntactic, syntactic, semantic, discourse and stylistic) amplifies the corpus's value by extending its functionalities and applications (McEnery *et al.*, 2006). One of many different definitions states: *A corpus is a large collection of language samples, suitable for computer processing and selected according to specific (linguistic) criteria, so that it represents an adequate language model.* (Koeva, 2010).

With the increased development of language technologies, the applications of corpora have been extended to all areas of computational linguistics and natural language processing (NLP). Corpora have become an indispensable resource for generating training sets for machine learning, language modelling, and machine translation. These developments have led to the necessity for reconsidering the traditional notions in corpus linguistics. As a result, we propose a corpus design based on automatic collection of very large monolingual and multilingual (and in particular parallel) corpora that cover a wide variety of styles, thematic domains, and genres.

This paper contributes to the discussion on the perspectives of corpus development in three ways: (i) by reconsidering several key traditional principles underlying corpus design, (ii) by proposing an approach in corpus design based on the revision of those fundamentals in light of recent advances in NLP technologies, (iii) by illustrating how the proposed model is applied in the Bulgarian National Corpus (BulNC).

The study is placed in the context of well-known corpora, both mono- and multilingual (Section 2), with an outline of their general features. The concepts of corpus size, balance, and representativeness are discussed in Section 3. In the same section we present our concept of corpora, which integrates the best practices of traditional corpus linguistics with the potential of the latest technologies for web crawling and language processing. Section 4 presents the process of compiling, structuring, documenting, and annotating the BulNC, followed by a brief evaluation of the quality of the corpus and an outline of some current applications.

2 OVERVIEW OF CONTEMPORARY MONOLINGUAL AND MULTILINGUAL CORPORA

The last decades have seen the compilation of large mono- and multilingual corpora for a lot of languages, including some less-resourced ones, Bulgarian among them. The brief overview illustrates the current standards in corpus design and compilation and provides a point of departure for comparison with the proposed paradigm.

2.1 *Large monolingual corpora*

1. At the time of its creation, the British National Corpus[1] (BNC) was one of the biggest (100 million words) existing corpora. Being compiled according to carefully devised principles and classification criteria[2], it set the standards for general monolingual synchronic corpora for quite some time. The BNC represents not

[1] http://www.natcorp.ox.ac.uk
[2] http://www.natcorp.ox.ac.uk/corpus/creating.xml

only written, but also spoken language, respectively 90% and 10% of the samples. It is POS-tagged, lemmatised, and supplied with detailed metatextual information. The corpus (text and annotated data) can be searched both online – through various search tools, and offline using XAIRA[3].

2. The Corpus of Contemporary American English[4] (COCA) is a 450+ million-word corpus currently in progress with an increase rate of 20 million words per year. The texts are evenly divided between 5 categories – spoken language, fiction, popular magazines, newspapers, and academic writing (Davies, 2010), each category currently containing 90 to 95 million tokens (as of June 2012). The corpus provides a web search interface (shared with the Google Books corpora) that allows searches for regular expressions and specifications for POS, lemma, collocations, frequency and distribution of synonyms. The queries may be refined in terms of genre or time period.
3. The Slovak National Corpus[5] (SNK) contains more than 719 million tokens[6]. The texts are divided into several categories with the following distribution: journalism (73%), literary texts (14%), professional texts (12%), and other (1%). A subcorpus of 1.2 million tokens, manually annotated with morphological tags, has also been compiled. The SNK and its subcorpora can be searched with a CQL (Corpus Query Language) compatible query syntax (Christ and Schulze, 1994) through a web interface or via the Bonito client[7], cf. the Czech National Corpus.
4. The Croatian National Corpus[8] (HNK) includes about 101 million words of mainly contemporary Croatian texts that cover different media, genres, styles, fields, and topics. They fall into the categories of informative texts (74%), fiction (23%), and mixed texts (3%), with further subdivision within these categories. The morphological tagset used in the HNK annotation is Multext-East-

[3] `http://www.natcorp.ox.ac.uk/tools/index.xml`
[4] `http://corpus.byu.edu/coca/`
[5] `http://korpus.sk`
[6] The version released at the beginning of 2011
[7] `http://korpus.juls.savba.sk/usage_en.html`
[8] `http://www.hnk.ffzg.hr/cnc.htm`

compatible, and the corpus can be searched offline through the Manatee/Bonito server-client[9].

5. The Russian National Corpus[10] (RNC) comprises more than 300 million words of texts ranging from the middle of the 18th century to the present day. The main part of the corpus, about 100 million words, consists of contemporary texts of three general categories: fiction (40%), non-fiction (56%) and recordings of public and spontaneous speech (4%), with a detailed internal classification[11]. The corpus has been automatically supplied with morphosyntactic annotation, and parts of it have been manually verified and disambiguated. A portion of the corpus has also been annotated with syntactic dependencies and semantic roles. Lexical-semantic information, covering taxonomic, mereological, topological and other features of words, has been assigned. The RNC provides a web interface for detailed search in the whole corpus and its subcorpora for words and phrases, grammatical (POS, morphology), syntactic, and semantic (taxonomy, evaluation and mereology) features.

6. The Czech National Corpus[12] (CNC) (Kocek *et al.*, 2000) was started in the 1990s. Since then it has been constantly growing and according to the latest published estimates currently amounts to 1.3 billion words. It consists of a number of subcorpora, among them several balanced subcorpora of 100 million words each, compiled every several years, the latest version being SYN2010. The distribution of texts across categories is as follows: fiction (40%), technical literature (27%) and journalism (33%), with more elaborate subdivision within these categories. Most of the written corpora in the CNC are annotated. The CNC can be searched for words and phrases using exact match and regular expressions both online and offline through the Corpus manager Manatee and the client Bonito[13].

[9] `http://www.hnk.ffzg.hr/pretraga_en.html`
[10] `http://www.ruscorpora.ru/`
[11] `http://www.ruscorpora.ru/en/corpora-stat.html`
[12] `http://ucnk.ff.cuni.cz`
[13] `http://www.textforge.cz/download`

7. The National Corpus of Polish[14] (NCP) (Bański and Przepiórkowski, 2010) contains fiction, daily newspapers, specialised periodicals and journals, transcripts of conversations and Internet texts, amounting to approximately 1 billion words. A balanced 250-million-word subcorpus extracted from the NCP has been compiled (Przepiórkowski, 2011), and part of the NCP, approximately 1.2 million words, was manually annotated. The corpus can be searched online through two search engines (Poliqarp and PELCRA) that allow queries for words and regular expressions; the former also searches for morphological tags and the latter offers collocation extraction. The search may be further refined with editorial and descriptive (genre or domain) metadata.
8. The German Reference Corpus[15] (DeReKo) amounts to 5.4 billion words (Bański *et al.*, 2012).The concept of the corpus explicitly rejects the feasibility of balance and representativeness (Kupietz *et al.*, 2010). The corpus is conceived as a versatile "primordial" sample from which specialised subsamples, or "virtual" corpora, are drawn. The development of the corpus is focused on the maximisation of size and stratification, rather than on the composition of specialised subsamples. The corpus includes POS annotation, partial morphological disambiguation, named entities, and syntactic dependencies. The corpus can be searched offline through the COSMAS II client[16].
9. A number of large corpora have recently come into existence, with size ranging from several (Baroni and Kilgarriff, 2006; Pomikálek *et al.*, 2009), through dozens (Pomikálek *et al.*, 2012), to hundreds of billions of words (Google Books Corpora, GBC[17], the largest being the 200-billion-word GBC of American English). What distinguishes these from the rest of the discussed corpora is that they represent a different type of approach to corpus creation, since they are collected fully automatically from web content. The GBC web search interface allows queries according to several criteria:

[14] `http://nkjp.pl`

[15] the Archive of General Reference Corpora of Contemporary Written German, `http://www.ids-mannheim.de/kl/projekte/korpora/archiv.html`

[16] `http://www.ids-mannheim.de/cosmas2/`

[17] `http://googlebooks.byu.edu/`

exact words or phrases, regular expressions, POS, lemma, collocations, frequency and distribution of synonyms, with further refinement in terms of genre or time period.

This brief outline shows that the dominant and constant tendency is for corpora to aim at a size ranging from several hundred million up to over a billion words.

All corpora are at least partly annotated and provide online or offline search interfaces. The differences lie in the quantity of the annotated data and the levels of annotation. The minimum annotation is generally POS tagging. Many corpora also include morphosyntactic annotation and lemmatisation, and some provide syntactic (e.g., DeReKo) or semantic annotation (e.g., COCA, GBC).

Some of the corpora discussed here follow predefined structure and classifications, whereas others abandon balance and representativeness in favour of size. The design criteria differ not only when it comes to coverage and distinction of textual categories and subcategories, but, more fundamentally, in the underlying assumptions. Balance is viewed as the equal representation of predefined text categories (Davies, 2010), or as a distribution of texts proportional to language production (Atkins *et al.*, 1991) or language reception estimated according to various criteria. Some authors, involved in the compilation of the previously discussed corpora, have proposed assessments of language reception on the basis of stylistic (Przepiórkowski *et al.*, 2010), sociological (Čermak and Schmiedtová, 2003), and marketing (Tadić, 2002) surveys.

The following trends emerge with respect to the relationship between size, balance and representativeness:

- Creation of corpora according to a predefined methodology that is considered sufficiently adequate to ensure corpus balance and representativeness (1-5).
- Development of large unbalanced corpora paired with static balanced subcorpora that are compiled in accordance with a carefully devised structure (6-7).
- Compilation of large unbalanced corpora that enables the extraction of subcorpora based on metadata description (8).

- Compilation of very large unbalanced corpora from the web whose structure and content are not concerned with balance and representativeness (9).

2.2 *Large parallel corpora*

1. Some of the major parallel corpora that have been largely drawn on by the NLP community are multilingual repositories of publicly available legal, administrative or journalistic texts, such as: the European Parliament Proceedings Parallel Corpus[18] (Europarl), the Canadian Hansard Corpus of parliamentary proceedings; the News Commentary Corpus[19]; the JRC-Acquis Multilingual Parallel Corpus[20] of legal texts, the EU Official Journal[21], MultiUN[22]. The OPUS collection[23] includes a set of various corpora – administrative (e.g., the EMEA corpus of administrative medical texts), news (including the SETimes corpus of news in eight Balkan languages and English), etc.
   These corpora are distinguished from traditional ones in that the data have been compiled for a different purpose and have subsequently been employed as corpora. Therefore not all of them are annotated. OPUS, EuroParl, and JRC-Acquis are tokenised, sentence-segmented and sentence-aligned. Parts of the OPUS collection are POS-tagged for some languages, with word alignment currently under way and dependency parsing envisaged in the near future. A part of the Hansard corpus is also sentence-split and aligned.
2. The Czech-English parallel corpus (CzEng) comprises 206.4 million tokens in Czech and 232.7 million tokens in English, distributed across 7 source domains: fiction, EU legislation, movie subtitles, parallel webpages, technical documentation, news, and texts from Project Navajo[24]. The predominant domains are fiction and legislation. The texts have gone through automatic sentence-

[18] `http://www.statmt.org/europarl`
[19] `http://www.statmt.org/wmt11/translation-task.html`
[20] `http://langtech.jrc.it/JRC-Acquis.html`
[21] `http://eur-lex.europa.eu/en/index.htm`
[22] `http://www.euromatrixplus.net/multi-un/`
[23] `http://opus.lingfil.uu.se/`
[24] `http://ufal.mff.cuni.cz/czeng/czeng10/`

splitting and alignment. Morphosyntactic tagging, lemmatisation, word alignment, surface and deep-level syntactic annotation are provided (Bojar *et al.*, 2012).

3. The Hunglish corpus[25] is a sentence-aligned parallel corpus of Hungarian and English containing 34.6 million Hungarian and 44.6 million English words. The texts cover a number of varied domains: literature, religion, international law, movie subtitles, software documentation, magazines, and business reports (Varga *et al.*, 2005). The corpus has been tokenised with the rule-based HunToken tokeniser and stemmed with the Hunmorph morphological analyser.
4. The Polish-Russian Parallel Corpus[26] consists of 50 million words equally divided between Polish originals with their Russian translations and the other way round. The corpus includes classical and modern literature as well as legal and journalistic texts. The texts are annotated according to the annotation schemes of the National Corpus of Polish and the Russian National Corpus.
5. The Japanese-English Bilingual Corpus of Wikipedia's Kyoto Articles[27] is a corpus of 440,000 parallel sentences made up of 12 million Japanese words and 11.5 million English words. The texts concerning Kyoto and other specific topics, such as traditional Japanese culture, religion, and history, are manually translated into English, aligned and verified. The corpus was used for the development and evaluation of Japanese-English machine translation systems in the Kyoto Free Translation Task (Neubig, 2011).

Many of the available parallel corpora are of modest size, especially in comparison with monolingual corpora, and as a rule they belong to a limited number of domains determined by the availability of parallel texts. For the most part these corpora are compiled automatically by web crawling or by downloading publicly available parallel collections. More varied content can be obtained from publishers or through manual compilation, but these methods are less efficient. A third source of parallel data has been the translation of monolingual corpora; Xu and Sun (2011), among others, have experimented with

[25] `http://mokk.bme.hu/resources/hunglishcorpus/`

[26] `http://www.pol-ros.polon.uw.edu.pl/`

[27] `http://alaginrc.nict.go.jp/WikiCorpus/index_E.html`

machine translation for increasing parallel data for less common languages.

Due to the limited domain and genre diversity of parallel texts, balance and representativeness are usually considered irrelevant. Three dominant patterns of parallel corpus design emerge:

- Acquisition of corpora from repositories of parallel content (1). Being publicly available, these collections are often reused in other corpora either as raw text or with the supplied annotation.
- Compilation (preferably automatic) of parallel corpora that aims at reflecting the diversity of monolingual corpora, possibly using readily available corpora (2-4).
- Construction of parallel corpora by means of human translation (5) or machine translation of the original content.

To conclude, there is considerable heterogeneity among the existing monolingual and parallel corpora in terms of size, design criteria, annotation principles, etc. At the same time, neither the possibilities of the modern technologies, nor the enormous amount of available data are used rationally enough to serve the needs of NLP. Moreover, traditional services for extraction of concordances and collocations fail to meet the needs of modern corpus linguistics and computational lexicography. The automatic collocation dictionaries extracted through "sketch grammars" and an algorithm for finding "good dictionary examples" allow a more efficient access to corpus data (Kilgarriff *et al.*, 2009).

2.3 *An overview of Bulgarian corpora*

The work on corpora for Bulgarian began in the 1990s with the compilation of relatively small text collections for specific purposes.

1. Two corpora of Spoken Bulgarian have been created in the 1990s[28] (Nikolova, 1987; Aleksova, 2000).
2. Further efforts were focused on building large reference corpora such as the BulTreeBank Text Archive (since 2000) with 15% of the texts coming from fiction, 78% from newspapers and about 7% excerpted from legal and government texts and others (Simov

[28] `http://folk.uio.no/kjetilrh/bulg/Aleksova/index.html` and `http://folk.uio.no/kjetilrh/bulg/Nikolova/`

et al., 2002). This corpus recently evolved into the Bulgarian National Reference Corpus[29]. The corpus interface executes queries allowing exact matches or regular expressions.

3. The "Brown" Corpus of Bulgarian[30] (BCB) (Koeva *et al.*, 2006), compiled in the period 2001 to 2005 as a general corpus of contemporary Bulgarian, is one of the Bulgarian corpora that closely follow a clearly established methodology, namely that of the Brown Corpus of Standard American English (Francis and Kučera, 1964). Text samples can be searched using queries for exact matches or regular expressions. The "Brown" Corpus of Bulgarian with full-length texts[31] (FullBrown), consisting of the originals from which the BCB 2000-word excerpts were sampled, is included as an integral part of the Bulgarian National Corpus and may be searched through its web interface.
   Concomitantly, a number of Bulgarian annotated corpora have been developed, covering POS tagging, word sense annotation, annotation of dependency structure, and sentence and clause alignment.
4. The Bulgarian POS-Tagged Corpus (BulPosCor) totals 174,697 words, each of them manually annotated with the context-relevant POS and morphosyntactic features.
5. The Bulgarian Sense-Annotated Corpus (BulSemCor) amounts to 95,119 lexical items, covering both single words and multiword expressions. Each of them has been POS-tagged, lemmatised, and assigned a synonym set from the Bulgarian Wordnet (Koeva *et al.*, 2006) that best corresponds to the sense of the lexical item in the particular context.
   Both BulPosCor and BulSemCor are integrated into the BulNC and can be accessed through its web search interface (see Section 4.6.1), as well as through specially developed interfaces[32].
6. The BulTreeBank is a syntactically annotated corpus developed within the HPSG framework (Simov and Osenova, 2004). Access to the data may be gained by submitting a contact form. The

[29] `http://www.webclark.org`

[30] `http://dcl.bas.bg/Corpus/home_en.html`

[31] `http://dcl.bas.bg/en/corpora_en.html`

[32] `http://dcl.bas.bg/poscor/en/`, `http://dcl.bas.bg/semcor/en/`

HPSG-based annotation has later been converted into syntactic dependency annotation covering 214,000 tokens, or slightly more than 15,000 sentences (Chanev *et al.*, 2006).

7. The Bulgarian-English Sentence- and Clause-Aligned Corpus (BulEnAC) (Koeva *et al.*, 2012a), a parallel sample from the Bulgarian National Corpus, comprises 176,397 tokens for Bulgarian and 190,468 for English. It is supplied with syntactic annotation for sentence and clause boundaries, relations between syntactically linked clauses (i.e., coordination or subordination) and clause-introducing words and phrases.

The main purpose of corpora 4 to 7 is to serve as training and test corpora in the development of various automatic annotation tools for multi-level annotation with sufficient accuracy and coverage. Most of the parallel corpora involving Bulgarian are purpose-driven and cover specific domains, such as administrative texts or fiction, which are widely available in parallel versions and hence easily collected.

The Bulgarian subcorpus in the JRC-Acquis corpus of EU legislation documents contains 16.1 million tokens (Steinberger *et al.*, 2006). The Bulgarian part of the SEE-ERA.NET Administrative Corpus (SEnAC) consists of excerpts from the Acquis communautaire, about 1.5 million tokens and 60,389 translation units, each containing one sentence translated into 8 languages (Tufiş *et al.*, 2009). The EuroParl Corpus of proceedings of the European Parliament includes approximately 6 million tokens in Bulgarian (Koehn, 2005).

The Multext-East corpus incorporates the original and translations into six languages of George Orwell's novel *Nineteen Eighty-Four*, with the Bulgarian part amounting to 54,823 tokens (Dimitrova *et al.*, 1998). In the SEE-ERA.net Fiction Corpus (SEnFC), consisting of translations of Jules Verne's novel *Around the World in 80 Days* into sixteen languages, the Bulgarian part adds up to 58,678 tokens (Tufiş *et al.*, 2009). The Cultural Greek-Bulgarian Corpus is a bilingual collection of literary and folklore texts containing approximately 350,000 tokens (Giouli *et al.*, 2009). The extended RuN-Euro Corpus includes a small Bulgarian part of 366,329 tokens (Grønn and Marijanovic, 2010), and ParaSol (von Waldenfels, 2006, 2011), a corpus of fiction texts, includes a Bulgarian subcorpus of over 2 million tokens as of June 2011. The Bulgarian-Polish-Lithuanian Parallel Corpus (Dimitrova *et al.*, 2009) contains more than one million words and combines texts from more than one domain – fiction texts and administrative texts (EU documents). Some parallel corpora in the OPUS collection (Tiedemann, 2009) include Bulgarian – medical documents by the European Medicines Agency, movie subtitles, and the SETimes news corpus.

Smaller and purpose-driven corpora, such as the *Nineteen Eighty-Four* (Multext-East) and the SEnAC and SEnFC corpora (SEE-ERA.NET), are tokenised, lemmatised, POS-tagged and aligned at sentence level. Annotation of larger corpora is usually limited to tokenisation, sentence splitting, and alignment, e.g. the OPUS collection, with the tendency to be extended to other levels of annotation.

Due to the limited amount of translations between particular pairs of languages, the interest in comparable corpora has been growing in the last decades. Still, only a small number of comparable corpora involve Bulgarian. The Multext-East comparable corpora with subcorpora of Bulgarian, Czech, English, Estonian, Hungarian, Romanian, and Slovene, include fiction and newspaper data (Dimitrova *et al.*, 1998). The Bulgarian-Croatian Comparable Corpus (Bekavac *et al.*, 2004) contains newswire texts, 393,000 tokens for Bulgarian and 1.3 million for Croatian. The Bulgarian-Polish-Lithuanian Comparable Corpus comprises fiction and electronic media documents balanced in size across the three languages (Dimitrova *et al.*, 2009).

This overview suggests that the existing Bulgarian corpora share most of the merits of the corpora compiled for other languages, and suffer from similar shortcomings, further aggravated by their smaller size and limited diversity, as well as the restricted availability of both monolingual and parallel data. On the positive side, most of the manually annotated corpora conform to the best annotation practices and have been employed in the development of various NLP applications for Bulgarian.

3 KEY FEATURES OF CORPORA

Apart from their use in traditional corpus linguistics and computational lexicography, contemporary corpora have been increasingly employed in developing language models, translation models and in training machine learning algorithms. However, despite the rapid development of technologies and the vast amount of electronic data, the available corpora largely adhere to long-established tradition: they aspire to represent a balanced sample of language and for that reason constitute collections of carefully selected, often fixed-size, text excerpts. They are being explored with outdated methods and tools, which limits their use to extraction of concordances and collocations.

In the context of the dynamically evolving web and with more and more mono- and multilingual corpora becoming available, the traditional understanding of corpus design has been undergoing reconsideration. Some of the most prominent corpus features: size, balance, and representativeness (Xiao, 2010) will be discussed in the following subsections. We then proceed to propose a general approach for corpus development based on *automatic compiling, detailed metadata description*, and *multiple annotation*. This, we believe, will result in dynamic enlargement and efficient management of corpus data.

3.1 *Corpus size revisited*

A corpus large enough for empirical studies on language might not contain sufficient occurrences of specific and rare language phenomena for drawing statistically valid conclusions (Banko and Brill, 2001; Keller and Lapata, 2003; Kilgarriff and Grefenstette, 2003). Consequently, for building probabilistic models, larger amounts of data are needed, as large data, even if they are noisy, yield more reliable models than estimates based on smaller, limited datasets. After exploring the performance of a number of machine-learning algorithms for disambiguation when the size of the training corpus was increased from a million to a billion words, Banko and Brill (2001) concluded that the performance of any algorithm improves with data size, although the optimal data size varies with different algorithms[33]. This assertion is reflected in the rationale behind the web-as-a-corpus framework (Kilgarriff and Grefenstette, 2003), where the case is made for the necessity of making vast amounts of Internet texts available for processing and querying. Scientists have long since realised that the largest corpus is the web and that what primarily keeps Internet data

[33] An important insight made by Curran and Osborne (2002) in criticising Banko and Brill (2001) is that the benefits of large amounts of data are better experienced when size is combined with sophisticated statistical language models.

from becoming a real corpus is the lack of linguistically focused metadata and annotation.

The major size-related concern for corpus linguistics is how to define optimality – in terms of corpus size and in terms of sample size. The criterion for optimal corpus size aims at ensuring adequate coverage of lexical diversity, estimated with respect to wordstock, thematic domains, genres or language phenomena, while the criterion for text sample size takes into account the balance between texts, as well as their diversity. Several attempts at approximating an "ideal" size and structure, defined intuitively or empirically, have been made. Yang *et al.* (2000) try to estimate a corpus size that would be sufficient for obtaining the core vocabulary, while Chevelu *et al.* (2007) propose an algorithm for calculating an optimal corpus design that ensures coverage of a preset description of phonological attributes. What qualifies as optimal corpus size is still an open question, contingent on the particular linguistic or lexicographic task.

We shall illustrate the relation between corpus size and lexical diversity by a comparison between the "Brown" corpus of Bulgarian and FullBrown. The former consists of around one million words in 500 fixed-size samples of approximately 2000 words with adjustment to sentence boundaries; the latter includes the full-length originals of the BCB excerpts and totals 4.5 million words. The Bulgarian "Brown" corpus has 112,130 unique tokens, of which 61,162 (6.12% of all corpus tokens) appear only once. FullBrown contains 256,413 unique tokens and 130,230 tokens (2.89% of all corpus tokens) have a frequency of 1.

The early corpus tradition used a fixed size of the text samples to ensure balance and diversity of data and to avoid the skewing that might result from including large texts. Although limiting the size of samples is still appropriate for balanced and domain- and purpose-specific corpora, the above example shows that the inclusion of full texts contributes to language diversity and helps overcoming data sparsity.

The approach we adopt is based on two assumptions: that larger corpora are better suited to language analysis, irrespective of the particular task; and, that these resources, if properly documented and annotated, may also serve as a reliable source from which smaller, uniformly processed, different-sized subcorpora can be extracted, thus eliminating the need for ad-hoc building of standalone fixed-structure corpora. Therefore we include the full versions of the texts in the corpus, as this allows us to extract comprehensive statistical metadata for the number of tokens, words, lemmas, clauses, sentences, and specific grammatical constructions that would enable further extraction of subcorpora, such as the one compiled for the development of the Bulgarian Sense-Annotated Corpus (BulSemCor; cf. Koeva *et al.* 2011).

3.2 *Balance and representativeness reconsidered*

The size of contemporary corpora comes at the expense of their structure, as they are usually created by collecting vast amounts of data at a fast rate. The predefined design criteria that used to be the organising principle of post-Brown corpora turn out to be empirically refuted and in need to be redefined in terms of the availability of various text types.

Representativeness is associated with the adequate coverage of the varieties of language use, while balance concerns the linguistically relevant distribution of texts across categories (Sinclair, 2005). Although these corpus features have been the focus of extensive study (Leech, 1991; Atkins, 1992; Biber, 1993; Sinclair, 2005; McEnery *et al.*, 2006), definitive qualitative or quantitative criteria for ensuring or evaluating them have not been convincingly established.

As a consequence, in traditional accounts, where the notions of balance and representativeness are defined in terms of supposedly relevant linguistic coverage and proportions of total language production, they remain tentative notions (Manning and Schutze, 1999; Kilgarriff and Grefenstette, 2003; Kupietz *et al.*, 2010). Moreover, defining them in this fashion is not adequate when it comes to the requirements posed to corpora by NLP. The new demands have called for a shift from compiling corpora that are carefully proportioned in terms of sample size and text types to expanding the quantity of the data.

Below, we attempt to redefine the relationship between size, balance, and representativeness in a data-driven perspective.

Representativeness is recast in terms of the range and diversity of text categories accompanied by enrichment of the sampling methodology. Since balance is hard to maintain for dynamic (constantly evolving) corpora, we suggest that instead of trying to maintain it for the whole corpus, we extract different balanced subcorpora based on a large set of criteria (both preset or user-defined) such as time period, thematic domain, genre, author, density or distribution of certain language phenomena, etc.

We focus on amassing large amounts of texts that cover a variety of languages, media type, styles, domains, genres, and topics. The dynamic enlargement of the corpus, including the growth rate, the range of samples, and their quantity, is determined by the availability of texts on the web rather than by a preset model. Corpus structure is ensured through detailed metadata organised in a comprehensive classification of categories. The detailed metadata description allows for easy compilation of general, domain- and purpose-specific subcorpora with a fixed structure or predefined features. The metadata classification scheme is flexible, in order to match the new texts that are constantly being included in the corpus.

3.3 *Extended metadata and linguistic annotation*

Metadata describe the properties of the text samples in the corpus and are external to the text itself. Burnard (2005) emphasises the importance of metadata and the need for them to be as detailed as possible so that one may be able to determine the relevance of a given linguistic resource to one's own purposes. In the proposed framework, the classification suggested by Burnard (2005) is adopted as a baseline description of the text metadata and the annotation of the texts.

1. Editorial – information about texts in relation to their original source (source, author, date of publishing, etc. Here we include information about language, direction of translation, name of the translator, etc.);
2. Descriptive – classificatory information such as style, domain, and genre;
3. Administrative – documentary information about the texts and the corpus, such as its availability, revision status, etc.;
4. Analytical – various levels of annotation;
5. Statistical – number of tokens, words, general words, domain-specific words, lemmas, noun phrases, phrases, clauses, sentences, etc. In addition to Burnard's classification we include various statistical information.

Extralinguistic metadata about the texts (types 1-3) are built through a combination of automatic and manual techniques with increasing application of the former. Extralinguistic metadata are derived automatically from the HTML markup of the original files or with various heuristics based, for example, on domain-specific or genre-descriptive keywords. Statistical data (type 5) are calculated before or after annotation.

We represent the metadata scheme as a graph (Figure 1) where the nodes are associated with metadata categories and the arcs with binary relations between the nodes, such as *style*, *domain*, and *genre*, etc. For some metadata relations, for instance *style*, the metadata categories are predefined; for others, such as *author*, the categories are an open set. The representation is simplified, e.g. authorship of the text is recorded only once for all kernel and satellite samples in different languages. As a further advantage, graph representation allows flexible extension with new relations and categories and shows where merging or splitting categories is permissible. For example, it is possible to merge the metadata with a database of books' descriptions allowing us to automatically assign publishing dates or obtain translations of the title in different languages. Different "graph mining" algorithms – common subgraph, shortest paths, minimum spanning trees, connectedness, etc. can be used when extracting subcorpora of different types.

Linguistic annotation increases the value of a corpus by making it more *usable*, as various kinds of information may be extracted, more *multifunctional*, as the corpus may be used for different purposes, and more *explicit* with respect to the analysed information (McEnery *et al.*, 2006, p. 30). In our approach, we adopt and supplement the criteria set out by McEnery *et al.* (2006) as follows:

- **Multi-layered** – the more richly annotated the corpus, the broader its range of applications for research and applied studies. Corpus processing needs to cover and accumulate as many levels of linguistic annotation as possible.
- **Compliance with standards** in data formatting and representation of annotation. Unification of various tagsets and data formats, including encodings, is enabled through easy and reliable conversion.

Figure 1: Example of the graph representation of corpus metadata.

- **Uniformity** – a common set of attributes and values for different languages and different media types – text, audio, image, video, and common techniques to manage (accumulate, combine, split, etc.) them. This will facilitate comparative studies and the application of language-independent tools.
- **Consistency** – as annotation of large amounts of texts in most cases is carried out automatically, it is necessary to provide means for validation and evaluation.

The following annotation principles are observed in general, both for manual and automatic annotation (Koeva *et al.*, 2010): the input text remains unchanged; the annotation is performed at consecutive stages and is accumulated as multi-level annotation; the annotation data are represented as attribute-value pairs. Each annotation level is independent, may be accessed separately and merged with other compatible annotation schemes.

For the abstract representation of annotation an attribute-value formalism is used, in which the attributes are different types of linguistic categories (i.e., word sense, syntactic category, grammatical gender) associated with a set of values, for example *shtastliv* (en: lucky) has the following attributes and values: word sense: *'having or bringing good fortune'*, syntactic category: Adjective, gender: masculine. Ambiguity is not accepted in annotation, so each attribute is assigned a single value. The set of attributes depends on the language features and the granularity of the annotation and is thus open. Binary relations may also be defined between attributes (i.e., common noun – concrete, animate – human), making graph representation possible.

Fully-automated annotation is faster and more consistent although its precision might be lower than manual annotation. Our approach employs primarily automatic annotation, at any level of monolingual and parallel linguistic representation, and to whatever extent possible. Subcorpora with a concentration of a particular grammatical feature (such as singularia tantum) or language construction (such as noun phrases with a prepositional complement) may be extracted on the basis of the annotation.

3.4 *A unified corpus approach*

The need for high-quality monolingual and multilingual corpora further necessitates adjustment of corpus design principles in order to ensure a uniform treatment of monolingual and multilingual corpus parts, with all texts being compiled, documented, processed and accessed within a common framework.

The main source for corpus compilation is and will be the *Internet*, through downloading of readily available text collections or by web crawling. Modern corpus development has to be based on *automatic (and semiautomatic) collection, documentation and annotation* of monolingual and multilingual corpora, while manual work is mainly reduced to defining metadata and annotation schemes, annotation tagsets and the development of gold-standard corpora for training and testing. The requirements for corpus development can be summarized as follows:

1. **Collection** – predominantly automatic compilation of full-text corpus samples by means of web crawling based on preliminary manual and automatic web mining; automatic cleaning of junk formatting, and elimination of duplicates;
2. **Documentation** – detailed metadata extracted from the mark-up of the Internet documents, from the raw data by means of document categorisation and information extraction, and from the annotation by means of statistical processing;
3. **Annotation** – largely automatic linguistic annotation covering different linguistic levels and conforming to uniformity with respect to different languages and different media types.

The corpus design requires a clear-cut structure based on an explicit description of sample categories and explicit mapping between parallel samples in different languages. On the other hand, the corpus structure has to be flexible enough to allow for reorganisation around different categories or languages. This is ensured by a *detailed and consistent metadata documentation* of corpus samples.

Another point of discussion has been whether corpus design should be based on linguistic or extralinguistic criteria (Atkins, 1992; Sinclair, 2005). We subscribe to the idea that text sampling should be based on external criteria derived from the text's communicative function (style, genre, domain, source, year of publication, etc.), rather than on internal criteria that reflect the features of the language of the text (Clear, 1992), since the former afford a more reliable classification, and also to a large extent predetermine the linguistic features of the texts.

The principles for corpus design we have adopted are reflected in the following requirements:

1. Task-independent design ensuring as many monolingual and multilingual data as possible, illustrating different media types with their styles, genres, and domains.
2. Extensibility of the corpus through the inclusion of newly emerging categories attested in language production.
3. Flexibility and robustness of the design in order to facilitate reconsideration and restructuring of classificatory information about the texts. Carefully designed mechanisms for reorganising should

ensure that already included texts are not misclassified after the changes.

4. Adoption of mechanisms for accommodating texts that belong to multiple categories while any additional information is also properly stored and remains accessible.
5. Easy access to the relevant documents, including simple and efficient extraction of information, as well as grouping and regrouping of texts into subcorpora.

This corpus design is proposed in order to maintain simultaneously monolingual and multilingual parallel corpora and allow them to be compiled, preprocessed, annotated, evaluated and accessed through common or compatible tools, compliant with metadata and annotation description schemes, as well as with common (or convertible) annotation tagsets. This approach ensures standardisation, reusability and automation at all stages of corpora development and usage.

Corpus development at the present time needs to take into account the fact that the main purpose of corpora is natural language processing, and should try to answer this field's growing needs of reliable, linguistically enriched multilingual resources. Fulfilling such functions, corpora can successfully serve both corpus linguistics and computational lexicography, as detailed metadata and annotation facilitate the compilation of various domain- and purpose-specific subcorpora.

4 THE BULGARIAN NATIONAL CORPUS

The Bulgarian National Corpus is designed according to the outlined approach. The corpus contains a large variety of texts of different size, media type (written and spoken), style, period (synchronic and diachronic), and languages (Koeva *et al.*, 2012b).

The BulNC started as a monolingual general corpus and has been enlarged constantly, with the latest effort focused on the collection and annotation of parallel data and resulting in the Bulgarian-X Language Parallel Corpus (Bul-X-Cor). The parallel corpora in the BulNC consist entirely of texts that have a Bulgarian counterpart (original or translation) and one or more foreign-language correspondences that can also be either original or translated. Both the Bulgarian and the foreign versions can be translations from a third language. Bulgarian serves as a pivot language for the parallel corpora, but any X-language is treated equally with respect to text type diversity, preprocessing, metadata scheme, general annotation principles, different levels of annotation, corpus quality evaluation and modes of access for (computational) research and implementations. The corpus may be used for tasks involving any pair of languages available in it. Applying the same principles and methodology used for the Bulgarian part of the BulNC and the Bul-X-Cor ensures, among other things, efficiency in terms of storage, as duplication of files between different parallel corpora is avoided and texts are stored and processed only once, unlike other corpora, such as the corpora in the OPUS collection.

4.1 *Compilation of the BulNC*

Three basic approaches have been applied in the compilation of both the kernel and the satellites:

1. **Using readily available text collections.** The kernel of the Bulgarian National Corpus was first compiled on the basis of the Bulgarian Lexicographic Archive and the Text Archive of Written Bulgarian, which together account for 55.95% of the corpus. Later, two domain-specific corpora from the OPUS collection were included, namely the EMEA corpus (medical administrative texts) and the OpenSubtitles corpus (film subtitles) representing respectively 1.27% and 8.61% of the kernel of the BulNC (see Figure 3). A large amount of news data in the Bulgarian Lexicographic Archive and the Text Archive of Written Bulgarian were provided by the publishers of various Bulgarian newspapers.
   The corpora were either obtained in plain text format or converted to it. Metadata were extracted automatically wherever possible, documented and verified manually in some cases. Full annotation was performed from scratch, even for already annotated texts (OPUS texts are tokenised and sentence-al-igned) to ensure conformity with the adopted principles and annotation standards.
2. **Manual compilation** by browsing the Internet. While being the primary approach in the past, manual collection has now been applied in a limited number of cases for small numbers of large

documents whenever the development of a focused crawler was deemed inefficient. Most of the previously developed corpora within the kernel of the BulNC were compiled manually, such as the Bulgarian "Brown" corpus. Recently, manual compilation has also been used for collecting parallel fiction texts in multiple languages, accounting for 3.70% of the kernel corpus.

3. **Automatic compilation** by web crawling is in general preferred. Some well-known and widely used approaches for automatic collection of corpora are adopted, tailored further to our specific needs and optimised with respect to the efficiency and precision of the output. Currently, automatically obtained subcorpora within the BulNC include a large amount of administrative texts, news from monolingual and multilingual sources, scientific texts and popular science (e.g., Wikipedia articles), altogether amounting to 30.47% of the Bulgarian kernel of BulNC.
   Manual and automatic web mining prior to the crawling process ensures crawling efficiency, as well as high-quality results when it comes to the validity of collected documents and the correspondence between parallel texts. As parallel resources involving Bulgarian are limited on the web, crawling was supported by direct targeting, automatic or manual, of the appropriate resources. The structure of source webpages is also considered when crawling, by applying either links traversal algorithms or URL templates as appropriate for each source.

Several crawling algorithms were examined (Paramita *et al.*, 2011) and the main technique chosen to be applied in the general crawler was the Breadth-First algorithm (Pinkerton, 1994). First, a generalised crawler with the main functionalities was developed. The crawler starts at the initial webpage of the respective collection of documents and either harvests the links recursively until the relevant pages containing the documents are reached, or uses URL templates to access the pages directly. In most cases, the websites containing parallel texts are very large[34] and a general (non-focused) crawler needs to process a very large amount of links and documents in order to select the relevant ones. The general crawler is therefore transformed into a focused crawler by adapting it to the structure of the source site

[34] http://eur-lex.europa.eu

as derived by automatic or manual web mining. The focused crawler either implements the link harvesting technique directly, or uses a particular set of URL templates specific for a given website. Next, the focused crawler ensures the relevance of the extracted documents by selecting only those texts that have Bulgarian equivalents. Some corpora are static and require a single run of the crawler, while others are dynamic (e.g., news websites) and need weekly or monthly crawls.

Procedures to verify the validity of the documents collected through automatic crawling are implemented: deletion of empty files obtained from either invalid or missing URLs, text size checks, and verification of encoding. Furthermore, genuine correspondence of parallel documents is checked by comparing URLs, file sizes, dates, etc. To conclude, focused crawling with preceding web structure mining (which considerably reduces the number of visited links) ensures high quality of the results and improves efficiency.

4.2 *Size of the Bulgarian National Corpus*

The kernel of the BulNC, consisting of all Bulgarian texts in the corpus, currently amounts to 979.6 million tokens. Although efforts have been made at ensuring the relative balance of the texts in terms of media type, written texts prevail significantly (91.11%), with spoken data representing only 8.89% of the tokens and being limited in variety – parliamentary proceedings, lectures, and subtitles.

At present, the Bul-X-Cor features 33 parallel corpora, the so-called satellites, adding up to 972.3 million tokens. The kernel and the satellites total 1.95 billion tokens altogether. Each parallel subcorpus within the Bul-X-Cor mirrors the structure of the kernel. Languages are not equally represented: the largest corpus is the Bulgarian-English parallel corpus (280.8 and 283.1 million words for Bulgarian and for English respectively); four other corpora comprise between 100 and 200 million tokens per language, sixteen parallel corpora are in the range of 30 to 52 million tokens per language, another seven in the range of 1 to 10 million tokens, and the rest are below one million, with the smallest ones being the Chinese, the Japanese and the Icelandic corpora with less than 50,000 tokens per language (Figure 2).

Figure 2: Largest Bulgarian-X language parallel corpora within the BulNC

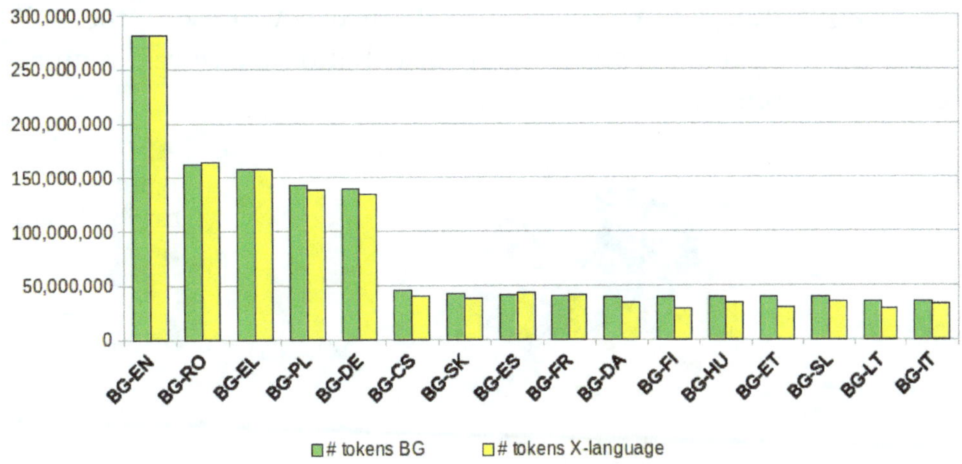

4.3 *Structure of the Bulgarian National Corpus*

The structure of the corpus adheres to three main principles: explicit definition of categories, clear-cut structure and structure flexibility. The structure is not rigid in the sense that it is not predefined. The corpus samples are supplied with extensive metadata, facilitating the extraction of subcorpora with specific structure and features.

Language reflects communication in the following aspects: function and roles of the participants (style), thematic content (domain), and compositional structure (genre). The realisation of their interconnectivity is essential in building a good model for text description and classification. The design of the corpus is therefore based on the three basic classificatory features of style, domain, and genre.

Style is defined as a general complex text category, which combines the notions of register, mode, and discourse. The proposed approach does not rely on a particular linguistic theory of style, but is based on the analyses of Todorov (1984) and Halliday (1985), among others, who consider the intrinsic characteristics of texts in relation to external, sociolinguistic factors, such as the function of the communicative act.

Different terms are used in the existing literature: speech genre (Todorov, 1984), text type (Biber, 1989), register (Crystal, 1991). We have adopted the term *style* in the sense of Crystal (1969) with a more complex meaning that combines the notion of register (various degrees of formality of language (Trudgill, 1992)), media type (spoken or written) and discourse (function and characteristics of the communicative situation as reflected in the text). At present, the BulNC includes texts from six styles. Their distribution measured in number of tokens is presented in Figure 3.

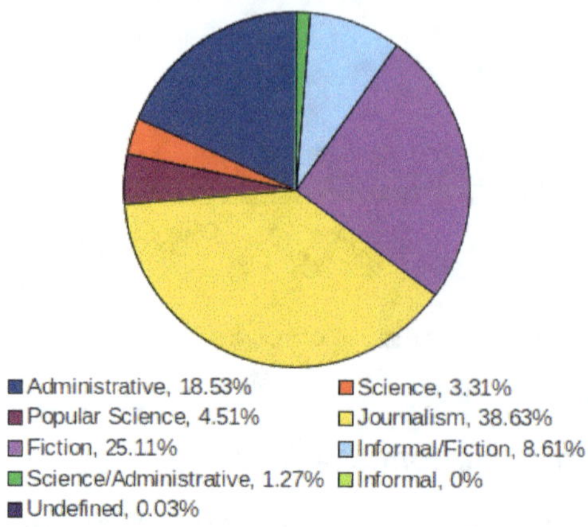

Figure 3:
Distribution of styles in the BulNC

A concise description of the text styles in the BulNC is presented in Table 1. Along with clear-cut styles, two complex styles are also included: Informal/Fiction and Science/Administrative. The former can be defined as informal texts within fiction (subtitles), and the latter as highly specialised (scientific, e.g., medicine) texts within the administrative style. Each of the complex styles exhibits features typical of both components and may share domains and genres with either of them.

Each style is subdivided into thematic domains. It is generally true that domains are style-dependent, although sometimes they are found across styles. For example, the scientific style is divided into categories according to scientific field, e.g., mathematics, economics, political science, etc. Some of the domains of journalistic texts are similar to those of scientific texts – politics, economy, etc.

The term genre also has multiple interpretations. For our purposes we accept the interpretation where genre is associated with the internal formal features of the text (Kress, 1993), although the notion is extended to all texts, both written and spoken. The classification of genres is also inconsistent across linguistic studies, and in particular in existing corpus descriptions (Lee, 2001). A general classification of genres based on style and a set of widely accepted genre types is used in the BulNC.

Table 1: Characteristics of styles in the BulNC

Style	Communicative situation	Function of the text	Features of the text
Administrative	Between official bodies and individual or legal subjects; official, formal, indirect, written	Establishing, regulating and maintaining formal relationships	Relatively strict form and structure, repetitive, ambiguity is avoided
Science	Between researchers and other specialists; formal, indirect, written	Communicating scientific facts	Strict form and structure, extensive use of specialised (domain-specific) language
Popular Science	Between researchers and the wider public; not strictly formal	Communicating scientific facts in accessible and understandable form	Freer form and structure, less specialised language
Journalism	Mainly between journalists and the general public; indirect	Providing information, news and commentary	Relatively stable form and structure, some emphatic elements (e.g., in structure or lexis)
Fiction	Between authors and the general public; indirect	Entertainment and conveying aesthetic and moral values	Free and varied structure, consistent genre-specific elements
Informal	Personal communication; more often direct, informal	Conveying personal message, sharing information	Free and varied structure, diversity in linguistic expression
Informal/ Fiction (Subtitles)	Informal situations within fictional work	Same as fiction; within the fictional framework – personal communication	Characteristics of both styles
Science/ Administrative	Administrative situations within highly specialised scientific domains	Same as administrative	Characteristics of both styles

Style	Number of domains	Number of genres
Administrative	11	16
Science	21	15
Popular Science	25	7
Journalism	19	12
Fiction	13	25
Informal	(not represented)	(not represented)
Informal/Fiction (Subtitles)	17	1
Science/Administrative	21	16

Table 2: Distribution of domains and genres across styles in the BulNC

Table 2 presents the number of domains and genres each style is divided into. Table 3 provides an example of the domains and genres for the Administrative style.

The distribution across domains of the samples in Bul-X-Cor is similar to the distribution in the kernel of the BulNC. The styles are represented as follows:

1. Administrative – EU legislation documents in 23 languages
2. Science/Administrative (Healthcare) – administrative documents from the European Medicines Agency in 23 languages
3. Journalism – news in 9 Balkan languages and English
4. Fiction – texts in Bulgarian, English, German, Romanian, Polish, Greek, Czech.
5. Informal/Fiction – subtitles of feature films, documentaries and cartoons in 29 languages.
6. Science – in Bulgarian and English.

Figure 4 illustrates the distribution of styles within the Bulgarian-English parallel corpus.

4.4 *Documentation and annotation*

The quality of corpus documentation and annotation has a major impact on the extent of its applications and usability. Therefore, great effort has been made to ensure that the documentation and annotation are accurate, well-structured and compliant with established stan-

Table 3:
Domains and genres for the Administrative style in the BulNC

Domains	Genres
Politics	debates
Law	contract
Education	report
Economy	application form
Health	interview
Military	commentary
Culture and arts	correspondence
Sports	law
Ecology	plan
Social policy	programme
Relations	minutes
Undefined	certificate
	directive
	proceedings
	information
	document
	undefined

Figure 4:
Distribution of styles in the Bulgarian-English parallel corpus

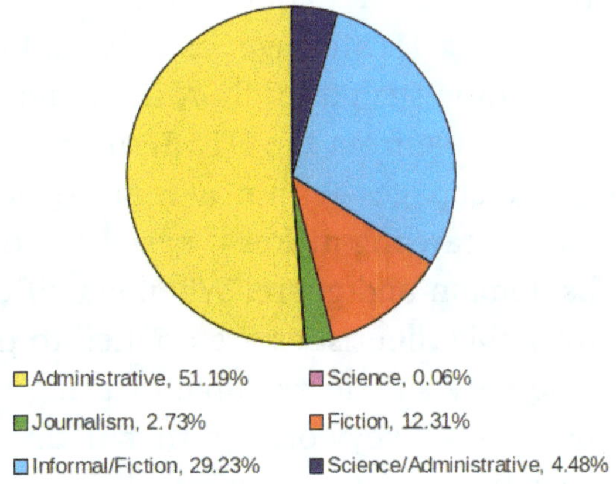

dards. Several levels of metadescription have been performed on the texts in the BulNC:

- Metadata documentation – metadata extraction and validation or metadata description of texts in any language;
- Monolingual annotation – processing of texts in any language at various linguistic levels;
- Multilingual annotation – alignment of parallel texts.

4.4.1 Text metadata

The metadata description of the texts in the BulNC is stored into 25 categories (Table 4) that are compliant with the established standards (Atkins, 1992; Burnard, 2005), although defined for the particular needs of the BulNC.

filename	path_to_file	date_added_to_corpus
author_info	author	translator_info
translator	text_info	title
year_of_creation	publishing_date	source_type
source	translated	medium
number_of_words	style	genre
genre_info	domain1	domain2
domain_info	notes	keywords
languages		

Table 4: Metadata in the BulNC

Metadata are mostly derived automatically, using two main techniques: (i) extracting information from the HTML or XML markup of the original files collected from the Internet, and (ii) keyword-based heuristics. HTML pages usually contain specifically tagged editorial information such as author, title, and date of publishing that are easily extractable from the HTML source.

Webpages within a website often contain similar texts, so focused crawling makes it easier to add classificatory information such as domain and genre. When classificatory information is not directly available, heuristics are applied to determine the domain and genre. One very simple example of using lists of domain-specific or genre-descriptive keywords is that if the title of a text contains a genre-specific word (e.g., *report*), it is assumed to denote the genre of the document.

The metadata are as detailed as possible in order to ensure easy text classification, corpus restructuring and evaluation, derivation of subcorpora based on a set of criteria (e.g., year of publication, domain). Some of the metadata categories, labelled with `_info`, are optional and contain additional details about the main category. A multiple domain description was also included to cater for the description of texts which have mixed domain features. So far, extensive metadata are provided for the Bulgarian and the English part of the BulNC, while the corresponding texts from the other languages share the common metadata (author, title, etc.) and inherit the classificatory information for style, domain, and genre.

4.4.2 Monolingual annotation

Until recently, parts of the BulNC, such as the Bulgarian POS-Tagged Corpus, the Bulgarian Sense-Annotated Corpus, the Bulgarian-English Sentence- and Clause-Aligned Corpus were manually annotated (see Section 2.3), while lately we have focused on automatic annotation of larger portions of the corpus.

The linguistic annotation in the BulNC is divided into: (i) general monolingual annotation (tokenisation and sentence splitting), available for all languages, and (ii) detailed monolingual annotation, available only for the languages for which the respective tools and resources are available: Bulgarian and English. The detailed annotation so far includes morphosyntactic tagging (POS tagging and rich morphological annotation), and lemmatisation. The annotation of Bulgarian texts is further extended by including word senses, synonyms, hypernyms and `similar_to` adjectives, noun phrases, and named entities.

The Bulgarian texts are annotated using the Bulgarian language processing chain[35]. It integrates a number of tools (a regular expression-based sentence splitter and tokeniser, an SVM POS-tagger, a dictionary-based lemmatiser, a finite-state chunker, and a wordnet sense-annotation tool), designed to work together and to ensure interoperability, fast performance and high accuracy. The training of the Bulgarian tagger is based on the following parameters: two passes in both directions; a window of five tokens, the currently tagged word being

[35] `http://dcl.bas.bg/dclservices/`

in second position; 2- and 3-grams of words or morphosyntactic tags or ambiguity classes; lexical parameters such as prefixes, suffixes, sentence borders, and capital letters. Lemmatisation is based on linking the tagger output to the Grammatical dictionary (75 word classes to 1029 unique grammatical tags in the dictionary)[36], while a number of rules and preferences are applied to resolve the ambiguities. The finite-state chunker is a rule-based parser working with a manually-crafted grammar designed to recognise unambiguous phrases and to exclude pronouns, adverbs, and relative clauses as modifiers. The context-dependent rules provide annotation for phrase boundaries and heads.

Apache OpenNLP[37] with pre-trained models and Stanford CoreNLP[38] are used for the annotation of the English texts – sentence segmentation, tokenisation, and POS tagging. OpenNLP could be trained and applied for other languages as well. There are also some pre-trained models for a number of widely used languages (German and Spanish, among others). Lemmatisation of the English texts is performed using Stanford CoreNLP and RASP (Briscoe, 2006). As we aim at high quality and consistency of the annotation, we examine various systems for processing English and other languages.

Uniformity in annotation for Bulgarian and other languages is achieved in either of two ways: (i) annotation of raw data from scratch, applying equal standards and principles, or (ii) conversion of already existing annotation. In each case the tagset and conventions accepted for the BulNC are followed. The different tagsets are mapped to the Bulgarian tagset, but any language-specific annotation is preserved. The design of the Bulgarian tagset provides a uniform description of the inflexion of Bulgarian words and multiword expressions (Koeva, 2006) based on morphological and morphosyntactic criteria[39]. The tagset is mappable to the Multext-East morphosyntactic descriptions (Erjavec, 2004; Chiarcos and Erjavec, 2011), which are valuable as a unified framework for many European languages, although some disadvantages have been discovered with regard to the set of descriptions, both on a general and a language-specific level (Przepiórkowski and Woliński, 2003).

[36] `http://dcl.bas.bg/est/dict.php`

[37] `http://incubator.apache.org/opennlp/`

[38] `http://nlp.stanford.edu/software/corenlp.shtml`

[39] `http://dcl.bas.bg/en/BulgarianTagset_en.html`

4.4.3 Multilingual annotation

Multilingual annotation includes alignment at different linguistic levels, currently sentence and clause level. Alignment at sentence level is essential for all parallel resources and it is therefore required for all language pairs. High-quality sentence segmentation is an important prerequisite for the quality of parallel text alignment. The vast majority of the errors that occur in sentence alignment follow from inaccurate sentence segmentation. Two aligners have been applied for parts of the corpus: HunAlign (Varga *et al.*, 2005) and Maligna[40]. The alignment is based on the Gale-Church algorithm, which uses sentence-length distance measure and is largely language-independent. Other alignment methods, such as the Bilingual Sentence Aligner (Moore, 2002) and the use of bilingual dictionaries, are envisaged as well. The aligners take as input texts with segmented sentences and produce a sequence of parallel sentence pairs (bi-sentences). At present, alignment is performed and tested on the Bulgarian-English Parallel Corpus. A further step in parallel corpora processing is automatic clause alignment (Koeva *et al.*, 2012a), currently under way.

4.4.4 Annotation formats

Each raw text in the corpus is in plain text format. The annotation tools exchange data in the so-called vertical format, which is converted into an XML format and then stored in a MySQL database. In the vertical format, the tokens are separated by a newline and the annotation tags by a tab character. Each tool accumulates tags in fixed positions in one or several columns (for tags with a complex structure). Tags can be associated with a single token or a group of tokens.

```
new            TOK_LAT      new          A
technologies   TOK_LAT      technology   Np
.              TOK_FS<S>    .            U
```

The XML format also provides flexibility for representing various levels of annotation in both flat form (as sequences of elements) or hierarchical form (as nested elements, particularly useful for syntactic annotation). In the flat XML format adopted so far the text is represented as a sequence of `words` with associated attributes and their values that store the annotation information.

[40] http://align.sourceforge.net/

```
<word w="new" l="new" sen="11439" pos="A">
<word w="technologies" l="technology" sen="11439" pos="Np">
```

4.5 *General evaluation of the BulNC*

The monolingual and parallel parts of the BulNC can be evaluated from several perspectives, either quantitatively or qualitatively.

- **Quality of compilation methods**
  The quality of the crawling is ensured by implementing several techniques: manual and automatic data mining prior to crawling, development of a focused crawler for efficiency, as well as methods for verification of the results.

- **Statistical methods for qualitative analysis and evaluation**
  The strategy to gather a greater variety of word-grams and their distribution rather than to achieve balanced text category distribution is dominant. The aim is to employ statistical methods for qualitative analysis and evaluation, e.g., the proportion between the number of unique tokens / lemmas in the corpus and their frequencies / coverage / distribution within different (combinations of) styles, domains, and genres. It is assumed that variety in word distribution presupposes variety in text categories. For example, sparsity is evaluated through Zipf's law for frequency distribution and type-to-token ratios between old and new words (Goweder and De Roeck, 2001), and violation of Zipf's law may indicate data sparsity.
  Word sequence distribution (higher-order N-grams) may be combined with smoothing and skipping techniques (i.e., calculation of conditional probability based on different context) and with word similarity measures for automatic word clustering (Koeva *et al.*, 2012a). In that respect, the new data not only contribute by adding new lexical units, but also by supporting the saturation of the language model based on the previously collected lexical units.

- **Quality of metadata and annotation**
  Effort is made to ensure high-quality annotation in terms of accuracy, variety and coverage. On the average, in each metadata record in the BulNC 17.79 categories are non-empty (71.16%), a

figure that shows a good overall coverage for the description of the corpus texts.

The POS and grammatical tagger included in the Bulgarian language processing chain (Koeva and Genov, 2011) performs with a precision of 96.58%. The precision reported for the pre-trained model of OpenNLP used for the POS tagging of the English texts is 96.59%. Access to the processing tools is provided through a web service[41] or a web interface for asynchronous tasks[42].

4.6 *Access and applications of the BulNC*

The BulNC has been developed and expanded primarily to meet the needs of natural language processing. Still, the broad range of areas of application of the corpus makes it well-suited for public availability.

4.6.1 Public access to the BulNC

As for the public access to the BulNC[43], we fully comply with Bulgarian and EU legislation concerning copyright and related rights. The law permits the use of copyrighted material for purposes of non-commercial scientific research and for education or private study. Where possible, we extract and store information about the source and the author's name and cite it accordingly. Several types of access to the corpus are provided: (i) download (limited); (ii) web search interface; (iii) collocation service; (iv) subcorpora selection; (v) frequency lists derived from the whole corpus or a given subcorpus.

Due to the inclusion of copyrighted material, the BulNC is not downloadable in full. For several style-specific subcorpora no redistribution limitations are in force, and these are available for download (registration required).

Like many of the large corpora presented in Section 2.1, the BulNC is supplied with a web interface for searching the corpus, as well as for building concordances and extracting collocations. The search system[44] (Figure 5) allows complex linguistic queries involving different levels of annotation combined in various ways. It is designed to support monolingual and parallel corpora in a uniform way. As compared

[41] http://dcl.bas.bg/dclservices/
[42] http://dcl.bas.bg/dclservices/admin/
[43] http://ibl.bas.bg/en/BGNC_access_en.htm
[44] http://search.dcl.bas.bg

to the CQL (Christ and Schulze, 1994), the implemented Designed query language (DQL) (Tinchev *et al.*, 2007) supports terms, such as: word – e.g. `word`; arbitrary word – e.g. `*{POS=A POS=ADV}`, relation – e.g. `word/F/`, and their combinations – e.g. `word/S/{POS=N}`. It is not restricted to a predetermined set of relations – at the moment queries for word forms, synonyms, hypernyms, and `similar_to` adjectives are supported. The atomic formulae allow both ordered and unordered queries, the latter being relevant for matching adjacent constituents with free word order, e.g., verbal clitics in Slavic languages. DQL is recursive and all Boolean combinations of formulae are formulae. This allows, among other things, disjunction of ordered queries, i.e., searching for paraphrases. The system also supports queries with regular expressions. For a given query the system retrieves matches in all documents regardless of language. Thanks to the alignment, the corresponding sentences in parallel documents are also accessible. The hits are paginated and the matches are highlighted. The user is able to view the detailed information for a given sentence in the hit set – the sentence metadata, its context, and correspondence(s) in the other languages.

The BulNC Collocation service employs the free NoSketchEngine[45], a system for corpora processing. The collocation service is a RESTful web service, supporting complex queries through HTTP and providing statistical information.

For instance, the query

```
http://dcl.bas.bg/collocations/?cmd=collocations&word=cat&cbgrfns=3td
```

returns statistical significance calculated with MI3, T-score, and logDice.

In accordance with our view that the corpus should allow for easy compilation of domain- and purpose-specific corpora compliant to a set of predefined criteria – e.g., synchronic, specialised, balanced subcorpora, we intend to provide a web interface for subcorpora selection, processing, and analysis. The extensive metadata ensures that a large set of criteria is available to cater for various research purposes and requirements. At present, we offer an offline request-based service for subcorpora selection and compilation of frequency lists[46].

[45] `http://nlp.fi.muni.cz/trac/noske`

[46] `http://ibl.bas.bg/en/BGNC_access_en.htm`

Figure 5: The BulNC search web service

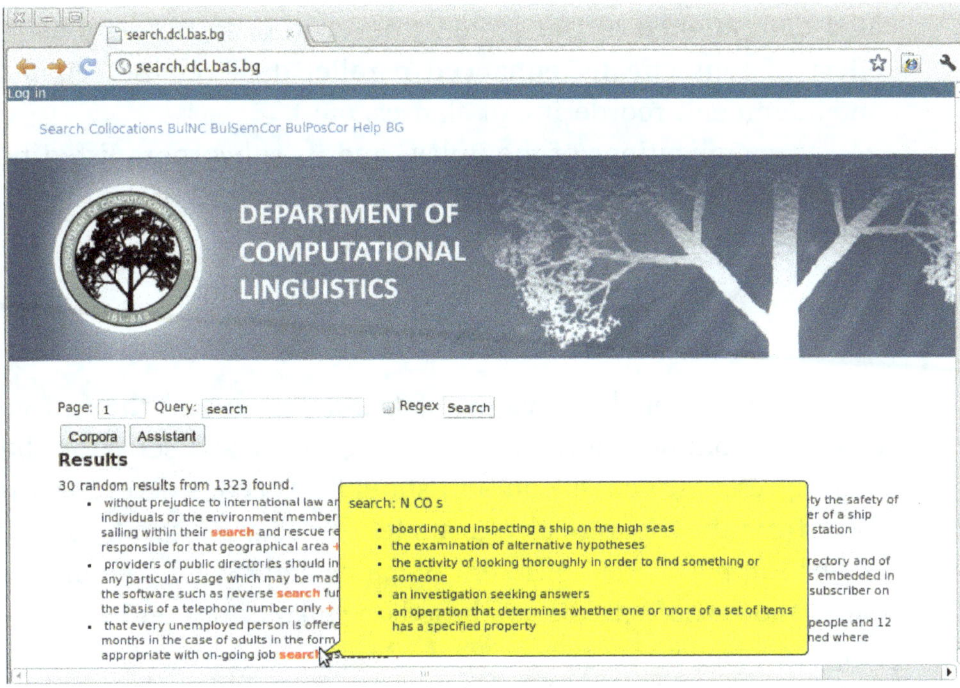

4.6.2 Specialised subcorpora

Manually annotated subcorpora of the BulNC have been used as training and testing resources in numerous studies and NLP tasks, among them theoretical linguistic research, lexicological and lexicographic studies, POS tagging, semantic annotation and disambiguation, MWE recognition, parallel text alignment, clause segmentation and alignment, and many others.

For example, parts of the BulPosCor were used as training and test corpora in the creation of the SVM POS-tagger. The principal application of the BulSemCor is in the training and evaluation of a multi-component word sense disambiguation system. The corpus Wiki1000+, which contains Wikipedia articles (part of the *Popular science* style), includes 13.4 million words. Wiki1000+ was used for the purposes of recognition and classification of multiword expressions. The Bulgarian Sentence- and Clause-Aligned Corpus has been used for the purposes of parallel text alignment at sentence and clause level. It has served as a training resource in the development of a tool for clause alignment (Koeva *et al.*, 2012a). Several Moses[47] models (Koehn and Hoang, 2007) have been built on a large amount of par-

[47] `http://www.statmt.org/moses/`

allel data aligned at the sentence level in order to demonstrate the effect of syntactically enhanced parallel data (clause segmentation and alignment, reordering of clauses, etc.).

The applications of the BulNC and its subcorpora listed here are only a few examples of the numerous applications of the BulNC in the field of natural language processing.

5 CONCLUSION

In the context of the advance of technologies and the fast-growing amount of online information, the notions of text selection, balance, and representativeness can and should be reconsidered, shifting the focus from the theoretically grounded expectation for the distribution of text samples across different domains and genres to more sophisticated and flexible prediction based on calculations and estimations of language usage.

The paper has outlined the main concepts in corpus compilation with an emphasis on the key issues related to the use of corpora for the purposes of NLP research and applications. The attempt at redefining these concepts draws upon a discussion of the principles adopted in the compilation of large monolingual and parallel corpora for various languages. At the present time, large monolingual and multilingual corpora are constructed mostly by amassing text archives, repositories of documents, and bulks of texts available on the Internet.

Against this background, we propose a clear-cut approach for the compilation of a large multilingual corpus and demonstrate it in the context of the Bulgarian National Corpus. Our approach emphasises the extensive metadata and multi-level annotation of very large automatically collected monolingual and multilingual corpora, as well as the uniform treatment of multilingual content with respect to compilation, documentation, annotation, processing, and access.

REFERENCES

Krasimira ALEKSOVA (2000), *Ezikat i semeystvoto. Kam metodikata za prouchvane na rechta v mikroobshtnostite (Language and the family. Towards a methodology for analysis of speech in micro social environments)*, Intervyu Press, Sofia.

Beryl Sue ATKINS (1992), Theoretical lexicography and its relation to dictionary-making, *Dictionaries: Journal of the Dictionary Society of North America*, 14:4–43.

Beryl Sue ATKINS, Jeremy CLEAR, and Nicholas OSTLER (1991), Corpus design criteria, `http://www.natcorp.ox.ac.uk/archive/vault/tgaw02.pdf`.

Michele BANKO and Eric BRILL (2001), Scaling to very very large corpora for natural language disambiguation, in *Proceedings of ACL 2001*, pp. 26–33.

Piotr BAŃSKI, Peter M. FISCHER, Elena FRICK, Erik KETZAN, Marc KUPIETZ, Carsten SCHNOBER, Oliver SCHONEFELD, and Andreas WITT (2012), The New IDS Corpus Analysis Platform: challenges and prospects, in *Proceedings of the Eighth International Conference on Language Resources and Evaluation (LREC 2012)*, pp. 2905–2911.

Piotr BAŃSKI and Adam PRZEPIÓRKOWSKI (2010), The TEI and the NCP: the model and its application, in *Proceedings of LREC 2010 Workshop on Language Resources: From Storyboard to Sustainability and LR Lifecycle Management (LRSLM2010)*, pp. 34–38.

Marko BARONI and Adam KILGARRIFF (2006), Large linguistically-processed web corpora for multiple languages, in *Proceedings of European ACL, Trento, Italy*, pp. 87–90.

Božo BEKAVAC, Petya OSENOVA, Kiril SIMOV, and Marko TADIĆ (2004), Making monolingual corpora comparable: a case study of Bulgarian and Croatian, in M. T. LINO, M. F. XAVIER, F. FERREIRA, R. COSTA, R. SILVA, C. PEREIRA, F. CARVALHO, M. LOPES, M. CATARINO, and S. BARROS, editors, *Proceedings of the Fourth International Conference on Language Resources and Evaluation (LREC 2004), Lisbon, Portugal*, volume IV, pp. 1187–1190.

Douglas BIBER (1989), A typology of English texts, *Linguistics*, 27:3–43.

Douglas BIBER (1993), Representativeness in corpus design, *Literary and Linguistic Computing*, 8(4):243–258.

Ondřej BOJAR, Zdeněk ŽABOKRTSKÝ, Ondřej DUŠEK, Petra GALUŠČÁKOVÁ, Martin MAJLIŠ, David MAREČEK, Jiří MARŠÍK, Michal NOVÁK, Martin POPEL, and Aleš TAMCHYNA (2012), The joy of parallelism with CzEng 1.0, in *Proceedings of the Eighth International Conference on Language Resources and Evaluation (LREC 2012)*.

Ted BRISCOE (2006), An introduction to tag sequence grammars and the RASP system parser, Technical report, University of Cambridge, Computer Laboratory Technical Report.

Lou BURNARD (2005), *Developing Linguistic Corpora: a Guide to Good Practice*, chapter Metadata for corpus work, Oxford: Oxbow Books, `http://ota.ahds.ac.uk/documents/creating/dlc/index.htm`.

František ČERMAK and Vera SCHMIEDTOVÁ (2003), The Czech National Corpus Project and lexicography, in M. MURATA, S. YAMADA, and Y. TONO, editors, *Asialex '03 Tokyo Proceedings: Dictionaries and Language Learning: How Can Dictionaries Help Human and Machine Learning?*, pp. 74–80.

Atanas CHANEV, Kiril SIMOV, Petya OSENOVA, and Svetoslav MARINOV (2006), Dependency conversion and parsing of the BulTreeBank, in *Proceedings of the LREC Workshop Merging and Layering Linguistic Information, Genoa, Italy, 2006*, pp. 16–23.

Jonathan CHEVELU, Nelly BARBOT, Oliver BOEFFARD, and Arnaud DELHAY (2007), Lagrangian relaxation for optimal corpus design, in *Proceedings of the 6th ISCA Tutorial and Research Workshop on Speech Synthesis (SSW6)*, pp. 211–216.

Christian CHIARCOS and Tomaž ERJAVEC (2011), OWL/DL formalization of the MULTEXT-East morphosyntactic specifications, in *Proceedings of the Linguistic Annotation Workshop 2011*, pp. 11–20.

Oliver CHRIST and Bruno M. SCHULZE (1994), *The IMS Corpus Workbench: Corpus Query Processor (CQP) User's Manual*, University of Stuttgart, Germany.

Jeremy CLEAR (1992), Corpus sampling, in G. LEITNER, editor, *New directions in English language corpora*, Berlin: Mouton de Gruyter.

David CRYSTAL (1969), *What is Linguistics?*, London: Edward Arnold.

David CRYSTAL (1991), *A Dictionary of Linguistics and Phonetics*, Cambridge, MA: Basil Blackwell.

James R. CURRAN and Miles OSBORNE (2002), A very very large corpus doesn't always yield reliable estimates, in *Proceedings of the 6th Conference on Natural Language Learning (CoNLL)*, pp. 126–131.

Mark DAVIES (2010), The corpus of contemporary American English as the First Reliable Monitor Corpus of English, *Literary and Linguistic Computing*, 25(4):447–465.

Ludmila DIMITROVA, Tomaž ERJAVEC, Nancy IDE, Heiki-Jan KAALEP, Vladimir PETKEVIC, and Dan TUFIŞ (1998), Multext-East: parallel and comparable corpora and lexicons for six Central and Eastern European languages, in C. BOITET and P. WHITELOCK, editors, *Proceedings of COLING-ACL'98: 17th International Conference on Computational Linguistics and 36th Annual Meeting of the Association for Computational Linguistics, Montréal, Québec, Canada*, pp. 315–319, San Francisco, Calif.: Morgan Kaufmann.

Ludmila DIMITROVA, Violetta KOSESKA, Danuta ROSZKO, and Roman ROSZKO (2009), Bulgarian-Polish-Lithuanian Corpus – current development, in *Proceedings of the International Workshop Multilingual resources, technologies and evaluation for Central and Eastern European languages in conjunction with International Conference RANPL 2009, Borovec, Bulgaria, 17 September 2009*, pp. 1–8.

Tomaž ERJAVEC (2004), MULTEXT-East Version 3: multilingual morphosyntactic specifications, lexicons and corpora, in M. T. LINO, M. F. XAVIER, F. FERREIRA, R. COSTA, R. SILVA, C. PEREIRA, F. CARVALHO, M. LOPES, M. CATARINO, and S. BARROS, editors, *Proceedings of the Fourth International Conference on Language Resources and Evaluation (LREC 2004), Lisbon, Portugal*, pp. 1535–1538.

Winthrop Nelson FRANCIS and Henry KUČERA (1964), Brown Corpus Manual, http://icame.uib.no/brown/bcm.html.

Roger GARSIDE, Geoffrey LEECH, and Tony MCENERY (1997), *Corpus Annotation: Linguistic Information from Computer Text Corpora*, London: Longman.

Voula GIOULI, Nikos GLAROS, Kiril SIMOV, and Petya OSENOVA (2009), A web-enabled and speech-enhanced parallel corpus of Greek-Bulgarian cultural texts, in *Proceedings of Workshop on Language Technology and Resources for Cultural Heritage, Social Sciences, Humanities, and Education (LaTeCH – SHELT&R 2009)*, pp. 35–41.

Abduelbaset GOWEDER and Anne DE ROECK (2001), Assessment of a significant Arabic corpus, in *Proceedings Workshop on Arabic Language Processing, 39th ACL, Toulouse.*

Atle GRØNN and Irena MARIJANOVIC (2010), Russian in contrast: Form, meaning and parallel corpora, *Oslo Studies in Language (OSLa)*, 2(1):1–24.

Michael HALLIDAY (1985), *An Introduction to Functional Grammar*, Melbourne: Edward Arnold.

Frank KELLER and Mirella LAPATA (2003), Using the web to obtain frequencies for unseen bigrams, *Computational Linguistics*, 29(3):459–484.

Adam KILGARRIFF and Gregory GREFENSTETTE (2003), Introduction to the special Issue on Web as Corpus, *Computational Linguistics*, 29(3):333–347.

Adam KILGARRIFF, Vojtěch KOVÁŘ, and Pavel RYCHLÝ (2009), Tickbox Lexicography, in *eLexicography in the 21st century: new challenges, new applications*, pp. 411–418, Brussels : Presses universitaires de Louvain.

Jan KOCEK, Marie KOPŘIVOVÁ, and Věra SCHMIEDTOVÁ (2000), The Czech National Corpus, in *Proceedings of EURALEX 2000*, pp. 127–132.

Philipp KOEHN (2005), Europarl: A parallel corpus for statistical machine translation, in *Proceedings of MT Summit*, pp. 79–86.

Philipp KOEHN and Hieu HOANG (2007), Factored Translation Models, in *Proceeding of the Conference on Empirical Methods in Natural Language Processing (EMNLP), Prague, Czech Republic, June 2007.*

Svetla KOEVA (2006), Inflection morphology of Bulgarian multiword expressions, in *Computer Applications in Slavic Studies*, pp. 201–216, Boyan Penev Publishing Center.

Svetla KOEVA (2010), Balgarskiyat semantichno anotiran korpus – teoretichni postanovki (Bulgarian semantically annotated corpus – theoretical concepts), in *Balgarskiyat semantichno anotiran korpus (Bulgarian semantically annotated corpus)*, IBL.

Svetla KOEVA, Diana BLAGOEVA, and Sia KOLKOVSKA (2010), Bulgarian National Corpus Project, in N. CALZOLARI, K. CHOUKRI, B. MAEGAARD, J. MARIANI, J. ODJIK, S. PIPERIDIS, M. ROSNER, and D. TAPIAS, editors, *Proceedings of the Seventh Conference on International Language Resources and Evaluation (LREC 2010)*, pp. 3678–3684.

Svetla KOEVA and Angel GENOV (2011), Bulgarian language processing chain, in *Proceedings of Integration of multilingual resources and tools in Web applications. Workshop in conjunction with GSCL 2011, 26 September 2011, University of Hamburg.*

Svetla KOEVA, Svetlozara LESEVA, Borislav Rizov RIZOV, Ekaterina TARPOMANOVA, Tsvetana DIMITROVA, Hristina KUKOVA, and Maria TODOROVA (2011), Design and development of the Bulgarian sense-annotated corpus, in *Las tecnologías de la información y las comunicaciones: Presente y futuro en el análisis de córpora. Actas del III Congreso Internacional de Lingüística de Corpus. Valencia: Universitat Politécnica de Valéncia*, pp. 143–150.

Svetla KOEVA, Svetlozara LESEVA, Ivelina STOYANOVA, Ekaterina TARPOMANOVA, and Maria TODOROVA (2006), Bulgarian tagged corpora, in *Proceedings of the Fifth International Conference Formal Approaches to South Slavic and Balkan Languages, Sofia, Bulgaria*, pp. 78–86.

Svetla KOEVA, Borislav RIZOV, Ekaterina TARPOMANOVA, Tsvetana DIMITROVA, Rositsa DEKOVA, Ivelina STOYANOVA, Svetlozara LESEVA, Hristina KUKOVA, and Angel GENOV (2012a), Application of clause alignment for statistical machine translation, in *Proceedings of the Sixth Workshop on Syntax, Semantics and Structure in Statistical Translation (SSST-6), 12 July 2012, Jeju, Korea.*

Svetla KOEVA, Ivelina STOYANOVA, Rositsa DEKOVA, Borislav RIZOV, and Angel GENOV (2012b), Bulgarian X-language parallel corpus, in N. CALZOLARI, K. CHOUKRI, T. DECLERCK, M. U. DOGAN, B. MAEGAARD, J. MARIANI, J. ODJIK, and S. PIPERIDIS, editors, *Proceedings of the Eighth International Conference on Language Resources and Evaluation (LREC 2012)*, pp. 2480–2486, `http://www.lrec-conf.org/proceedings/lrec2012/pdf/587_Paper.pdf`.

Gunther KRESS (1993), Against arbitrariness, *Discourse and Society*, 4(2):169–191.

Marc KUPIETZ, Cyril BELICA, Holger KEIBEL, and Andreas WITT (2010), The German Reference Corpus DEREKO: A Primordial sample for linguistic research, in N. CALZOLARI, K. CHOUKRI, B. MAEGAARD, J. MARIANI, J. ODJIK, S. PIPERIDIS, M. ROSNER, and D. TAPIAS, editors, *Proceedings of the*

Seventh conference on International Language Resources and Evaluation (LREC 2010), pp. 1848–1854.

David LEE (2001), Genres, registers, text types, domains and style: clarifying the concepts and navigating a path through BNC jungle, *Language Learning & Technology*, 5(3):37–72.

Geoffrey LEECH (1991), The state of the art in corpus linguistics, in *English Corpus Linguistics: Linguistic Studies in Honour of Jan Svartvik*, pp. 8–29, London: Longman.

Christopher MANNING and Hinrich SCHUTZE (1999), *Foundations of Statistical Natural Language Processing*, MIT Press.

Tony MCENERY, Richard XIAO, and Yukio TONO (2006), *Corpus-Based Language Studies. An Advanced Resource Book*, Routledge.

Charles F. MEYER (2002), *English Corpus Linguistics. An Introduction*, Cambridge University Press.

Robert C. MOORE (2002), Fast and accurate sentence alignment of bilingual corpora, in *AMTA'02: Proceedings of the 5th Conference of the Association for Machine Translation in the Americas on Machine Translation: From Research to Real Users*, pp. 135–144, London, UK: Springer-Verlag.

Graham NEUBIG (2011), The Kyoto Free Translation Task, `http://www.phontron.com/kftt`.

Cvetanka NIKOLOVA (1987), *Chestoten rechnik na balgarskata razgovorna rech (A Frequency Dictionary of Colloquial Bulgarian)*, Sofia: Nauka i izkustvo.

Monica PARAMITA, Ahmet AKER, Robert GAIZAUSKAS, Paul CLOUGH, Emma BARKER, Nikos MASTROPAVLOS, and Dan TUFIŞ (2011), Report on methods for collection of comparable corpora, ACCURAT – Analysis and Evaluation of Comparable Corpora for Under Resourced Areas of Machine Translation.

Brian PINKERTON (1994), Finding what people want: Experiences with the WebCrawler, in *Proceedings of the First World Wide Web Conference, Geneva, Switzerland*, `http://thinkpink.com/bp/webcrawler/www94.html`.

Jan POMIKÁLEK, Miloš JAKUBÍČEK, and Pavel RYCHLÝ (2012), Building a 70 billion word corpus of English from ClueWeb, in N. CALZOLARI, K. CHOUKRI, T. DECLERCK, M. U. DOGAN, B. MAEGAARD, J. MARIANI, J. ODJIK, and S. PIPERIDIS, editors, *Proceedings of the Eighth International Conference on Language Resources and Evaluation (LREC 2012)*, pp. 502–506.

Jan POMIKÁLEK, Pavel RYCHLY, and Adam KILGARRIFF (2009), Scaling to billion-plus word corpora, *Advances in Computational Linguistics. Special Issue of Research in Computing Science*, 41:3–14.

Adam PRZEPIÓRKOWSKI (2011), Linguistic annotation of the National Corpus of Polish, FDSL 9, `http://www.uni-goettingen.de/de/document/download/cbcf2e9ded91b3c41d0c460c31d1d9bb.pdf/nkjp.pdf`.

Adam PRZEPIÓRKOWSKI, Marek ŁAZIŃSKI, Rafał L. GÓRSKI, and Barbara LEWANDOWSKA-TOMASZCZYK (2010), Recent developments in the National Corpus of Polish, in N. CALZOLARI, K. CHOUKRI, T. DECLERCK, M. U. DOGAN, B. MAEGAARD, J. MARIANI, J. ODJIK, and S. PIPERIDIS, editors, *Proceedings of the Seventh conference on International Language Resources and Evaluation (LREC 2010)*, pp. 994–997.

Adam PRZEPIÓRKOWSKI and Marcin WOLIŃSKI (2003), The unbearable lightness of tagging: A case study in morphosyntactic tagging of Polish, in *Proceedings of the 4th International Workshop on Linguistically Interpreted Corpora (LINC 2003), EACL 2003*, pp. 109–116.

Kiril SIMOV and Petya OSENOVA (2004), A hybrid strategy for regular grammar parsing, in M. T. LINO, M. F. XAVIER, F. FERREIRA, R. COSTA, R. SILVA, C. PEREIRA, F. CARVALHO, M. LOPES, M. CATARINO, and S. BARROS, editors, *Proceedings of the Fourth International Conference on Language Resources and Evaluation (LREC 2004), Lisbon, Portugal*, pp. 431–434.

Kiril SIMOV, Petya OSENOVA, Sia KOLKOVSKA, Elisaveta BALABANOVA, Dimitar DOIKOFF, Krassimira IVANOVA, Alexander SIMOV, and Milen KOUYLEKOV (2002), Building a linguistically interpreted corpus of Bulgarian: the BulTreeBank, in *Proceedings of the Third International Conference on Language Resources and Evaluation (LREC 2002), Canary Islands, Spain*, pp. 1729–1736.

John SINCLAIR (2005), *Developing Linguistic Corpora: a Guide to Good Practice*, chapter Corpus and text – basic principles, Oxford: Oxbow Books, `http://ahds.ac.uk/linguistic-corpora/`.

Ralf STEINBERGER, Bruno POULIQUEN, Anna WIDIGER, Camelia IGNAT, Tomaž ERJAVEC, Dan TUFIŞ, and Daniel VARGA (2006), The JRC-Acquis: A multilingual aligned parallel corpus with 20+ languages, in *Proceedings of the Fifth International Conference on Language Resources and Evaluation (LREC 2006)*, pp. 2142–2147.

Marko TADIĆ (2002), Building the Croatian National Corpus, in *Proceedings of the Third International Conference on Language Resources and Evaluation (LREC 2002), Canary Islands, Spain*, pp. 441–446.

Jörg TIEDEMANN (2009), News from OPUS – A collection of multilingual parallel corpora with tools and interfaces, in N. NICOLOV, K. BONTCHEVA, G. ANGELOVA, and R. MITKOV, editors, *Recent Advances in Natural Language Processing*, volume V, pp. 237–248, Amsterdam/Philadelphia: John Benjamins.

Tinko TINCHEV, Svetla KOEVA, Borislav RIZOV, and Nikola OBRESHKOV (2007), System for advanced search in corpora, in *Literature and Writing in Internet*, pp. 92–111, Sofia: St. Kliment Ohridski University Press.

Tzvetan TODOROV (1984), *Mikhail Bakhtin: The Dialogical Principle*, Minneapolis: University of Minnesota Press.

Peter TRUDGILL (1992), *Introducing Language and Society*, London: Penguin.

Dan TUFIŞ, Svetla KOEVA, Tomaž ERJAVEC, Maria GAVRILIDOU, and Cvetana KRSTEV (2009), ID10503 Building Language Resources and Translation Models for Machine Translation focused on South Slavic and Balkan Languages, in *Scientific results of the SEE-ERA.NET Pilot Joint Call, Vienna*, pp. 37–48.

Dániel VARGA, Lásló NÉMETH, P'eter HALÁCSY, András KORNAI, Viktor TRÓN, and Viktor NAGY (2005), Parallel corpora for medium density languages, in *Proceedings of the RANLP 2005*, pp. 590–596.

Ruprecht VON WALDENFELS (2006), Compiling a parallel corpus of Slavic languages. Text strategies, tools and the question of lemmatization in alignment, in B. BREHMER, V. ZHDANOVA, and R. ZIMNY, editors, *Beiträge der Europäischen Slavistischen Linguistik (POLYSLAV) 9*, pp. 123–138, München: Sagner.

Ruprecht VON WALDENFELS (2011), Recent developments in ParaSol: Breadth for depth and XSLT based web concordancing with CWB, in Daniela M. and R. GARABÍK, editors, *Natural Language Processing, Multilinguality. Proceedings of Slovko 2011, Modra, Slovakia, 20-21 October 2011*, pp. 156–162.

Richard XIAO (2010), Corpus creation, in *The Handbook of Natural Language Processing*, pp. 147–165.

Jia XU and Weiwei SUN (2011), Generating virtual parallel corpus: a compatibility centric method, in *Proceedings of the Machine Translation Summit XIII*.

Dan-Hee YANG, Pascual Cantos GOMEZ, and Mansuk SONG (2000), An Algorithm for Predicting the Relation between Lemmas and Corpus Size, *ETRI Journal*, 22(2):20–31.

Permissions

All chapters in this book were first published in JLM, by Institute of Computer Science of the Polish Academy of Sciences; hereby published with permission under the Creative Commons Attribution License or equivalent. Every chapter published in this book has been scrutinized by our experts. Their significance has been extensively debated. The topics covered herein carry significant findings which will fuel the growth of the discipline. They may even be implemented as practical applications or may be referred to as a beginning point for another development.

The contributors of this book come from diverse backgrounds, making this book a truly international effort. This book will bring forth new frontiers with its revolutionizing research information and detailed analysis of the nascent developments around the world.

We would like to thank all the contributing authors for lending their expertise to make the book truly unique. They have played a crucial role in the development of this book. Without their invaluable contributions this book wouldn't have been possible. They have made vital efforts to compile up to date information on the varied aspects of this subject to make this book a valuable addition to the collection of many professionals and students.

This book was conceptualized with the vision of imparting up-to-date information and advanced data in this field. To ensure the same, a matchless editorial board was set up. Every individual on the board went through rigorous rounds of assessment to prove their worth. After which they invested a large part of their time researching and compiling the most relevant data for our readers.

The editorial board has been involved in producing this book since its inception. They have spent rigorous hours researching and exploring the diverse topics which have resulted in the successful publishing of this book. They have passed on their knowledge of decades through this book. To expedite this challenging task, the publisher supported the team at every step. A small team of assistant editors was also appointed to further simplify the editing procedure and attain best results for the readers.

Apart from the editorial board, the designing team has also invested a significant amount of their time in understanding the subject and creating the most relevant covers. They scrutinized every image to scout for the most suitable representation of the subject and create an appropriate cover for the book.

The publishing team has been an ardent support to the editorial, designing and production team. Their endless efforts to recruit the best for this project, has resulted in the accomplishment of this book. They are a veteran in the field of academics and their pool of knowledge is as vast as their experience in printing. Their expertise and guidance has proved useful at every step. Their uncompromising quality standards have made this book an exceptional effort. Their encouragement from time to time has been an inspiration for everyone.

The publisher and the editorial board hope that this book will prove to be a valuable piece of knowledge for researchers, students, practitioners and scholars across the globe.

List of Contributors

Alistair Kennedy
School of Electrical Engineering and Computer Science University of Ottawa, Ottawa, Ontario, Canada

Stan Szpakowicz
School of Electrical Engineering and Computer Science University of Ottawa, Ottawa, Ontario, Canada
Institute of Computer Science Polish Academy of Sciences, Warsaw, Poland

Richard Moot
LIRMM, Montpellier University, CNRS

Tobias Denkinger
Faculty of Computer Science Technische Universität Dresden Germany

Simon Dobnik and Robin Cooper
Department of Philosophy, Linguistics & Theory of Science (FLOV) Centre for Linguistic Theory and Studies in Probability (CLASP) University of Gothenburg, Sweden

Manex Agirrezabal, Aitzol Astigarraga and Bertol Arrieta
University of the Basque Country (UPV/EHU), Department of Computer Science, 20018 Donostia, Spain

Mans Hulden
University of Colorado Boulder, Department of Linguistics, Boulder, Colorado (USA)

Timm Lichte
University of Düsseldorf, Germany

Simon Petitjean
Université d'Orléans, LIFO, France

Svetla Koeva, Ivelina Stoyanova, Svetlozara Leseva, Tsvetana Dimitrova, Rositsa Dekova and Ekaterina Tarpomanova
Department of Computational Linguistics, Institute for Bulgarian Language, Bulgarian Academy of Sciences, Sofia, Bulgaria

Index

www.ingramcontent.com/pod-product-compliance
Lightning Source LLC
LaVergne TN
LVHW080609210926
848485LV00003B/127